THE ROUTLEDGE COMPANION
TO THEATRE AND PERFORMANCE ✳

What is theatre? What is performance? What connects them and how are they different? How have they been shaped by events, people, practices and ideas in the twentieth century? And where are they heading next?

The Routledge Companion to Theatre and Performance offers some answers to these big questions. It provides an accessible, informative and engaging intro-duction to important people, events, concepts and practices that have defined the complementary fields of theatre and performance studies. Three easy-to-use alphabetized sections include more than 120 entries on topics and people ranging from performance artist Marina Abramović, to directors Vsevolod Meyerhold and Robert Wilson, the Living Theatre's *Paradise Now*, the haka, multimedia performance, political protest and visual theatre. Each entry includes crucial historical and contextual information, extensive cross-referencing, detailed analysis and an annotated bibliography.

The Routledge Companion to Theatre and Performance is a perfect reference guide for the keen student and the passionate theatre-goer alike.

Paul Allain, Professor of Theatre and Performance at the University of Kent, is author of *The Art of Stillness: The Theatre Practice of Tadashi Suzuki* (Methuen, 2002), and has published extensively on Polish theatre and performer processes.

Jen Harvie of Queen Mary, University of London is author of *Staging the UK* (Manchester, 2005), and has published widely on the relationships between contemporary performance and cultural identities, especially national and gender identities.

Also available from Routledge

Fifty Key Theatre Directors
Edited by Shomit Mitter and Maria Shevtsova
0–415–18732–X

Fifty Contemporary Choreographers
Edited by Martha Bremser
0–415–10364–9

Who's Who in Contemporary World Theatre
Edited by Daniel Meyer-Dinkegräfe
0–415–14162–1

THE ROUTLEDGE COMPANION
TO THEATRE AND PERFORMANCE

Paul Allain and Jen Harvie

Routledge
Taylor & Francis Group

LONDON AND NEW YORK

First published 2006
by Routledge
2 Park Square, Milton Park, Abingdon, Oxon, OX14 4RN

Simultaneously published in the USA and Canada
by Routledge
270 Madison Avenue, New York, NY 10016

Routledge is an imprint of the Taylor & Francis Group

© 2006 Paul Allain and Jen Harvie

Typeset in Times New Roman by
Keystroke, Jacaranda Lodge, Wolverhampton
Printed and bound in Great Britain by
MPG Books Ltd, Bodmin, Cornwall

British Library Cataloguing in Publication Data
A catalogue record for this book is available from the British Library

Library of Congress Cataloging in Publication Data

ISBN 0–415–25720–4 (hbk)
ISBN 0–415–25721–2 (pbk)

ISBN13: 9–78–0–415–25720–6 (hbk)
ISBN13: 9–78–0–415–25721–3 (pbk)

For Joanna Labon,

and

for my mother, Judy Harvie,
and in memory of my father,
Eric A. Harvie

CONTENTS

Part III Concepts and practices   **125**

CONTENTS

ACKNOWLEDGEMENTS

We would like to warmly thank the following: Talia Rodgers who commissioned the book, Rosie Waters who steered it patiently towards production, and David Avital and Andrea Hartill for the final push. We are grateful to Sunja Redies and Diane Parker for their eager readiness to help, and all the marketing team at Taylor & Francis working behind the scenes. We are especially indebted to the many anonymous readers whose reports shaped our entries and selection of contents and who often helped our task beyond the call of duty. For giving us the time needed to research and write this *Companion*, we would both formally like to thank the Arts and Humanities Research Council as well as our respective institutions, past and present: the University of Kent, Queen Mary, University of London, and Roehampton University. For reading and commenting on specific entries we are grateful to Jason Arcari, Christopher Baugh, Honor Ford-Smith, Adrian Heathfield, Peggy Phelan and John Rudlin. We thank Maggie B. Gale, Patrice Pavis, Simon Shepherd and Heather Smyth for their help in diverse ways, as well as colleagues and students at Queen Mary, University of London, Kent and Roehampton. Paul is also grateful to Ken Pickering for his friendly discussions. Finally, though not least, we are immensely grateful to Joanna Labon and Deb Kilbride for their patience and support throughout.

INTRODUCTION

This book accessibly provides critical description and analysis of important people, events, concepts and practices in the fields of contemporary and twentieth-century theatre and performance. It aims to be useful for students, theatre-goers, scholars, teachers, theatre-makers and artists. But it is also for anybody who is interested in engaging with these fields of cultural practice at a time when theatre and other forms of live performance continue to thrive and expand – both despite and because of the proliferation of recorded media – and when performance has become one of the most influential contemporary paradigms for understanding identities and how we interact with and in the world.

This *Companion* is organized primarily into three A–Z lists of entries on people, events and concepts. Entry topics are selected to reflect a broad-based intercultural interdisciplinarity and focus largely – though not exclusively – on Western performance from the twentieth century. The entries aim to provide information and to answer questions, but they also ask questions, pointing out the critical issues that each entry raises within the academic disciplines and artistic practices of theatre and performance, and suggesting where readers could pursue further research on each topic. Each entry thus includes crucial historical and contextual information but also extensive cross-referencing, detailed analysis and an annotated bibliography. Part I, People, includes entries on theorists, performers, directors, designers, artists, teachers and writers who have made a defining contribution to the fields of theatre and performance. Part II, Events, selects a small sample of theatre performances and other events that are either important in themselves or exemplify the ways particular kinds of activities have shaped theatre and performance and their significance in the twentieth century. The third and largest part, Concepts and practices, introduces practices and ideas that are central to these fields, both in making theatre and performance and in their analysis. Throughout, the book integrates practice, theory and history, framing these areas as necessarily complementary rather than exclusive and separate.

This introduction develops two important frameworks for understanding what we have aimed to do in this book and the critical issues we have had to address. First, it considers why we have written the book the way we have, selecting certain topics and omitting others, making choices about structure, and including sections on chronology and bibliography, for example. Second, it explores some of the critical issues that we have had to attend to in writing the book, such as issues of canon formation, critical bias, disciplinary boundaries and, as the twenty-first

1

century progresses, where the practices of theatre and performance and the fields of theatre and performance studies are going.

THE ENTRIES

Before we began writing this *Companion*, we proposed notional word lengths for each entry, both to contain them and to help us project how many entries we could include and how they should be balanced. Entries then expanded or contracted, largely as we responded to the interest different topics have elicited among scholars, practitioners and audiences, but also as we developed a sense of dialogue with – and within – the book. An entry's length should not, therefore, be equated with its importance as some kind of objective rule, though we recognize that entry length does articulate at least one of the book's structural logics. In content, each entry is designed to provide both description and analysis. In practice, we have also tried to let each entry dictate its own particular needs and shape.

The entries in the 'People' section provide basic biographical data, list some key productions, practices, achievements, or writings where relevant, and mention antecedents, influences, collaborators and followers. More importantly, they try to present the main debates, ideas and practices that have gathered around each of the people, plotting how these have evolved with time (or not) and tracking their subsequent influence.

The list of people in this section includes a range of mostly twentieth-century theatre and performance practitioners, artists and theorists. The prominence and influence of directors in theatre from the late nineteenth century throughout the twentieth compelled us to include many of them. In response both to the rise of performance art in the twentieth century and to the distinctiveness of its practices – within theatre and fine art – we also include many performance artists. Closely following are the writers and theorists, though we have largely omitted those who are known predominantly as playwrights, another large area of influence which we could not address in these pages. Those playwrights we have included, like Hélène Cixous and Wole Soyinka, are acclaimed as much for their ideas on the theatre or the social role and function of writing as for their works and craft. This is not to deny the impact and importance of many playwrights and their plays, but we wanted to focus on the live event and those who have somehow commented on or inspired it, rather than considering the theatre as a primarily literary domain. Our theorists have analysed theatre practice, performance, performance studies, and more. Some people to whom we have given space – like Erving Goffman, Mikhail Bakhtin and Judith Butler, to cite three examples – were or are not principally theatre or performance scholars. We have included them because their ideas have had profound influence on performance studies and have even affected theatre practice, although this may be less immediately apparent. Many of the people chosen for inclusion in this section are the usual suspects, but we hope we have also included some surprises. Our participants hail from Asia, Africa, Europe and the Americas, though the nature of their acclaim means nearly all of them have travelled widely and often relocated from their birthplace or been educated elsewhere, like Rustom Bharucha and Wole Soyinka. In this section, we also include companies whose work is recognized collectively rather than simply through their figureheads. Finally, we have included las Madres de la Plaza de Mayo who are united not by their artistic vision or theatrical practice but by their desire to make known – through their actions – the terrible and often uncertain fate of their own families. As well as illustrating their own tragic case, las Madres demonstrate the ascendance of performative protest throughout the twentieth century and into the twenty-first. The list of entries in this section is diverse, indicating the broad range of activities encompassed by the theatre – and especially performance.

The 'Events' entries briefly introduce the event itself and its documentation (if any exists), and chart the impact it has had by explaining its significance, be it for other practitioners, theories of performance, or communities of audiences or participants. As history reveals, some events pass by and are paid scant attention, while others, like Lady Diana's funeral, are important partly because of the attention given to them at the time. Others still, like the opening of the Cabaret Voltaire in 1916, have gained importance by being treated subsequently as defining moments. Performance is extended and elaborated by its aftermath and context, its writings and reflections, as well as its subsequent provocations to action or to thought. This helps to explain why so many of the practices of performance analysis are derived from other disciplines like sociology, anthropology, cultural studies, and increasingly the hard sciences, though this research is very much still in its infancy. We need to consider so much more than just the event itself in its own narrow time frame – the study of any performance needs to take in what happened prior to and after the event, as much as during it. Some events stay with us all our lives, shaping our personalities and even our daily reflexes, impacting well beyond the specialist discourses of academia. Others are forgotten the moment we leave the auditorium or begin the journey home. But while theatre has fairly clear parameters, performance also includes how we play, rest, interact, present ourselves to each other or strive to change our society and surroundings. Accordingly, some of the events entries deal with one moment in time, others reflect on ongoing processes and some are concerned with manifestations of human behaviour that are culturally, politically or socially highly charged. We refer to theatrical events – including plays that have been particularly influential, usually exploring them through première performances. But we also look at real-life expressions and activities that might be informed by political or social imperatives. And we look at cultural or social events (raves, sports meetings or protests) that function as public spectacles, many on a global scale.

The range of work we might have included in this section is of course vast. But the parameters of the book as a *Companion* rather than a dictionary were a given, and this set some limits. We felt that some events had to be included because they have become central to discourses on performance and the theatre. Others are well-recognized landmarks in theatre or performance history. Others still, we believe, exemplify the kinds of activities that are increasingly important to theatre and performance scholarship and help us indicate broader trends in interest and critical approach. As well as being wary about trying to include too much, we were also concerned not to present a list of events as definitively the most important. This kind of canon formation raises questions about the bias of any given selection and the risks of devaluing things by excluding them. We therefore include in our selection of defining and influential moments and practices, both past and continuing, some which are firmly established and some which lie on the periphery of both academic and public consciousness of theatre and performance.

Interestingly, we have seen live, witnessed or participated in hardly any of the chosen events ourselves. But live experience of given events is not essential to analysing them in our field (as demonstrated by the huge discipline of theatre history), even though many scholars are primarily concerned with this very issue and the question of what it means to be present at a work live rather than experiencing it through mediation. This very presence or liveness is also crucial because it distinguishes our discipline from film, media, television or literary studies. The complexities of liveness aside, the twenty-eight events represent for us those occasions in the twentieth century that have partly defined our fields, their questions and their practices. We include nothing from this century, perhaps because less than a decade into it we cannot yet see, or have not yet experienced, what will shape or is shaping it. '9/11', as it is known in the United States and many other places, was obviously a serious contender for inclusion and has been much discussed in academic and social circles. Its influence has been monumental. But it is not yet clear how it has altered the ways we do and think performance and theatre. There are nascent signs of a renewed politicization of practice, and of playwriting especially. At the time of writing, though, it is hard to gauge the long-term significance of this development.

In 'Concepts and practices', the largest part, there is even more variability in content and format. Some terms, such as presence or puppetry, are only briefly discussed because they are also addressed within more complex entries on liveness or masking. Some entries are necessarily largely pragmatic, like lighting and sound, though we never address practical issues without exploring contextual ones. Other entries are more abstract and try to clarify thinking or extrapolate central concerns. With many entries in this part – like theatre, performance, acting and dance – the field opened up vast before us as we attempted definitions and tried to rein them in. The terms theatre and performance are so embedded throughout this *Companion* that we decided not to include them in bold for cross-referencing. It is, though, through the complexity of cross-referencing, as well as in the specific context of these terms' usage, that these crucial words start to build real value and meaning.

Throughout, the book treats performance mostly as it relates to theatre, though it also refers at times to dance, performance art and fine art. It was often impossible to completely separate these disciplines, particularly in the 'Concepts and practices' section. The same argument can also be made about music, though not to the same degree. The category of music *as* music is not something we particularly address here, however central it is to the range of practices that constitute performance. For example, we exclude pieces that may have defined or pushed back the parameters of musical performance, like Igor Stravinsky's *The Soldier's Tale* (1918). There is no space to analyse such innovations here, despite their influence and significance. But we have included music-based practitioners like John Cage and Laurie Anderson, whose works have addressed issues and techniques of performing that cut right across disciplinary boundaries. Anderson's cross-media work shifts into acting with her construction of multiple stage personas. The beguiling 'silence' of Cage's *4'33"* (1952) articulates as much about the acts of playing, performing, listening, the audience, liveness and presence as it says something about music itself.

OUR SELECTIONS, PERSPECTIVES AND PRACTICES

We realize that readers will be drawn to consider what we have left out as much as what we have included. This *Companion* is neither an encyclopedia nor a dictionary and makes no claims to be comprehensive. Due to restricted space, we have included a selective and limited range of entries in an expanding field of activities and theories. This is necessarily partial and suggestive, a way of mapping the main trajectories. We avoided the word 'key' to clarify that we do not aim to present a canonical selection. Performance is about play and fluidity more than fixity of terms; canons soon become out of date or at least set themselves up to be challenged; and most importantly, theatre and performance are both living practices that are in process, evolving. We aim to convey this sense of our fields' dynamism by including entries that are both recognized as important and ones which might be seen as emergent or indicative, and by acknowledging the limits and selectivity of our coverage. This book invites the reader to examine theatre and performance through ideas, through people, and by describing the significance of certain events that have shaped these fields. But we emphasize the limits of what we have included here and encourage the reader to see our entries as only a portion of what might be considered. We also appreciate that those included did not work alone. More than most disciplines and arts, ours are truly collaborative.

We have not tried to mask or ignore our biases, which have been made highly evident to us throughout the process, especially through anonymous readers' responses as we have drafted the *Companion* and their suggestions regarding what else we might include. We acknowledge that we are writing from particular positions and with particular interests and we have tried to capitalize on these to produce a *Companion* that benefits from the enthusiasms, commitments and knowledge we can bring to it. However, we have also tried to acknowledge and explore our own prejudices and subjective interests and to go beyond them: through our collaboration; through responding to readers' reports and the editors' insightful suggestions; and through our university teaching, which keeps us aware of developing curricula as well as students' interests. To further offset the limitations of our biases, we would encourage you as readers to actively search for our prejudices and positions, take issue with our emphases, challenge our synopses, and form your own opinions about the main components that comprise our fields. Write between the lines and the entries in the white spaces that surround them. Fill the gaps in the chronology and bibliography. This is a *Companion* designed to travel with you rather than to sit idly on the reference shelf.

The selection process was one challenge, while another was to synthesize without oversimplifying. We wanted to limit jargon, while being able, still, to articulate the specificities, complexities and contradictions of our fields. We also acknowledge this complexity by marking cross-references in bold, opening each individual entry beyond its own narrow terms. The annotated bibliographies suggest further reading and explain briefly why we consider certain texts useful or important. Our bibliographies focus largely on books rather than articles, primarily to prioritize material that is most widely available. Again, these are highly selective and suggestive, hopefully encouraging further reading and research. The Bibliography at the end of the *Companion* primarily collates from individual entries that have general rather than specific application but also adds some more of interest while still maintaining the *Companion*'s focus. The Chronology is drawn from the entries and materials mentioned in the book but also includes major world events. These additions should therefore be seen not as serving theatre and performance in general, but as providing another way of approaching the book's content. Reading the chronological time line in one sweep puts back the linear shape on a history that we have broken into three categories and disorganized by alphabetization. Through the Chronology's mapping you can read clusters of activity, strange conjunctions of births and deaths, and feel the sweep of change in the twentieth century.

The *Companion* is inevitably informed by the fact that we have written it in Britain in the first years of the twenty-first century. We thought hard about the geographical scope of the book and its historical focus. Restrictions needed to be set, though these did not necessarily reflect our own personal tastes or desires. As theatre and performance scholars, our research has drawn us frequently to other countries' practices, especially in Canada, Poland and Japan, as much as to practices in Britain. Our choices and writing are inevitably informed, though, by living and working in Britain, even if this is not explicit in the content of our selections. Our own interests in international work aside, performance practice and study in Britain have been wide-ranging and cross-cultural for decades, even if the language to describe such interculturalism only developed fully as late as the 1990s. The primacy of the playtext and the playwright has shifted with the growing interest in devising and visual approaches to performance-making. Dance has continued to encroach on theatre's territory. The technologies of multimedia performance have eroded the mimetic tradition that dominated for so long, overtly showing representation as multiple and fractured and revealing the processes by which performance is made. Similarly, performance art has laid bare the theatre's tools and techniques, discarding many of them on the way and inventing its own.

In the light of such developments in theatre and its practices, it is alarming that British theatre is still rarely identified as European. Quite why is seldom discussed, but is clearly problematic and tied into complex questions of national identity, cultural histories and cultural investments. There is no denying British theatre's recent impact on mainland European theatre, through interest in the work of Sarah Kane, Mark Ravenhill and Caryl Churchill. The backward flow into Britain is equally evident in the influence of Jacques Lecoq, Jacques Copeau and Jerzy Grotowski. Festivals like the Edinburgh International Festival, BITE at London's Barbican Centre and the London International Festival of Theatre have opened up British theatre thinking and practice by bringing the best of world performance to Britain. One result is that the study of plays as the primary focus of theatre or drama studies has been increasingly challenged as being far too limited. However, we still need to articulate more accurately these national and cultural differences and similarities, as well as focusing on the rich cross-currents. The vexed questions about European theatre and the United Kingdom's place in it are only implicit in these entries and their selection, but they have been present throughout the book's process. We have attempted to speak from our own locales and preoccupations without being parochial, while honouring the trajectories of the past and anticipating the potentials of the future.

Our book might be founded on Western practices, principles and theories, even if we ourselves are caught somewhere between Europe and North America. But just as our histories are inseparable from American as well as continental European practices and concepts, nor has it ever been possible in the twentieth century as well as this one to isolate ourselves from African, Asian or Australasian performance, even if we had wanted to. We have not had space to focus specifically on non-Western practices *per se*, but we have occasionally stepped outside our declared focus – in the entries on Motokiyo Zeami, Wole Soyinka and the haka, for example – to question the hegemonies and priorities we are reproducing. Tadashi Suzuki is a world director as much as a Japanese one, partly because of the widespread influence of his training method and his writings as they are published in English. Where, too, does Soyinka belong? Our small provocations are a reminder that the frames this book uses are only a structure we have created, driven by the demands of such a publication. Such rigidity must not carry over into the freer domain of thinking. We welcome the new eclecticism of our fields and their much wider cultural, geographical and disciplinary purview, while recognizing the (particularly academic?) need to limit, catalogue, archive, document and list.

We also had to limit our historical parameters. Writing at the start of a new century made the process of retrospection neater and logical. The scope of the twentieth century also allowed us to explore the great changes wrought by the movement from modern to postmodern ways of thinking and the impact this had on making performance work.

THEATRE STUDIES AND PERFORMANCE STUDIES

However we now define it, and wherever we locate the cause, there is no denying that the field of theatre studies has undergone a paradigm shift. The advent of theatre studies was already an innovation beyond the study of drama because it emphasized that theatre's meaning is produced not just through its texts but through all its significations and practices – including training, uses of space and technology, performance style and scenography, for example. Beginning in the United States in the 1970s – but burgeoning in the 1980s and 1990s and moving well beyond the US – performance studies began to explore non-theatrical cultural practices that shared performance characteristics with theatre. This was partly motivated by expanding interdisciplinary links that proposed new ways of understanding things, and by growing interest in redressing theatre studies' potential focus on cultural practice that was both elite and Western. In one direction, led by Richard Schechner at New York University, this new scholarship explored links with anthropology in particular; examined such activities as religious and other social rituals, including rites of passage and sporting events; and observed performance practices in Asia and in Native American communities. In another direction, led by scholars at Northwestern University in Chicago, performance studies developed out of speech communication studies to examine such things as rhetoric and graffiti. Performance studies also responded to the increasing diversification of performance practices, especially the rise of performance art and body art and the growth of installation art. In this context, again, performance studies was interdisciplinary, crossing over with fine art and various critical fields such as feminism, sociology and philosophy. Finally, performance studies introduced new critical concerns that were shared by new forms of performance as well as more traditional theatre forms. These concerns include liveness and the ephemerality of performance, the politics of protest, and new critical practices such as performative writing. Performance studies has received much criticism – for proposing too vast a field, for dehistoricizing and taking things out of their social context, and for being amateur in its efforts to practice interdisciplinarity. But it has also demonstrated the profound resonance of thinking of a huge range of cultural practices as performance, and it has greatly expanded the strategies through which we can think about performance.

Whether the paradigm shift from theatre to performance studies has ended or is still just beginning is hard to tell. In Britain, performance studies appears to be in its infancy in relation to the large family of drama and theatre departments that exist. Yet, whatever the titles of the courses on which we teach, there is no denying the substantial impact this shift from theatre to performance – to put it at its most crude – has had. In this book, the 'broad spectrum' approach of performance studies has encouraged us to include such entries as raves, sports and the Olympics within our 'Events' section. The 'Concepts and practices' section includes numerous terms derived from the study of performance, rather than the theatre as such. Since its commissioning, the book's working title has changed, from a *Companion to Performance* to a *Companion to Theatre and Performance*. This might seem to argue against the increasing dominance of performance just outlined. But paradoxically, it in fact attests to the deepening entrenchment of performance and performance studies in Britain. The extent of this swing has meant that we wanted to reinstate the theatre at the centre of our *Companion*, to locate the book within a practice which is partly our history and in which performance studies' development is deeply embedded. Even if our writing is located in a field that at present is increasingly hybridized and all the more exciting for that, we can ignore neither the theatre's history before performance studies nor performance studies' practical and conceptual links to theatre. Finally, because we wanted this *Companion* to be as useful as possible for its readers, we felt it must recognize and demonstrate the current co-dependence of theatre studies and performance studies.

We have also not ignored the professional context in which we and our students now operate. Almost as striking as the paradigm shift from theatre to performance studies is the fact that the boundary between theatre and performance's makers and thinkers has become increasingly thin in British higher education. Residences, artists' fellowships, the growth of practice-as-research and the very practical nature of many university programmes have all eroded mutual suspicions and doubts. We wanted to address a range of audiences in this *Companion*, but even if we hadn't, it is now impossible to separate thinkers from doers. The two are inextricably linked.

With a growing university-level student body in Britain and the rapid expansion of our subject fields, there has recently been a fervent publication of readers, dictionaries, sourcebooks and guides to theatre and performance. It is important to ask why there have been so many such books of this sort. The growth and change in the discipline sketched here have resulted in a greater need for orientation. And no two books are the same when they try to cover wide ground. Many of the books that already exist are either theatre dictionaries or edited collections of theoretical texts. Few have attempted to make such an overt bridge between the two fields of theatre and performance studies, or have embraced practice and theory as closely as we do here, combining the pragmatic and the analytical.

It might be tempting to try to define what performance and theatre are, to close down. This is not a book of definitions, however, but a guidebook. Our subject is currently too open and its practices too dynamic to be best served by prescriptive statements. We want the entries, the networks and links these create, and the map they draw, to be a topography to guide you through a quickly shifting and enlarging field which now has a well-established and well-documented history and has come of age as an academic subject, but is moving on.

HOW TO USE THIS BOOK

Words that have their own entry are normally indicated in bold in their *first* reference in any individual entry. There are exceptions to this rule. As mentioned above, because the words *theatre* or *performance* occur so frequently through-out the book, we have decided not to put them in bold, except where they are part of a composite term. We also do not put entry words in bold when we are using them in ways not implied by the entry. Finally, we have chosen to put in bold words which are variations on entry titles; for example, we sometimes put the word *devised* in bold although the actual entry is titled *devising*.

Paul Allain and Jen Harvie,
Canterbury and London,
February 2005

Part I
PEOPLE

PEOPLE

ABRAMOVIĆ, MARINA (SERBIAN PERFORMANCE ARTIST/ TEACHER, 1946–)

Calling herself the grandmother of **performance art**, Abramović has made work since the 1970s that is intimate, physically and emotionally exposing, dangerous, and which extrapolates such practices of **everyday life** as walking, screaming and simply existing to explore their latent power. In work that bears some resemblance to that of fellow **body artists Orlan** and **Stelarc**, she has pushed the limits of her body's endurance, art practice, and the relationship between performer and **audience**, consistently investigating the social responsibilities of art, artist and audience.

Some of her earliest work was probably the most dangerous because it invited not only audience participation but potential violence as well. In *Rhythm 0* (1974), she invited her audience to do what they wanted to her using a selection of seventy-two available objects, ranging from the relatively benign (a feather, lipstick, honey), to the potentially harmful (matches, scissors, knives, a whip, a saw, an axe), to the potentially lethal (a bullet, a gun). Concerned spectators halted the performance after six hours, by which point all of Abramović's clothes had been cut off, she had been cut, painted, cleaned and decorated, and a loaded gun had been held to her head. As **Richard Schechner**'s Performance Group discovered in *Dionysus in 69* (1968–69), breaking conventional performer/ audience boundaries can produce exciting, unexpected outcomes, but it can also expose the performer to uncontrollable risks.

In subsequent performances, Abramović reduced her audience's potentially sadistic access to her, but continued to explore the limits of her endurance as well as her own masochism, her audience's relationship to it, and the powers of endurance to transform – physically, emotionally and psychically. Throughout 1975, she performed several body art pieces that tested physical limits: screaming until she lost her voice in *Freeing the Voice*; running repeatedly into a wall until she collapsed in *Interruption in Space*; and using a razor to cut a five-pointed star into her stomach, whipping herself, and lying on a cross of ice for thirty minutes in *Lips of Thomas*. Clearly these works staged violent physical transformations, but they also explored the potential for these somewhat **ritualized** acts to effect less visible psychic transformation, both for Abramović as actor and for her audience as witness.

From 1976 to 1988, in one of contemporary art's most famous long-term collaborations, Abramović continued to test the limits of endurance with her partner, the East German artist known as Ulay (Uwe Laysiepen). After a long series of works that continued to explore the endurance of pain, the couple shifted to making work that required them more obviously to endure time. In *Night Sea Crossing* (1981), performed in various locations around the world, they sat still, silent, and without eating, facing each other across a table for seven to twelve hours at a time over several days. The culmination of their collaborative endurance art was *The Lovers: Walk on the Great Wall* (1988, China). Over ninety days, she walked from the eastern end of the wall, he from the western end, to meet in the middle, where they ended their relationship. Here, they staged endurance in time and **space**, literally and metaphorically enacting their journey/life together as at once shared, separate and separating.

In the 1990s and into the twenty-first century, Abramović continues to make durational work but often with a much more explicitly social reference than in her earlier work. *Balkan Baroque* (1997) referred directly to the ethnic cleansing of the recent wars in her homeland. The **installation** juxtaposed a triptych of videos showing her parents and herself, three copper vessels, and a pile of 1,500 beef bones. For six hours a day over five days she sat on the bones and scrubbed them with disinfectant. As in her earlier work, Abramović's enactment explored physical and emotional pain as well as feelings of shame, using video to contextualize her live actions and religious references to suggest confession and the potential of forgiveness. Again, *Balkan Baroque* challenged her audience to witness and take responsibility for the violence she committed against herself. In a shift from the predominantly personal references of her earlier work, however, *Balkan Baroque* also challenged her audience to take responsibility for the larger political contexts to which it referred. In 2002, she performed *The House with the Ocean View*, living without talking or eating for twelve days in a New York Gallery installation of three exposed rooms elevated 1.5m above the floor and 'approached' only by ladders with butchers' knives for rungs. (The piece gained notoriety not least because it featured in the HBO television programme *Sex and the City* in 2003.) Audiences were asked to keep silent but to participate in what Abramović called an 'energy dialogue', in which she engaged the gaze of individual audience members one at a time. At the end of the work, she explained that it was a response to the events of 11 September 2001, and was dedicated to the people of New York. Again, she used personally depriving durational work to stage personal and social contemplation, reflection and – possibly – transformation.

While she may have shifted her media and strategies over the years, Abramović has remained relentlessly committed to exploring art and performance as means for expressing and encountering violence and pain, as media for challenging the limits of conventional performer/audience boundaries and possibilities of communication, and as ritual acts that might effect personal and social psychic transformation.

Bibliography

Abramović's *Artist Body* briefly describes her works, illustrates them with photos and provides commentary and biography. Goldberg and Warr's books provide useful context. Iles collects several critical articles and is extensively illustrated.

Abramović, Marina (1998) *Artist Body: Performances 1969–1998*, Milan: Charta.
—— (2003) *Marina Abramović: The House with the Ocean View*, Milan: Charta.
—— and Dobrila De Negri (1998) *Performing Body*, Milan: Charta.
——, Germano Celant and Sergio Troisi (2001) *Public Body*, Milan: Charta.
Goldberg, RoseLee (1998) *Performance: Live Art Since the 60s*, London: Thames and Hudson.
Iles, Chrissie (ed.) (1995) *Marina Abramović: Objects, Performance, Video, Sound*, Oxford: Museum of Modern Art.
Warr, Tracey (ed.), survey by Amelia Jones (2000) *The Artist's Body*, London: Phaidon.

ANDERSON, LAURIE (AMERICAN MULTIMEDIA PERFORMANCE ARTIST/COMPOSER/MUSICIAN/WRITER/ VISUAL ARTIST/FILMMAKER, 1947–)

Laurie Anderson works across a range of media to tell stories in which she observes society and makes social critiques – gently and with humour, but pointedly. She consistently challenges performance's conventional forms, combining and juxta-posing its media to make theatre/concerts, 'talking books' and technological **body art**. She rejects **realism** to produce dreamlike disembodied voices, androgy-nous bodies, large-scale, **surreal** stage pictures, and **postmodern** non-linear series of observations, thereby provoking her **audiences** to look and listen anew. From within her strange but generally calm, even languid, performances, she subtly explores themes of power, gender relations, communication and technological development, often focusing on apparent social contradictions such as her own impulses to be both private (for example, to whisper) and public (to perform), and American culture's simultaneous propensity for both puritanism and violence.

Although her initial training was in sculpture, Anderson quickly shifted into **performance art** when she began incorporating **sound** and herself into her work. In the **happening** *Duets on Ice* (1974–75), she wore skates embedded in blocks of ice and played her self-playing violin – fitted with a speaker and playing recordings of cowboy songs – in various public settings until the ice melted. Minimalist works like this explored properties of sound, time, **site-specificity**, balance and contrast, and challenged the autonomy of the art object and artist by opening the piece up to chance and outside influences, like **John Cage**'s *4′ 33″*. It also deliberately placed Anderson outside of the institutions and economies of fine art. Although her subsequent work moved indoors and onstage and took on a larger scale and more technology, it retained the surprise of her early work because it pioneered **multimedia** performance, combining live performance, video and slide projections, synthesized music, and amplified and/or sonically altered monologues. Her stock of signature eerie and disembodied sounds includes her own voice, deepened an octave, slowed and amplified through a vocoder to produce what she has called 'the voice of authority' (subversively mimicking a male voice). Along with sound, her performances characteristically distort **space** (especially scale), often by placing her as the tiny and lone live performer in an oversized suit on a large stage dominated by outsized furniture or gigantic rear-projected silhouettes or videos. Through sonic and spatial juxtapositions like this, Anderson happily explores technology's pleasures and potentials but she does not sell out to it, because she simultaneously scrutinizes its dominance over humans, especially in contemporary American culture. She also explores the **performativity** of identity, speaking and appearing as male and female, human and cyborg. And she simultaneously exploits and challenges the apparent value of **liveness** by technologically mediating her own performance.

Anderson's ongoing sonic and spatial experiments further indicate her dedication to exploring new ways of communicating with audiences. While her early small gallery exhibitions and handmade books used intimacy and contact to effect communication, subsequent live shows such as *Songs and Stories from Moby Dick* (1999) use altered instruments, songs such as 'O Superman' (1981) tap into popular music markets, and her **internet** and CD-ROM work uses electronic and cyberspatial interactivity (for example, the CD-ROM *Puppet Motel*, 1994). Her foray into popular **musical performance** probably garnered her biggest audience but nevertheless remained experimental. 'O Superman', which she first performed in an early version of the performance *United States* (1980), reached the Number 2 spot in British pop music charts but was – atypically for the charts – eight minutes long. Her dual commitment to experimentation and communication has led her to collaborate with some of the twentieth century's most famous innovative artists. For example, she has produced sound for choreographer Trisha Brown's *Set and Reset* (1983), Robert Wilson's production of *Alcestis* (1986) and **Robert Lepage**'s solo show *The Far Side of the Moon* (2000).

Much of her earliest work was predominantly autobiographical and often explicitly **feminist**. Throughout her work, Anderson advocates the expression of personal feelings, dreams and aspirations even as she appraises society (for example, American politics and culture from the era of Reagan to that of George W. Bush). Although, as she claims in *Stories from the Nerve Bible*, she 'ran out of stories' and switched from talking about 'I' to talking about 'you', her work maintains an ethereal, dreamlike quality and intimacy (see **psychoanalysis**). For example, her famous 'performance portrait of the country', the eight-hour *United States, I–IV* (1983), coupled social critique with observations of **everyday** events, autobiographical material and personal expression. Anderson continues to perform internationally and to explore innovative means of expressing personal feelings as well as social analysis. In particular, she continues her strongly ambivalent relationship with technology, having accepted a position as NASA's first artist-in-residence.

Bibliography

Stories from the Nerve Bible idiosyncratically documents Anderson's artwork from the 1970s into the 1990s. Howell, Jestrovic and McKenzie all provide suggestive analyses of her work. Goldberg's book provides extensive photographs, long sections of performance text, commentary, biography and a bibliography.

Anderson, Laurie (1984) *United States*, New York: Harper and Row.
—— (1994) *Stories from the Nerve Bible: A Retrospective, 1972–1992*, New York: Harper Perennial.
Goldberg, RoseLee (2000) *Laurie Anderson*, London: Thames and Hudson.
Howell, John (1992) *Laurie Anderson*, New York: Thunder's Mouth Press.
Jestrovic, Silvija (2004) 'From the Ice Cube Stage to Simulated Reality: Place and Displacement in Laurie Anderson's Performances', *Contemporary Theatre Review* 14.1: 25–37.
McKenzie, Jon (1997) 'Laurie Anderson for Dummies', *The Drama Review* 41.2: 30–50.

ARTAUD, ANTONIN (FRENCH ACTOR/THEORIST/WRITER, 1896–1948)

There is no denying how central Artaud has been to the development of twentieth-century performance, with his advocacy of physical, visual and non-verbal aspects of theatre. Artaud's main theoretical investigations concentrate on his notions of 'Theatre of Cruelty' and theatre as a 'plague', contained within his writings in *The Theatre and Its Double*, published in 1938. Though an actor, his actual practice is minimally articulated and offers few concrete techniques. The essay 'An Affective Athleticism' depicts a systematic **training** of breathing, based partly on theories from the Jewish Cabala, through which an actor can supposedly tap into emotional memories rooted in the body. But beyond this rather esoteric hypothesis there are few indications of what the performer might actually *do* in Artaud's theatre, though he did chart some basic staging scenarios as well as **scenographic** and aural possibilities. It is predominantly his theories, therefore, that have driven forward later investigations. Many of his ideas were visionary and ahead of his time and it is only posthumously that Artaud has achieved great acclaim.

Artaud worked at a time of economic hardship between the two world wars as he witnessed the departure of mass **audiences** from theatres into cinemas and the music hall. He therefore championed the theatre's role as providing a liberating and purgatory experience that could cleanse society of its violent excesses through a kind of 'soul therapy'. Operating almost as a contagion or plague that subconsciously passes out into the world through mass audiences, theatre could reveal society's hidden side. Artaud believed that performance could tap into the kinds of energies and unconstrained behaviour that a plague unleashes, as people struggle for survival against all odds. The physicality of the theatre event should wake audiences up, sensitize them and penetrate beneath the skin, enlivening their 'hearts and nerves' by attacking and stirring their unconscious. Artaud was strongly influenced by Sigmund Freud's **psychoanalytic** theories about the unconscious as well as the **surrealists**, with whose philosophies and aesthetics he identified. Another important inspiration was Alfred Jarry, the author of ***Ubu Roi*** (1896) – in 1926, Artaud co-founded the Alfred Jarry Theatre, with which he worked for three years.

Artaud berated the limitations of **naturalism** for appealing only to our rational verbal side. Instead he argued for a **ritualistic** form of communication where words could operate as incantation rather than meaning. The Cambodian and then **Balinese dance-theatre** that he saw in 1922 and 1931 respectively provided a model for this, though he mistakenly conceived the very precise symbolic gestures and *mudras* (or hand gestures) of the Balinese dancers as non-specific communication with their gods. But the synthesis of **music**, **dance**, elaborate costuming and **mask** all helped Artaud to forge his vision of a total theatre.

Artaud advocated seating the audience in revolving chairs so that they could take in the action surrounding them as the actors moved throughout the auditorium. They would then also witness their fellow audience's responses rather than just seeing the backs of heads (as in proscenium arch theatre), endorsing his notion of contagion. Giant **puppets** were to appear alongside the actors in a **mise en scène** that emphasized rhythm, **movement** and complex theatre technologies based on **lighting and sound** effects. This interest in current technology was inspired in part by Artaud's acting in films such as Abel Gance's epic *Napoléon* (1927). The subject matter of the performances he described was to be drawn from real-life events (tales of love, crime, invasions and war), with actors and puppets enacting violent actions or murders. These stories of grand historical figures should become as vivid as dreams or visions, so that the stage event has a sort of hyperrealism. This is Artaud's 'double': theatre should recall those moments when we wake from dreams unsure whether the dream's content or the bed we are lying in is our reality. The theatre could mirror life but also move on from naturalism's mimetic representation to appeal also to our unconscious, thus revealing life in its totality. In a response to Artaud, Jacques Derrida developed this concept in relation to deconstruction in his much-discussed essay 'The Theatre of Cruelty and the Closure of Representation' (1978). He extended Artaud's attack on the facile and passive mimesis of naturalism, questioning whether representation in the theatre is actually possible.

Artaud's understanding of cruelty must not be oversimplified. He is referring as much to rigour, precision and the demands made on the actors and audience – questions of process – as to the style or content of performance. He stated that people had forgotten how to scream, and that the actor had an imperative to use his or her entire physical resources to make contact with a hidden 'ur-self' in order to express primal emotions and touch the spectator. His desire to reconfigure the theatre event necessitated redefining the spectator's as much as the performer's role. Although he directed few productions himself, he did put his ideas into practice in productions of August Strindberg's *The Dream Play* (1928) and much more emphatically in Percy Bysshe Shelley's *The Cenci* (1935). His theories can also be read through his short plays like *A Spurt of Blood* (1925).

Following *The Cenci's* failure, in 1936 and 1937 Artaud made journeys to Mexico, Brussels and the Aran Islands in Ireland, after which he was confined as a patient in a Paris mental institution for several years. Poor mental health afflicted him for much of his life. He then became a heavy drug user (including opium and heroin), which further destabilized him. Many of his written statements, manifestos and letters are couched in a complex and meandering language, which is undeniably passionate, if at times frustrating in its abstraction. His ideas have most tangibly been put into practice by those who came after him. This influence was particularly strong in the 1950s and 1960s in **happenings**, in the dedicated work of **Jerzy Grotowski**'s actors, in the **spatial** and experiential experiments of the Living Theatre and pieces like *Paradise Now* (1968), and in **Peter Brook**'s 1964 Theatre of Cruelty season in London. Following on from these theatrical experiments, **performance and body artists** like **Stelarc**, **Marina Abramović** and Ulay have, with their extreme physical plundering of the body's resources and limitations, explored what cruelty means on quite a personal and embodied level, often citing Artaud as a direct influence, while Orlan read his texts during her surgical operations (*Reincarnation*, 1990–93). The spectacular events and **multimedia** performances by groups like La Fura dels Baus, popular at the end of the twentieth century, even if not 'Artaudian' *per se*, also show how pervasive Artaud's vision of a total theatre still is.

Bibliography

Artaud's writings appear in various places in English, from *The Theatre and Its Double* to Sontag's collection. Barber and Esslin introduce his life in accessible ways, and the 2001 collection has a very helpful commentary.

Artaud, Antonin (1970) *The Theatre and Its Double*, trans. Victor Corti, London: Calder and Boyars Ltd.

Barber, Stephen (1993) *Antonin Artaud: Blows and Bombs*, London: Faber and Faber.

Derrida, Jacques (1978) *Writing and Difference*, trans. Alan Bass, Chicago: University of Chicago Press.

Esslin, Martin (1976) *Antonin Artaud, the Man and His Work*, London: John Calder.

Schumacher, Claude and Brian Singleton (eds) (2001) *Artaud on Theatre*, London: Methuen.

Sontag, Susan (ed.) (1988) *Antonin Artaud: Selected Writings*, trans. Helen Weaver, Berkeley: University of California Press.

BAKHTIN, MIKHAIL (RUSSIAN LITERARY CRITIC, 1885–1975)

Bakhtin is best known in the West for his theories of dialogism, polyphony and **carnival**. All of these are concerned with literary, linguistic and cultural forms and their ideological effects, especially the potential resistance they offer to authoritarian control.

Bakhtin argued that one of the ways official culture attempts to assert its control is through monologic discourse – language and expression that appear to be coherent, unified in voice, and 'the last word'. Dialogism, on the other hand, admits and articulates differences, combining a number of independent voices, consciousnesses and styles, and incorporating laughter, irony and indeterminacy. Polyphony, similarly, describes the inclusion – but not assimilation – of many voices or, literally, many sounds. Although this many-voiced-ness might seem to be most characteristic of drama with its numerous characters, Bakhtin claimed that drama assumes a monologic authorial voice, which quells difference. He argued that the quintessential dialogic form was the novel, with its contradictory, contesting, overlapping voices, and its author's and characters' discourses interacting on equal terms (most impressively, for Bakhtin, in the novels of Dostoevsky). Despite his dismissal of drama, Bakhtin's theories of dialogism have been recuperated for drama and performance, particularly as a means of exploring the anti-authoritarian impulses and variegated forms of much modernist and **post-modernist** performance (in, for example, **Dada** and the work of **Bertold Brecht**, the **Wooster Group**, **Guillermo Gómez-Peña** and **Laurie Anderson**).

Probably more influential in performance studies, however, is Bakhtin's theory of carnival developed in his book on early Renaissance writing, *Rabelais and His World*. For Bakhtin, the term 'carnival' could describe the fair, its environment and its participants' behaviours, but also unconventional or lowbrow behaviour more broadly: colloquial language, bawdy humour and scatological references to bodily functions, whether these were experienced in real life or through fiction like Rabelais'. Bakhtin's central concern with carnival was with its social function, especially its relationship to dominant cultures. On one hand, carnival could be seen to disrupt and challenge authority by being other – unruly, indecorous and transgressive. On the other hand, because carnival was socially sanctioned or allowed to happen – through the granting of permits for carnivals proper, for example – its ability to break and challenge rules was always contained and, therefore, ultimately ineffectual. For Bakhtin, carnival's social role was ambivalent, *both* transgressive and contained, something that challenged cultural limits and simultaneously enforced them. It is this dynamic, ambivalent social effect of carnival that many have used to think about the social function of theatre and performance, from the official (for example, 'national' theatre and state **parades**) to the subcultural (street **festivals** and **raves**).

Bakhtin wrote many of his most influential texts in the 1920s and 1930s. However, their influence was delayed initially because of censorship in Stalin-era Russia (in 1929, Bakhtin was sentenced to six years' exile in Soviet Central Asia). His work was only rehabilitated in the Soviet Union in the 1960s and 1970s and translated into English in the 1980s. Since then, however, critics across a range of disciplines – from linguistic and literary studies, to philosophy, ethics, cultural studies and **feminist** and postcolonial studies – have found in his writings excellent tools for exploring the social production of meaning and the political potential of expressive activities, including performance.

Bibliography

Bakhtin, M. M. (1981) *The Dialogic Imagination*, ed. Michael Holquist, trans. Caryl Emerson and Michael Holquist, Austin: University of Texas Press.
—— (1984) *Rabelais and His World*, trans. Hélène Iswolsky, Bloomington: Indiana University Press.
Holquist, Michael (1990) *Dialogism: Bakhtin and His World*, London: Routledge.
Lechte, John (1994) *Fifty Key Contemporary Thinkers: From Structuralism to Postmodernity*, London: Routledge.

BARBA, EUGENIO (ITALIAN DIRECTOR/THEORIST, 1936–)

Since the mid-1960s, Barba has **directed** numerous performances while simultaneously developing sophisticated theoretical models for analysing processes of performing, performer **training** and dramaturgy. Barba's theatrical explorations began in Opole, Poland, where he worked as assistant director to **Jerzy Grotowski** from 1960 to 1964. Barba's apprenticeship with Grotowski led to a rich relationship that Barba has described as being akin to that between a master and his disciple. In 1968, Barba edited Grotowski's *Towards a Poor Theatre* under the auspices of his own company, Odin Teatret, which he founded in Oslo in 1964, with **actors** rejected from Oslo's drama schools. Since 1966 Odin has been situated in the small town of Holstebro, Denmark. Barba was instrumental in introducing the work of Grotowski to an international public and his practices drew closely on the Laboratory Theatre's approach. This can be seen explicitly in early performances such as *Kaspariana* (1967), *My Father's House* (1972), but even in later pieces like *The Castle of Holstebro* (1990). Odin's productions have toured to great acclaim, praised in particular for the immense technical ability of the highly trained actors. Some of these, like Iben, Nagel Rasmussen, Torgeir38
Wethal and Elsa Marie Laukvik, have worked with Barba from the beginning.

As well as touring performances to international theatre **festivals**, Barba has taken his work to south Italian villages and to the Yanomami native Indians in the Amazon, leading what he calls 'barters'. These involve the cultural exchange of training exercises, songs and performances. For Barba, it is not the quality or value of the goods exchanged that counts, but the action of exchange itself. Although the interaction is always performance-based, outcomes might be more concrete or permanent: in one Italian village the **audience** gained access to Odin's performance not with tickets but by bringing books, thereby starting a local community library which the village desperately needed. Barba frequently leads exchanges with 'third theatre' groups, whom he defines as those working on the margins of society, often with minimal infrastructure and high artistic ideals, and whose primary motivation is experimentation. Odin Teatret's own emphasis on research and a broad notion of collaboration has enabled company members to develop solo pieces and specialisms, be they documentary filmmaking, vocal training or organizing the large company archive.

Barba has attempted to create a working vocabulary to discuss performance (and especially **performing**), under the umbrella of **theatre anthropology**. He invented this term to examine what lies behind performance and performer techniques from a broad international spectrum of performance modes and cultures. He has articulated the findings of his research through regular meetings of the International School of Theatre Anthropology (ISTA), founded in 1979. These events have hosted performers from a range of disciplines and from East and West, to demonstrate and share the principles that underlie their work. Barba has considered such techniques to be pre-expressive, focusing on that which is happening before (but also at the same time as) a performer expresses him- or herself in a particular role. Pre-expressivity emphasizes how the performer stands, the **space** the body occupies, and even involuntary physical processes such as the pulse rate, which all affect the performer's communication. It concerns the energy (or *bios* as Barba prefers to call it) that exists even before the performer has any intention to express herself. Pre-expressive principles are thus part of a panoply of techniques that might be called pre-cultural, or which are at least not culturally encoded or located.

Barba has shown numerous performances at ISTA events, sometimes as barters. ISTA productions have included the multicultural performance sequence *Theatrum Mundi* (1982), which places performers from different countries alongside each other in an integrated cross-cultural practice and attempts to apply techniques and principles from diverse disciplines in performance. The importance of these pieces is still to be fully articulated, but they demonstrate Barba's ability to negotiate new terrains and terminologies for examining the nature and craft of performance as well as pre-performance techniques.

With his emphasis on the pre-cultural, interest in **intercultural** and cross-cultural theatre, seen in his invention of terms like 'Eurasian theatre', Barba has frequently been attacked by critics like **Rustom Bharucha** for ignoring cultural and social conditions. Barba maintains that his perspective is only one way of deconstructing performance and in his numerous articles and books he has argued that his approach has pragmatic value for performers. It is also an antidote to the distance with which **Asian performance** is often viewed and, importantly, has shown what performing arts across cultures have in common – what unites rather than separates them. Through his range of practices, Barba has made a significant contribution to broadening the parameters of Western performance and experimentation, helping to refine not only performance craft but also studies of performance.

Bibliography

Turner and Watson provide useful background and contextual information, including on Odin Teatret. Several videos are commercially available about the company's different modes of work, especially from the 1970s. Details of these can be found on their website.

Barba, Eugenio (1979) *The Floating Islands: Reflections with Odin Teatret*, Denmark: Thomsens Bogtrykheri.

—— (1985) *Beyond the Floating Islands*, Denmark: H. M. Bergs Forlag.

—— (1994) *The Paper Canoe – A Guide to Theatre Anthropology*, trans. Richard Fowler, London: Routledge.

—— and Nicola Savarese (eds) (1991) *A Dictionary of Theatre Anthropology: The Secret Art of the Performer*, London: Routledge.

Odin Teatret. Online. Available <http://www.odinteatret.dk> (accessed 20 November 2004).

Turner, Jane (2004) *Eugenio Barba*, London: Routledge.

Watson, Ian (1993) *Towards a Third Theatre: Eugenio Barba and the Odin Teatret*, London: Routledge.

—— and colleagues (2002) *Negotiating Cultures – Eugenio Barba and the Intercultural Debates*, Manchester: Manchester University Press.

BAUSCH, PINA (GERMAN CHOREOGRAPHER/DANCER, 1940–) AND THE WUPPERTAL DANCE THEATRE

Although she is a **dance** choreographer, Bausch has been profoundly influential in theatre as well as through her pioneering work in the hybrid form of dance theatre. Her choreography's ongoing emphasis on social experience and emotional expression has successfully challenged the formalism, abstraction and aestheticism typical of much ballet and contemporary dance. And her demonstration that performing bodies (and not just voices) can be acutely expressive, both emotionally and socially, has provoked theatre-makers to develop their use of performers' bodies and **movement** to produce both emotional expression and social critique.

Bausch's fundamental interest in the expressive potential of the body was established early through **training** with **expressionist** choreographer Kurt Jooss in Germany. Following further training in New York at the Juilliard School of Music, Bausch returned to Germany in 1962 to work as a solo dancer and, later, a choreographer. The Wuppertal Opera Company, in Germany's industrial Ruhr Valley, invited her to choreograph in 1972 and appointed her director in 1973. She promptly changed the company name to Wuppertaler Tanztheater (Wuppertal Dance Theatre) and, soon after, to Tanztheater Wuppertal Pina Bausch.

In making these name changes, Bausch signalled the company's movement away from the conservative classical dance – whether ballet or modern – that was predominant in Germany at the time. What she was moving towards was both a different kind of dance – or content – and a different kind of performance event – or form. She revived German traditions of expressionism, notably *Ausdruckstanz*, or expressive dance, which had been popular in the interwar years and had influenced her early training, and she sought in **everyday** movement a physical vocabulary for expressing personal experience. Using performers' autobiographical material, her dances are **devised** through **improvisation**. Sequences within each dance may appear elegant, heroic and *extra*ordinary, but they are just as likely to appear fatigued, defeated and ordinary, expanding the emotional range of dance movement. She also aimed to develop dance's theatrical potential, most importantly **scenographic** and costume design, 'non-dance' movement, and the use of the spoken word, sometimes in direct address. Often, the 'theatricalization' of the event facilitates the expressiveness of the dance. For example, Bausch's settings in real elemental materials – with floor coverings of a layer of earth in *Rite of Spring* (1975), dead leaves in *Blue Beard* (1977), carnations in *Nelken* (1982), and ankle-deep water in *Arien* (1985) – provoked different (including everyday) movements from her dancers as well as emotional responses from her **audiences**. Norbert Servos has called Bausch's sets like these 'poetic playgrounds' (see **visual theatre**).

Bausch's shows characteristically use montage and repetition and are several hours long, circling around themes of love, loneliness, fear and exploitation in a style reminiscent of dreams, everyday life and popular cultural forms such as music hall. In these and many other respects, Bausch's dance aims to be democratic, using material devised by her international dancers, many of whom are long-time collaborators, and developing a form and a physical vocabulary that is not elite, like ballet's, but is inspired by everyday contexts, movements and music. Her familiar costumes of satin evening gowns and tuxedos are reminiscent of social dance as distinct from theatrical dance, and she sources music from 1930s and 1940s popular culture. While Bausch's dance aims to explore democratic expressiveness, however, part of what it demonstrates is that individual expression is profoundly controlled – or, more precisely, produced – by material conditions (physical obstacles), social expectations (taboos and codes of dress and behaviour) and social contexts (the group). Movement may be expressive but, because it is socially conditioned, it is rarely genuinely spontaneous. Identity, likewise, is shown to be 'accumulated' through the **performative** repetition of patterns of social movement, **play** and games, **rituals** and – in this context, of course – dance sequences.

Bausch's dance has aesthetic appeal – being by turns beautiful, harrowing, kinetically exciting, eccentric and funny. But she is not satisfied with providing attractive, escapist illusions, and her work is designed more precisely to provoke emotional reactions. She admits she is less interested in *how* people move than in *what* moves them. Thus she aims to articulate and challenge some of the problems of daily life, especially those arising from gender relations. By repeatedly costuming her female performers in stereotypical social costumes of high heels and cocktail dresses and her male performers in suits, for example, her work evokes the oppressions of gender categories even as it stimulates nostalgia for them (see **feminism**). Further, she challenges her audience to engage with and respond to her work by provoking them out of passivity, whether by using iconoclastic movements, sets, costumes or music and sometimes **surreal** compositions, or by making her shows overlong or open-ended (see **postmodernism**). By constantly invoking the dress and music of the 1930s and staging her work in landscapes that frequently end up devastated, she also invites her audiences to think about historical events and transitions, especially in Germany.

Bausch's demonstration of dance theatre's potential has inspired many other choreographers and companies – including London-based DV8 Physical Theatre – to adopt and develop the form, and has inspired many theatre **directors** to enhance their use of the body in performance. Her work is known and celebrated internationally, not least through her company's long-time touring to major world **festivals**. She continues to be a pre-eminent pioneer of dance theatre.

Bibliography

For analysis, see Cody, Fernandes, Gradinger and Mulrooney. Servos provides lavish photographic illustration and Gradinger offers an extensive bibliography.

Cody, Gabrielle (1998) 'Woman, Man, Dog, Tree: Two Decades of Intimate and Monumental Bodies in Pina Bausch's Tanztheater', *TDR: The Drama Review* 42.2 (*TDR* 158): 115–31. Reprinted in Rebecca Schneider and Gabrielle Cody (eds) (2002) *Re:Direction: A Theoretical and Practical Guide*, London: Routledge, pp.193–205.

Fernandes, Ciane (2001) *Pina Bausch and the Wuppertal Dance Theater: The Aesthetics of Repetition and Transformation*, New York: Peter Lang.

Gradinger, Malve (1999) 'Pina Bausch', in *Fifty Contemporary Choreographers*, Martha Bremser (ed.), London: Routledge, pp.25–29.

Mulrooney, Deirdre (2002) *Orientalism, Orientation and the Nomadic Work of Pina Bausch*, New York: Peter Lang.

Pina Bausch. Online. Available <www.pina-bausch.de> (accessed 25 February 2005).

Servos, Norbert (1984) *Pina Bausch Wuppertal Dance Theater, or, The Art of Training a Goldfish: Excursions into Dance*, trans. Patricia Stadié, Cologne: Ballett-Bühnen Verlag Rolf Garske.

BHARUCHA, RUSTOM (INDIAN THEATRE DIRECTOR/ THEORIST, 1946–)

Bharucha has had an influential impact on **intercultural** theories and practices, questioning the motives and processes of the likes of **directors Jerzy Grotowski**, **Richard Schechner**, **Eugenio Barba** and **Peter Brook**. He has harshly exposed misrepresentations and mystifications of **Asian performance** and culture in their performances and research processes, particularly regarding Brook's *Mahabharata* (1985). His views have themselves been strongly criticized. He has also decried what he considers the biases and shortcomings in Western (though not exclusively) scholars' and practitioners' attempts to mix cultures or develop theories based on cross-cultural principles and methodologies. His materialist approach has led him to refute the acultural thinking and claims for universalism of many intercultural projects, recently turning his attention to the problematics of work by Singaporean company Theatreworks. Too much theorizing and too many performances, he has argued, are apolitical, and ignore the specificity of local culture, local interests and needs, as well as overriding the specific traditions in which performers might be based. Bharucha takes issue with Barba's notion of Eurasian theatre, arguing that

Barba misleadingly conflates culturally and socially specific processes in a way that ignores historical and gender difference, for example. His most notable condemnation of Western thinkers and practitioners appeared in his collection of essays *Theatre and the World* (published in 1990 in India). This book also describes an Indian intracultural project that looked to local grassroots sources and influences as a model of good practice.

A product of cultural mixing, Bharucha taught for several years in New York, though he has worked and lived predominantly in India, where he has led his own dramaturgical and creative projects. He has often **directed** classical Western and Indian plays, searching for Asian and especially Indian traditions of **acting** that can be used in the performance of European texts, like his realization of Franz Xavier Kroetz's *Request Concert* (1986–89). Interestingly, these creative works have recieved little critical attention in Western circles, and nothing like that he has paid to others' work.

Bibliography

Bharucha has written several books and articles about Indian theatre and cultural traditions and politics, as well as works like *Theatre and the World* that are known more widely in the West.

Bharucha, Rustom (1993) *Theatre and the World: Performance and the Politics of Culture*, London: Routledge.

—— (1997) 'Somebody's Other: Disorientations in the Cultural Politics of our Times', in *The Intercultural Performance Reader*, Patrice Pavis (ed.), London: Routledge, pp.196–212.

—— (1999) *In the Name of the Secular: Contemporary Cultural Activism in India*, Delhi and New York: Oxford University Press.

—— (2000) *The Politics of Cultural Practice: Thinking Through Theatre in an Age of Globalization*, London: Athlone.

—— (2004) 'Foreign Asia/Foreign Shakespeare: Dissenting Notes on New Asian Interculturality, Postcoloniality, and Recolonization', *Theatre Journal* 56: 1–28.

BOAL, AUGUSTO (BRAZILIAN THEATRE DIRECTOR/ TEACHER, 1931–)

Boal has consistently attempted to demonstrate that theatrical action has the potential to make a social and political impact. His work has catalysed the theatre's struggle to maintain a political focus in what has been called a **postmodern** age, after the fervent agitation of the 1960s. Boal was initially a **director** at the Arena Theatre in São Paulo, Brazil, where he produced international classic plays, but he soon became concerned to find a theatre language that was accessible to the illiterate and poor masses in the Latin American countries where he worked. He argued that Aristotle's system, based on the three unities of time, **space** and action as well as catharsis, was 'coercive'. He believed that catharsis, like **carnival**, is a device that maintains the status quo and keeps the oppressed passive by encouraging a controlled dispersal of 'steam' or tension. Inspired by the educationalist Paolo de Freire and his book *Pedagogy of the Oppressed* (1970), Boal drew on **Bertold Brecht**'s theories and practices, especially when his work moved out of theatre buildings and away from traditional performance structures. Under the umbrella of the **theatre of the oppressed**, he has developed several techniques and modes of performance that can operate in theatrical and non-theatrical milieus.

After being exiled from Brazil and then Argentina in 1971, Boal moved to Europe and settled in Paris, where he invented the idea of the 'cop-in-the-head'. This was to denote the oppression of self-censorship and social control which is more familiar in the West and is very different from the more overt forms of demagogy found in Latin America. After his return to Brazil in 1986, he became a Member of the City Council for Rio de Janeiro in 1992, where he has been encouraging groups to suggest the implementation of new laws through his 'Legislative Theatre' practice. This involves the use of forum techniques with active 'spectactor' participation to pinpoint, discuss and refine potential legislation to support local communities.

Boal has published books in several languages, documenting both his techniques and his theories. Partly as a consequence of this wide dissemination of his ideas, his practices have been adopted by many groups, ranging from the homeless in London to communities of Canada's First Nations who have explored problems with sexual abuse. His **paratheatrical** work borders on therapy, though the emphasis is on communal rather than individual healing. For him the theatre must question and engage with real, often external, issues and situations and attempt to help resolve them, thereby attempting to empower people. While his utopianism has been inspirational for many, his detractors have questioned the relevance of his approach in a European (rather than Latin American) context, where political and social polarities and oppressions are less clearly defined. Detractors aside, his work has been fundamental in breaking down notions of where and with whom theatre can happen, in investigating the boundaries between art and **everyday life**, and in maintaining a politicized theatre practice.

Bibliography

The best access to Boal's work is through his own texts, which illustrate the development of his theories with practical examples. The Schutzman and Cohen-Cruz collection illuminates the wider application of Boal's ideas. Babbage presents a good introduction to Boal and his practices as well as ways to apply his techniques.

Babbage, Frances (2004) *Augusto Boal*, London: Routledge.
Boal, Augusto (1979) *Theatre of the Oppressed*, trans. Charles A. and Maria-Odilia Leal McBride, London: Pluto Press.
—— (1995) *The Rainbow of Desire*, trans. Adrian Jackson, London: Routledge.
—— (1998) *Legislative Theatre*, trans. Adrian Jackson, London: Routledge.
—— (2001) *Hamlet and the Baker's Son: My Life in Theatre and Politics*, trans. Adrian Jackson and Candia Blaker, London: Routledge.

—— (2002) *Games for Actors and Non-Actors*, trans. Adrian Jackson, 2nd edition, London: Routledge.
Schutzman, Mady and Jan Cohen-Cruz (eds) (1994) *Playing Boal: Theatre, Therapy and Activism*, London: Routledge.

BREAD AND PUPPET THEATRE COMPANY (AMERICAN VISUAL AND ENVIRONMENTAL THEATRE GROUP, 1961–)

Bread and Puppet came to the fore of American experimental theatre in the late 1960s and 1970s with **protest and demonstration** performances such as *A Monument for Ishi* (1975) that utilized giant **puppets**, **parades** and symbolic **masks**, amongst other **popular theatre** devices and forms. Many early works were protests against the Vietnam War – for example, *Fire* (1966) – but they also addressed other social issues including the growth of materialism and increasing technological mechanization. Founded by German Peter Schumann in New York in 1961, the group's name refers to the company's practice of inviting **audiences** after performances to share bread baked by the company. Schumann's premise was that theatre should be as essential to life as bread. Such symbolism and the use of simple allegorical narratives has given his work what many have perceived as a **ritual** and spiritual dimension.

The collective are still active today on their farm in Vermont, USA, and lead workshops and create performances, such as the annual local piece *The Domestic Resurrection Circus and Pageant*, which ran from 1970 to 1998. Their performances happen on a vast scale often on outdoor sites, utilizing simple but bold **expressionistic** designs and community participation, either in the making and manipulation of the puppets and objects, through wearing masks, or through the communal eating of bread. Bread and Puppet's performances have a strong ideological basis (Schumann is a pacifist) and often address regional or topical issues such as environmental waste or nuclear power, as well as the impact of global problems on local groups. These issues alter to address ongoing or new social concerns as they arise. Bread and Puppet's **visual and environmental theatre** practice epitomizes a politically and socially engaged mode of **carnivalesque** street presentation and demonstration and has attracted many imitators.

Bibliography

Brecht's two-volume title provides a wealth of information on the company. Shank places their work in the broader context of American theatre experimentation.

Bread and Puppet. Online. Available <http://www.gpdesigns.com/puppets/> (accessed 20 February 2005).
Brecht, Stefan (1988) *The Bread and Puppet Theatre*, 2 vols, London: Methuen.
Shank, Theodore (2002) *Beyond the Boundaries: American Alternative Theatre*, revised and updated edition, Ann Arbor: University of Michigan Press.

BRECHT, BERTOLD (GERMAN THEATRE DIRECTOR/WRITER/THEORIST, 1898–1956)

Brecht was a major reformer of several aspects of twentieth-century theatre. He created an **acting** process, theories of dramaturgy and performance, a performance style, and wrote hundreds of plays and poems, many informed by his strong belief in Marxism. His works were meant to instruct as well as move, a defining principle of his creative output, and they promoted a Marxist vision. Over time this conviction relaxed a little as he shifted from a didactic stance to a more open investigation of possibilities. Early plays such as *The Mother* (1932) were starkly polemical in their presentation of political crises and potential solutions. This approach was epitomized in his *Lehrstücke*, or learning plays, such as *The Measures Taken* (1930), several of which were targeted at theatre workers to instruct them in the aesthetics and techniques of Brecht's theatre as well as ways of thinking. His later and better-known plays such as *The Caucasian Chalk Circle* (1954) and *Mother Courage* (1949) presented dilemmas for the **audience** to consider, putting the onus on the spectator to question and evaluate potential means to make redress for the characters' plights. Brecht demanded a critical response from the spectator, an active intellectual engagement which he found lacking in the closed cycle of **naturalism**. In naturalism, the audience is expected to empathize with the characters on stage but is not necessarily expected to think how their situation might be altered. The process therefore ends as the play closes. Brecht wanted to break down the 'fourth wall' through various devices: revealing decisions his characters made and the context in which they did so; making narrative techniques overt; and exposing the processes by which performances are constructed, even showing the actor to be aware on stage of the artifice of his or her role. These notions of public participation in change and an emphasis on process rather than product are as fundamental to Brecht's aesthetic vision as they are to Marxism.

Brecht was aware of the increasing danger of his position as a Marxist and public figure and so fled Germany in 1933. He left Europe in 1941 and went into exile in North America. He continued to write there, including a first draft of *The Caucasian Chalk Circle* and *The Life of Galileo* in 1947, the year when he was famously questioned about his Communist connections by the House Un-American Activities Committee. He returned to a Communist East Germany in 1948 and a year later, with his wife, Helene Weigel, founded the still-extant Berliner Ensemble. Under his charge this became one of the most influential theatre groups in Europe, contributing to the politicization of writers and theatre artists worldwide. The development of poetic plays by the likes of British playwright John Arden, for example, followed the ensemble's visit to the United Kingdom and London's Palace Theatre in 1955.

Of all Brecht's theatrical strategies, the most widely known is alienation or the *Verfremdungseffekt*. This is more appropriately translated as 'distancing' or 'distantiation', alluding primarily to the critical perspective with which an audience should engage with the production as well as the attitude an actor might have towards his or her role. It was inspired in part by the non-illusionistic nature of Chinese theatre and especially Beijing Opera, to which Brecht was introduced when he met the actor Mei Lan Fang (1894–1961) in 1935 in Moscow. The *Verfremdungseffekt* was made possible by many techniques, most notably *Gestus*. Actors should recognize a play's key *Gestus*, or those actions which have social-political resonance and implications. Such awareness should help make visible the central dilemma of any one moment within a production. An example is Helene Weigel's silent scream in *Mother Courage* when she hears of her son's death but must hide her response for her own safety. Such techniques might seem at first sight overcomplicated and difficult to embody, but Brecht wanted his plays also to exude a sense of fun (*Spass*), inspired in part by his contact with the thriving world of German cabaret in the 1920s and 1930s. Frequent assumptions about Brecht's work include the misunderstanding that he did not want his audience to feel any emotion. Rather, Brecht wanted the spectators to rationalize their emotional responses and to evaluate the stage action objectively in order to ascertain the social foundation of the characters' motivations and their own reactions to these. To further separate the actors from their textual material and encourage objectivity, Brecht wrote parts for narrators or storytellers, and used *Sprachgesang*, or half-spoken, half-sung text. Many of the songs in his plays were written by the celebrated composer Kurt Weill. Such **popular theatre** devices made his work accessible, thereby replacing the bourgeois as the dominant audience in the theatre in pre-Second World War Weimar Germany with a more representative cross-section of society and especially the working class. Brecht also collaborated with the designer Caspar Neher to create a **scenography** with functional rather than decorative props, which showed realistically how people worked and lived. Neher constructed simple locations for each scene and emblematic scenographic items such as Mother Courage's cart. His style integrated a spartan playing **space** – a boxing ring of sorts – with appropriate and telling gestic detail.

Brecht's reflections on and theories of performance are most clearly expressed in the 'Short Organum for the Theatre' (1948) and in short pieces such as *The Street Scene* (1938), which describes how different witnesses at an accident narrate the same event from alternative perspectives that combine to make up the whole picture. He differentiated between his Epic Theatre and naturalism's Dramatic Theatre. Epic Theatre relies on narrative rather than plot, the action unfolding in self-contained scenes that make up the total story, each of which might be introduced by a slogan or a sign. It depicts social and political processes, whereas naturalism shows people governed by natural laws and evolutionary determinism, unalterable and beyond the sway of reason. Brecht's ability to articulate his playwriting and **directing** practice succinctly and with passion, along with the model books (*Modellbücher*) which he left (these are photographic and textual documents of his stagings and their **mise en scène**), has meant that his ideas have been, and will continue to be, at the centre of politically motivated theatre practices, like those of **Augusto Boal**, for a long time to come.

Bibliography

There are numerous books on Brecht, including useful edited works like the Thompson and Sacks *Companion*, Wright's recontextualization, and the Routledge sourcebook, as well as the controversial Fuegi biography.Willett's translations and analyses have become the authoritative texts on Brecht's life and works.

Brecht, Bertold (1965) *The Messingkauf Dialogues*, London: Methuen.
—— (1970–present) *Collected Plays*, 10 vols, London: Eyre Methuen.
Fuegi, John (1994) *Life and Lies of Bertold Brecht*, London: HarperCollins.
Martin, Carol and Henry Bial (eds) (1999) *Brecht Sourcebook*, London: Routledge.
Thomson, Peter and Glendyr Sacks (eds) (1994) *The Cambridge Companion to Brecht*, Cambridge: Cambridge University Press.
Willett, John (1959) *The Theatre of Bertold Brecht*, London: Methuen.
—— (ed.) (1964) *Brecht on Theatre*, London: Methuen.
Wright, Elizabeth (1989) *Postmodern Brecht: A Re-Presentation*, London: Routledge.

BROOK, PETER (ENGLISH THEATRE DIRECTOR/ THEORIST, 1925–)

Peter Brook has combined successful international productions of classical texts with experimental **devised** pieces, as well as lectures and writing. He worked initially as a director in Britain where, in a short space of time and at an early age, he directed a large body of work, including classical European plays, Shakespeare and opera. He was dubbed a 'boy wonder' after successful productions like *King Lear* at the Royal Shakespeare Company with Paul Scofield (1962). During the 1960s his work became more experimental, and in collaboration with director Charles Marowitz he produced the 1964 'Theatre of Cruelty' season at the Royal Shakespeare Company's Aldwych Theatre in London. This was an attempt to put **Antonin Artaud**'s theories into practice, an important research project even if some of the results were considered disastrous. Other notable productions from this period include Peter Weiss's *Marat-Sade* (1964) and the devised piece *US* (1966), both of which showed influences from **Bertold Brecht**. The latter production (ambivalently titled either '*us*' or '*US*' as in the United States), questioned the Vietnam War and interrogated the individual's responsibility in the face of such devastation. For this production, Brook invited **Jerzy Grotowski** and his lead **actor** Ryszard Cieślak to work briefly with his actors. Their close relationship founded on mutual support and interest in research processes lasted until Grotowski's death in 1999.

In 1968, Brook wrote *The Empty Space*. This book launched a scathing attack on 'deadly theatre', or moribund commercial productions and received ways of directing Shakespeare, balanced against the commendation of theatre that unites the rough, the immediate and the invisible (or an otherworldly metaphysical dimension). *The Empty Space* was influenced partly by the Polish critic Jan Kott's book *Shakespeare Our Contemporary* (1964), which argued for the possibility of making classical works up to date. This notion was embodied in Brook's highly influential 1970 production of *A Midsummer Night's Dream* set in a white box – as opposed to the more familiar black studio-theatre – and designed in part like a **circus** or playground. This production was critically acclaimed for its inventiveness and playfulness, though, ironically, it heralded Brook's departure from Britain to Paris. Here he first set up the CIRT (Centre International de Recherche Théâtrale) and then CICT (Centre International de Créations Théâtrales), as he shifted his focus away from laboratory work, replacing 'Recherche' with 'Créations'. In Paris, with more support for experimentation than he felt he could muster in Britain, he employed a multicultural group of performers and musicians to research the universality of performance, not only through their own sharing of techniques in **rehearsal** and workshop but also through their productions. Notable among these were: *Orghast at Persepolis* (1971), which utilized **sounds** 'written' (or rather scored) by British poet Ted Hughes, in part based on the ancient Persian language Avesta; the African project, which was a tour to tiny rural communities in sub-Saharan Africa in 1972 with **improvised** presentations; and a performance based on a Sufi poem, both titled *The Conference of the Birds* (1979). As well as his opera productions, innovative, simply staged productions of classics like *The Tempest* (1983), and films like *Lord of the Flies* (1961), Brook directed the Indian epic *The Mahabharata* (1985), which aroused controversy for supposedly exploiting Indian culture, mythology and practitioners, a charge levelled most notably by **Rustom Bharucha**. Others such as Una Chaudhuri presented a more balanced view, and critics in the press were mostly highly positive about the piece. Brook has attracted similar criticisms for what many have considered his eclectic 'piracy' and minimal recognition of cultural difference in his **intercultural** projects, which he strongly refutes.

As well as this extensive practice, Brook has elaborated on the art of the performer through lectures and writing, attempting to define how the 'invisible can be made visible'. He has frequently attempted to reveal his processes and debunk myths, claiming – as in the title of one of his books – that 'There are no secrets'. His performances are recognized for their simplicity of staging and what he calls an 'absence of style'. He often uses the central **scenographic** device of a carpet, laid down in an African village or more often in the middle of his Paris theatre Les Bouffes du Nord, its simplicity compatible with the few representative props, a low-key mode of speaking and understated performances. Critics (and notably Kenneth Tynan) have found this simplicity uninspiring, though such complaints detract only marginally from his status as a theatre innovator of international renown. Most recently, Brook has been exploring the intricacies of the human psyche in *The Man Who* (1993), based on neurologist Oliver Sacks' book *The Man Who Mistook His Wife for a Hat* (1985), and in *The Tragedy of Hamlet* (2000). Brook's beginnings in classical European theatre have always provided his textual base and he repeatedly returns to the vitality of Shakespeare's language and the Elizabethan theatre event as points of departure. He has pushed at the borders of twentieth-century theatre, trying to find a performance aesthetic that transcends cultures, attracting controversy but more frequently acclaim.

Bibliography

Brook's own writings mostly have an accessible style, often drawing on examples from his own productions. Williams has collated many of these and has also commented on much of Brook's oeuvre, especially post-1970. Croyden and Reeves and Hunt give useful ways into Brook's praxis.

Brook, Peter (1968) *The Empty Space*, London: McGibbon and Kee.
—— (1988) *The Shifting Point*, London: Methuen.
—— (1993) *There Are No Secrets: Thoughts on Acting and Theatre*, London: Methuen.
Chaudhuri, Una (1998) 'Working out (of) Place: Peter Brook's *Mahabharata* and the Problematics of Intercultural Performance', in *Staging Resistance: Essays on Political Theater*, Jeanne Colleran and Jenny S. Spencer (eds), Ann Arbor: University of Michigan Press, pp.77–97.
Croyden, Margaret (2004) *Conversations with Peter Brook*, London: Faber and Faber.
Reeves, Geoffrey and Albert Hunt (1993) *Peter Brook*, Cambridge: Cambridge University Press.
Williams, David (ed.) (1988) *Peter Brook – A Theatrical Casebook*, London: Methuen.
—— (ed.) (1991) *Peter Brook and* The Mahabharata*: Critical Perspectives*, London: Routledge.

BUTLER, JUDITH (AMERICAN ACADEMIC/PHILOSOPHER, 1956–)

Butler is a philosopher, **feminist** and queer theorist whose ideas have been groundbreaking and hotly debated across a broad range of disciplines, from performance and literary theory to law, sociology, film and cultural studies. A prolific writer, her most influential work for performance studies is *Gender Trouble* (1990). Here she argues that gender identity is not biologically given but socially constructed through repeated performed acts. Thus, although most cultures explicitly and implicitly enforce very strict definitions of what is female and what is male, individuals can nevertheless be understood to have at least some control over how they enact their gender identities. By disrupting the sets of repeated acts which are usually taken to signify male or female, enactments of gender that are parodic or simply unusual can subvert dominant understandings of gender, sex and sexuality as well as the oppressions those understandings can produce. Butler's theorization of gender as **performative** was extremely influential – it enabled gender and queer theorists and activists to pose identity as something that is actively chosen rather than passively suffered and to reclaim formerly pejorative characterizations such as 'queer'.

Many critics felt that *Gender Trouble*'s theory bore little relation to actual, material bodies. Butler responded to this criticism in *Bodies that Matter* (1993), arguing that, while the body may be material and given (if not unchanging), its meanings are nevertheless discursively or performatively constructed and understood. Sex as well as gender, therefore, is a performative act. In *Excitable Speech* (1997), Butler explores various acts of speaking and what their potential legal and social effects for identity have been and might be. She continues to publish extensively on theories of the subject, gender identity, social oppression and political agency, notably – for theatre and performance studies – through a sustained reading of Sophocles' *Antigone* in *Antigone's Claim* (2000). Her work is indicative of a 1990s trend for theorists from a range of disciplines to use ideas of **performing** and performativity to help articulate understandings of the subject's political agency.

Bibliography

Butler, Judith ([1990] 1999) *Gender Trouble: Feminism and the Subversion of Identity*, London: Routledge.
—— (1993) *Bodies that Matter: On the Discursive Limits of 'Sex'*, London: Routledge.
—— (1997) *Excitable Speech: A Politics of the Performative*, London: Routledge.
—— (2000) *Antigone's Claim: Kinship Between Life and Death*, New York: Columbia University Press.
—— (2004) *The Judith Butler Reader*, Oxford: Blackwell.
—— (2004) *Undoing Gender*, London: Routledge.
Salih, Sara (2002) *Judith Butler*, London: Routledge.

CAGE, JOHN (AMERICAN MUSICIAN/COMPOSER/THEORIST 1912–92)

John Cage is a founding father of **performance art**, a figure of enormous imagination and influence. Working predominantly in the field of experimental **music** and performance, Cage studied with composer Arnold Schoenberg before the Second World War, after which he embarked as a composer on the pieces that made his name, many of which have gained mythological status. While a tutor at Black Mountain College, North Carolina, just after the Second World War, Cage devised the 'prepared piano'. He placed objects inside a piano that interfered with the sound of the strings, creating additional percussion when the piano was played. Works like this were influenced deeply by Marcel Duchamp, whom Cage knew and admired, and whose hallmark **surrealist** work of a urinal titled *Fountain* (1917) had questioned what art is. Although there was an interventionist approach in Cage's piano, this later gave way to the concept of chance in artistic processes of which he was a primary proponent. Cage argued that intention got in the way of the creative act and that the artist should merely divert the **spectator**/auditor's attention to what already exists in nature. He did not mean nature in a purist sense but encompassed human and technological developments too, be it raindrops, an audience breathing, the sound of a car horn, or the noise of tuning in twelve radios, as in *Imaginary Landscapes No. 4* (1951). This non-intentionality evolved from a fascination with Buddhism and Zen that Cage sustained throughout his long life. Perhaps the best example of this approach is his musical piece *4' 33"* (1952), whose impact was enormous. The scandal it sparked helped broaden notions both of what constitutes **performing** and what music can be.

Cage's work was entirely non-representational and arhythmical, as well as being conceptually demanding, leaving the audience to construct meaning and significance if this was their wont – a truly collaborative act. Although his early explorations saw him tossing coins in order to randomly construct his notation and orchestration, Cage also wrote music in a more orthodox sense, though often for an unorthodox mix of instruments, using synthesizers and other modes of technological mediation or pre-recorded sounds. His career centred on an enduring fifty-year collaboration with **dancer** and choreographer **Merce Cunningham**. Together they created many performances, espousing the importance of collaboration (his music was always conceived to be performed with a significant theatrical dimension), while stressing the need for their respective art forms to remain autonomous. In one case, Cage wrote music for a Cunningham dance piece (*Points in Space*, 1986, subsequently filmed), of which he knew nothing in advance about the content except its duration. Music and choreography came together for the first time in the première performance, conjoined by the dancers. It was a device they used frequently and that helped to keep their collaboration alive. Cage inspired many artists working in the United States in the 1960s and 1970s, including **Robert Wilson**, Yvonne Rainer, choreographer of *Trio A* (1966), and other members of the Judson Church Group, who were exploring the boundary between dance and **everyday** movement. He listed among his friends and collaborators the prominent visual artists Robert Rauschenberg and Jasper Johns, as well as pianist David Tudor, names that show the breadth of Cage's practice and ideas.

Bibliography

Cage articulated many of his complex and controversial ideas in writing, both creative and theoretical. These have offered great scope for academic analyses like those listed below, which are just a small sample of the many available studies. Kaye and Zurbrugg show the impact of Cage's ideas on **postmodern** thinking and practice.

Cage, John (1967) *A Year from Monday; New Lectures and Writings*, Middletown, CN: Wesleyan University Press.
—— (1968) *Silence: Lectures and Writings*, London: Calder and Boyars.
Fetterman, William (1997) *John Cage's Theater Pieces*, Amsterdam: Harwood.
Kaye, Nick (1994) *Postmodernism and Performance*, London: Macmillan.
—— (1996) 'John Cage', in *Art into Theatre*, Nick Kaye (ed.), Amsterdam: Harwood Academic Publishers, pp.14–24.
Kostelanetz, Richard (ed.) (1993) *Writings About John Cage*, Ann Arbor: University of Michigan Press.
Zurbrugg, Nicholas (1993) *The Parameters of Postmodernism*, London: Routledge.

CHRISTO (BULGARIAN/AMERICAN ARTIST, 1935–) AND JEANNE-CLAUDE (FRENCH/AMERICAN ARTIST AND PRODUCER, 1935–)

Husband-and-wife artistic team Christo and Jeanne-Claude are most famous for their wrappings – **site-specific** buildings, objects and environments which they temporarily enclose, surround or cover for a period of days or weeks in enormous quantities of fabric. Some of their most famous works include: *Valley Curtain, Rifle, Colorado, 1970–1972* (first planned in 1970 and realized in 1972), a 417-metre-wide orange nylon curtain suspended across a valley; *Surrounded Islands, Biscayne Bay, Greater Miami, Florida, 1980–1983*, where they framed eleven islands with 600,000 square metres of bright-pink fabric; *The Umbrellas, Japan – USA, 1984–1991*, where they erected more than three thousand 6m-high umbrellas in the countrysides of Japan and California; and *Wrapped Reichstag, 1971–1995*, where they wrapped Berlin's famous government building in 100,000 square metres of high-strength polypropylene aluminium-coated fabric. Their work is monumental, in both planning and execution: *Wrapped Reichstag* was planned over twenty-four years, and *The Umbrellas* cost US$26 million and required the permission of forty-four government authorities and approximately 450 farmers and landowners.

Christo and Jeanne-Claude's wrappings compel us to look anew at our **everyday** surroundings and to reconsider relationships between what is natural and what is man-made, commercial or packaged. They turn functional buildings into luminous, ghostly spectres, suggestively haunting urban and rural sites. Their use of fabric evokes classical art's fascination with drapery's lightness, darkness, form and volume. It also recalls conventions of wrapping bodies in fabrics, whether to conceal or enhance, in simple daily dressing or, more emotively, in swaddling babies, veiling brides and widows or shrouding corpses. The work raises issues about art's commodification. Christo's preparatory drawings, collages and books illustrating the **installations** are portable, durable, saleable as commodities, and raise the couple's CVJ Corporation millions of dollars. The installations, however, resist commodification. Paid for by the CVJ Corporation, they offer free access to the public, are temporary, and their materials are recycled, not sold. Although the work is generally attributed to a single artist, Christo, its actual requirement of many people's labour, commitment and campaigning testifies to its social functions. It can stimulate international collaboration (*The Umbrellas*), provoke thought about borders (*Valley Curtain*) and facilitate a community's efforts to redefine itself. In the context of German reunification after 1989, supporters of *Wrapped Reichstag* argued that the German government's agreement to the project demonstrated the country's renewed open-mindedness before the international media **audience** that Christo and Jeanne-Claude's work attracts.

This work is performance not least because it combines **scenography**, **space** and event. Its monumental scenography uses objects and **lighting** to produce awesome visual effects and to alter environments and landscapes radically. It is an event as its fabrics are unfurled, as long as it lasts, and as it is dismantled – in all of the contexts in which passers-by engage with it, whether by helping to construct it, moving around or through it, viewing it or witnessing it through the media. It becomes performance by compelling passers-by to perform differently in its presence than they probably would do in the same space were it 'unwrapped'.

Bibliography

Christo and Jeanne-Claude's book documents *Wrapped Reichstag*, *The Gates* project for New York's Central Park and *Over the River* for the western USA. Baal-Teshuva includes analysis and extensive photographic illustration. Vaizey's book is mostly a picture catalogue.

Baal-Teshuva, Jacob (1995) *Christo and Jeanne-Claude*, Köln: Benedikt Taschen.
Christo and Jeanne-Claude (1995) *Three Works in Progress*, London: Annely Juda Fine Art.
Christo and Jeanne-Claude. Online. Available <http://www.christojeanneclaude.net/> (accessed 28 January 2005).
Vaizey, Marina (1991) *Christo*, London: Academy Editions.

CIXOUS, HÉLÈNE (FRENCH ACADEMIC/WRITER OF CRITICISM, PLAYS, FICTION AND MEMOIR, 1937–)

Cixous is a pioneer of **feminist** thought, artistic practice and activism. A prolific writer across a range of genres (which she playfully combines), she is probably best known in English translation for her theorization and practice of *écriture féminine* (feminine writing). Because she believes patriarchal writing functions to contain its subjects, she does not precisely define this term but attempts, instead, to enact it. Thus her writing is characterized by poetry, excess, repetition, word **play**, and an emphasis on affect or feeling, including sexual feeling.

In her writing for theatre, Cixous experiments with these features and also with the apparent linearity of time and the truth of narrative. For example, in *Portrait of Dora* (1976), her revision of a Freudian case study, she gives equal import to memory, fantasy and dream as well as 'real' present-time action. In early theoretical writing such as '*Aller à la mer*' and 'The Laugh of the Medusa', she argued that dominant classical theatre objectifies and victimizes not only its heroines – such as Electra and Ophelia – but also its female **audiences**, and she has experimented in freeing her female characters and audiences alike from these positions.

Her more recent work in theatre has shifted from an emphasis on the personal and the unconscious to an emphasis on public history, focusing more explicitly on issues of race and colonialism while maintaining a commitment to feminism. Born a Jew in colonial Algeria, she has explored the links between patriarchal and colonial oppression especially through the epic history plays she has written since 1980 for the Paris-based collective theatre company, the Théâtre du Soleil, **directed** by Ariane Mnouchkine (for example, *The Terrible but Unfinished Story of Norodom Sihanouk, King of Cambodia* [1985] and *The Indiad, or the India of their Dreams* [1987]).

Importantly, the distinctions made above between Cixous' theoretical and fictional writing are probably not ones she would make herself, because she abjures conventional writing categories, combining, like **Peggy Phelan**, theory with fiction and autobiography in a **performative** writing practice.

Bibliography

Cixous and Calle-Gruber's book includes a long interview, biographical information and an extensive bibliography. Sellers' collection includes several writings on theatre. Penrod, Shiach and Dobson all discuss Cixous' writing for theatre.

Cixous, Hélène ([1975] 1980) 'The Laugh of the Medusa', trans. K. and P. Cohen, in *New French Feminisms*, Elaine Marks and Isabelle de Courtivron (eds), Brighton: Harvester, pp.245–64.
—— ([1977] 1984) '*Aller à la mer*', trans. Barbara Kerslake, *Modern Drama* 27.4: 546–48.
—— (2003) *The Plays of Hélène Cixous*, London: Routledge.
—— and Mireille Calle-Gruber (1997) *Hélène Cixous, Rootprints: Memory and Life Writing*, trans. Eric Prenowitz, London: Routledge.
Dobson, Julia (2002) *Hélène Cixous and the Theatre: The Scene of Writing*, Oxford: Peter Lang.
Penrod, Lynn Kettler (1996) *Hélène Cixous*, New York: Twayne Publishers.
Sellers, Susan (ed.) (1994) *The Hélène Cixous Reader*, London: Routledge.
Shiach, Morag (1991) *Hélène Cixous: A Politics of Writing*, London: Routledge.

COPEAU, JACQUES (FRENCH THEATRE DIRECTOR/TEACHER, 1879–1949)

Copeau's approach to making theatre in the early decades of the twentieth century was exploratory and consistently challenging to established models. It became the bedrock for later innovations in mime, physical theatre and body-based performance. But before becoming a **director**, Copeau was for many years a theatre critic, and throughout his career he continually supported new writing, translated plays into French, and adapted a range of materials, equally at home with Molière or Aeschylus as well as Noh-inspired plays. His nephew Michel Saint-Denis brought such ideas and practices to the United Kingdom through what became the Old Vic Theatre School and as an early director of the Royal Shakespeare Company (1961).

In spite of this avid support and interest in playwrighting and the text, the primary focus of many of Copeau's productions and his **training** processes was **acting**. He was critical of the theatre's conventions and stylistic tricks and advocated simple staging over decorous **scenography**. This emphasis on corporeal training inspired several people who collaborated directly with him, including Charles Dullin, Jean Dasté, Louis Jouvet and Etienne Decroux. His teaching was also formative for practitioners like **Jacques Lecoq** and Jean-Louis Barrault, who did not have direct contact with Copeau himself, but worked with his students or colleagues. Through such broad transmission, Copeau achieved widespread recognition in France and beyond.

Copeau founded the Vieux Colombier theatre in Paris in 1913 as a site to produce his own plays. He was never happy in Paris, though, and was vehemently opposed to what he considered the artifice of its theatre, a view shared by **Edward Gordon Craig**, whom he met in 1915. Having established a reputation as a director, in 1921 Copeau founded a school for his actors, to give them the additional skills and resources needed to work in an exploratory way. In 1924, he boldly closed down the Vieux Colombier and relocated the school to Burgundy in rural France with co-teacher Suzanne Bing (who did most of the coaching) and other collaborators. Here his training focused on simplicity, **improvisation**, **play** and honesty in performance, notions which he had also investigated during **rehearsals** on an earlier retreat in rural France in 1913. To achieve these qualities he attempted to strip his actors of any pretensions or assumed conventions, using noble **masks** (later termed 'neutral' masks by Lecoq), and working with a bare stage without decor. The local natural environment played a large role in this process, with much work conducted outdoors and in the community.

In Burgundy, Copeau turned to what might be considered popular theatre forms such as commedia dell'arte, Greek tragedy and medieval theatre as theatrical sources for his new works. His company Les Copiaus performed in village squares and at **festivals** in outdoor **spaces**, using inspiration gathered from the area, its people and the rural culture. He looked to **rituals** to help establish theatre's place in French society, fuelled partly by his conversion to Catholicism in 1925. He balanced his belief in training the body with cultural, moral and social education of his troupe, who lived communally in what Copeau described as a 'brotherhood'. For some, his approach was too prescriptive and his devout faith and discipline led to tensions within the school. Les Copiaus disbanded in 1929 and reformed as La Compagnie des Quinze, without Copeau.

Copeau worked continually as a freelance director until 1940, when he was made director for a few months of France's most prominent and long-established national theatre, the Comédie Française. Copeau's research with popular performance, choral and mask work, his emphasis on physicality in performance and training and his belief in establishing alternative ways of making theatre have all left an influential legacy in European theatre, impacting as much on textual as well as body-based approaches to performance.

Bibliography

Rudlin and Paul have collated primary sources, whereas the other texts adopt biographically based analyses. Kurtz's book is based on personal acquaintance with Copeau. Rudlin's book is much more comprehensive.

Kurtz, Maurice (1999) *Jacques Copeau: Biography of a Theater*, Carbondale and Edwardsville: Southern Illinois University Press.
Rudlin, John (1986) *Jacques Copeau*, Cambridge: Cambridge University Press.

—— (2000) 'Jacques Copeau: The Quest for Sincerity', in *Twentieth Century Actor Training*, Alison Hodge (ed.), London: Routledge, pp.55–78.

—— and Norman H. Paul (ed. and trans.) (1990) *Copeau: Texts on Theatre*, London: Routledge.

CRAIG, EDWARD GORDON (ENGLISH DESIGNER/ PRODUCER/ACTOR/THEORIST, 1872–1966)

Gordon Craig has been instrumental in shaping the trajectory of twentieth-century performance through his imaginative championing of **scenographic** innovation and his rejection of the **naturalistic** actor, focusing rather on the actor's **movement** and bodies in **space**. His vivid and sweeping simple stage designs rejected naturalism's detail and representational illusionism, creating environments and moods through various devices, most notably the play of light and shadow, large painted flats or cloth hangings and bold constructions such as stairways. These provided spaces in which the actor and large massed choruses could move, illuminated by swathes of demarcating light or spotlights. Craig's hallmark was symbolism, and he pared his designs to the bone as in his 1912 *Hamlet* for **Konstantin Stanislavsky** at the Moscow Art Theatre, where large screens suggestively hinted at the metaphysical dimension of the play.

In one of his many treatises, Craig promulgated the idea that mimetic actors were prey to their emotions, often vain and lacking in creativity, and that the '*Übermarionette*', or giant **puppet**, should replace them. He suggested that this godlike figure would be able to work with more control and without the intrusion of the ego, and would remind the **audience** of the power and mystery of ancient **ritual** performances. Craig championed a demagogic **director**/scenographer figure in order to oversee this actor-less vision. His ideas and techniques have influenced **Tadeusz Kantor** and **Bread and Puppet Theatre** amongst many others. Following the path laid before him by his famous theatrical lineage (his mother was the celebrated actress Ellen Terry and his father the architect and theatre enthusiast Edward William Godwin), Craig is one of the twentieth century's first theoretical practitioners and innovators. As well as setting up his own theatre school in Florence, he published many of his views in books and in the long-running journal, the *Mask*, that he founded and edited, and whose motto was 'After the practice, the theory'.

Bibliography

The amount of writing about Craig is not commensurate with the influence he has had and the volume of writing he himself produced, of which the most notable texts are in his 1911 collection. Bablet and Innes offer general overviews on Craig's life and work, while Walton focuses more on Craig's theatrical principles.

Bablet, Denis (1966) *The Theatre of Edward Gordon Craig*, London: Heinemann Educational Books.

Craig, Edward Gordon (1911) *On the Art of the Theatre*, New York: Theater Arts Books.

Innes, Christopher (1983) *Edward Gordon Craig*, Cambridge: Cambridge University Press.

Walton, Michael J. (1983) *Craig on Theatre*, London: Methuen.

CUNNINGHAM, MERCE (AMERICAN CHOREOGRAPHER/ DANCER/TEACHER, 1919–)

Cunningham has made a lasting impact on contemporary **dance**, creating pieces that have expanded the boundaries of form in modern choreography and question how dance is made, especially through his collaboration with composer **John Cage**. Cage was Cunningham's principal collaborator, and together they created many pieces that tested the limits of each other's disciplines. Their cooperation was exemplary, revealing how collaboration works best not as compromise but when two autonomous forms and approaches maintain and also enhance their own values and strengths. This notion of the autonomy of artistic elements has underpinned all Cunningham's work, even though he has consistently collaborated with other artists, too. These include American visual artist Robert Rauschenberg, who designed several early dance pieces like *Summerspace* (1958), and Charles Atlas and Elliot Caplan, both filmmakers. With these two, Cunningham shot several innovative works for film and television, notably *Walkaround Time* (1973) with Atlas and *Points in Space* (1986) with Caplan, which also had **music** by Cage.

Most of Cunningham's output has been with the Merce Cunningham Dance Company, which he founded in 1953, initially with John Cage and David Tudor as musicians. This was after a six-year spell as a lead dancer in Martha Graham's company, then time spent pursuing his own experiments at Black Mountain and Bennington colleges. His company still operates today, frequently touring internationally. In his work, Cunningham expresses the importance of dance for dance's sake and rarely choreographs for pre-existing music. This shifts emphasis away from the expressivity and intention of **movement** and the idea that dance has to be thematic or generate meaning, to focus on the form and practice itself. Such a strategy pushes responsibility on to the **audience**, suggesting that it is up to them to find meaning in his works. This was furthered as he explored (like, and with, Cage) chance processes for choreographic purposes, most notably early on in his career in *Sixteen Dances for Soloist and Company of Three* (1951).

Cunningham has kept abreast of technological developments, as a pioneer of integrating electronic music into dance, and by leading explorations with Motion Capture and LifeForms software, which allows the choreographer to manipulate 3-D human forms on computer and thus choreograph in virtual space. He exploits the differences and discrepancies between animated and live movement as he transfers his choreography from screen to the studio. Cunningham also teaches extensively, including what has become known as 'Cunningham technique', which (in spite of its name) emphasizes personal expression over technical precision. He has received numerous awards and has an almost legendary status as a pioneer in contemporary dance. Cunningham's works have been danced by companies all over the world.

Bibliography

There is a vast body of works on Cunningham's decades of practice, from articles to videos to interviews to books, a very small sample of which is listed below. These range from Vaughan's (the Cunningham company's archivist) beautifully illustrated insider perspective, to the more objective analyses of Klosty and Kostelanetz.

Cunningham, Merce with Frances Starr (1968) *Changes: Notes on Choreography*, New York: Something Else Press.
Klosty, James (ed.) (1975) *Merce Cunningham*, New York: Dutton.
Kostelanetz, Richard (ed.) (1992) *Merce Cunningham/Dancing in Space and Time*, New York: a capella books.
Merce Cunningham. Online. Available <http://www.merce.org> (accessed 21 February 2005).
Vaughan, David (ed.) (1997) *Merce Cunningham: Fifty Years*, New York: Aperture Foundation.

GOFFMAN, ERVING (CANADIAN SOCIOLOGIST/SOCIAL ANTHROPOLOGIST, 1922–82)

Although not involved directly in performance as either a practitioner or thinker, Goffman has made a deep and long-lasting contribution to theoretical debates in performance studies through his sociological investigations into the 'presentation of self in **everyday life**'. This phrase is also the title of one of his major books, published in 1959, which analyses social interactions using terminology derived from theatrical performance, such as 'character', 'props' and 'setting'. Although the model of theatre with which he illustrates his theories seems to derive from **naturalism** – he refers to 'settings' rather than **scenography**, for example – the broad application of these theories allows us to go beyond models of behaviour and character enshrined in mimesis. His ideas have gained currency for their appreciation of the power dynamics of social interactions, particularly focusing on how people present a 'front' or **mask** and adopt roles within particular social groupings and situations. In defining this **performative** behaviour as a 'front', Goffman demonstrates how specific modes of self-organization and presentation (or traits) might be agreed amongst a group or within an institution either implicitly or explicitly. This front also impacts of course on an **audience** or the person with whom the 'performer' is interacting, as it is read by them. Their behaviour might be seen as being in character or in keeping with someone's profession, or it might be construed that it in fact masks an alternative reality. This response to, and the effect of, one's daily 'theatrical' self-presentation is the focus of much of Goffman's work. While he is careful to note that theatre is not the same as real life, observing that it is so much more planned, **rehearsed** and intentional, he asserts that theatre provides a vital conceptual model for revealing that how we are perceived does not always tally with what we are attempting to show. He thus articulated in an original way the gap in reception between the performer and the spectator which occurs in real life as much as in performance.

Goffman has looked at other performative aspects of daily human behaviour in his celebrated works *Stigma* (1963), *Behaviour in Public Places* (1963) and *Encounters* (1961), which have expanded on his performative analysis of human interaction. *Stigma* considers how those whom society might conceive as marginal figures manage their positions as outsiders and resist the oppression of that position through seeking and **performing** new identity traits that consolidate an otherwise obscure characterization. **Camp** behaviour is one example. Goffman has also written about the framing of performance, in an attempt to ascertain at what point human behaviour becomes performance. These questions and Goffman's fieldwork and analyses still provide a firm and authoritative base for theoretical investigations into what performance and performing are.

Bibliography

Goffman, Erving (1959) *The Presentation of Self in Everyday Life*, New York: Doubleday.
—— (1963) *Stigma*, New Jersey: Prentice-Hall.
—— (1974) *Frame Analysis*, Cambridge: Harvard University Press.

GÓMEZ-PEÑA, GUILLERMO (MEXICAN WRITER/ PERFORMANCE ARTIST/CULTURAL ACTIVIST, 1955–)

Born in Mexico and living and working primarily in the USA since 1978, Gómez-Peña is a prolific writer and **performance artist** whose work explores and interrogates the experience of being a migrant and living in culturally hybrid communities. Describing himself as 'a migrant provocateur', he explores the marginalized and oftentimes oppressed status of the immigrant and provokes his audiences to confess and address – verbally, in writing or via the **internet** – the fears that produce cultural and racial stereotypes (for example, in *The Temple of Confessions*, 1994–97). He also works to promote alternative understandings of cultural differences that do not seek to contain those differences, and it is in this spirit that his work celebrates hybridity, particularly hybrid art forms and identities. He works across media – in print, **installation**, radio, film and the internet – but most often makes live performances. These frequently take the form of living dioramas, interactive performances/installations which display him and his collaborators – in a cage in *Two Undiscovered Amerindians Visit Spain* (1992), in Plexiglas boxes in *The Temple of Confessions* – wearing hybrid costumes and surrounded by pseudo-ethnic artefacts, soundscapes and backdrops. The complexity and apparent confusion of the material in these dioramas (including their live 'specimens') work to question the efforts of traditional anthropology to classify identity into discrete categories. Identity – be it national, racial, sexual, religious or otherwise – is not presented as unified and static, as it might be in a conventional **museum display**, but rather as hybrid, dynamic and **performative**. These living dioramas also challenge the benevolence often assumed by anthropological display by showing what museums often exclude (such as expressions of racism) and by directly returning the potentially voyeuristic gaze of the **spectator**. The self-consciously presentational form of Gómez-Peña's **intercultural** displays also problematizes global culture's commodification of identities – especially ethnic identities.

Other hybrid aspects of Gómez-Peña's performances include: their languages, which are usually at least bilingual; their 'high' and 'low' cultural sources, which range from religious iconography to popular films to create characters like the immigrant superhero El Mad Mex; their authorship, as Gómez-Peña frequently collaborates with other artists, including Roberto Sifuentes, Coco Fusco and choreographer Sara Shelton Mann; their sites, both within conventional performance and art venues and in outside **spaces**, in public plazas or on a beach; and their borderland relationship to art, **ritual** and activism. Committed to a politically engaged art, Gómez-Peña problematizes borders, be they territorial, disciplinary, artistic or between performers and **audiences**. His work is well-known within performance studies partly because he has been working for many years pioneering a **postmodern** performance activism. He has performed and exhibited across the Americas and worldwide, and has published profusely, in books, in journals and online.

Bibliography

All of Gómez-Peña's writing and his films demonstrate his activist, interventionist politics. For examples of artists influenced by Gómez-Peña, see Fusco.

Fusco, Coco (ed.) (2000) *Corpus Delecti: Performance Art of the Americas*, London: Routledge.
Gómez-Peña, Guillermo (1993) *A Binational Performance Pilgrimage*, Manchester: Cornerhouse.
—— (1996) *The New World Border: Prophecies, Poems and Loqueras for the End of the Century*, San Francisco: City Lights Books.
—— (2000) *Dangerous Border Crossers: The Artist Talks Back*, London: Routledge.
——, La Pocha Nostra and associates (2004) *Ethno-Techno: Los Video Graffitis*, vol.1. DVD.
Temple of Confessions, The. Online. Available <http://www.echonyc.com/~confess/> (accessed 21 January 2005).

GROTOWSKI, JERZY (POLISH THEATRE DIRECTOR/ THEORIST, 1933–99)

Jerzy Grotowski is recognized as one of the major theatre **directors** of the twentieth century who has continually challenged and extended what theatrical activity comprises through a rigorous focus on **acting** and investigations into performance **space** and the actor–**audience** relationship. His most influential period was the 'production phase', based in Opole and then Wrocław in Poland during the 1950s and 1960s. During these years he created internationally acclaimed productions, such as: *Akropolis* (1962), set in a concentration camp and designed by Auschwitz survivor Józef Szajna; *Dr Faustus* (1963), based on Christopher Marlowe's text; **The Constant Prince** (1965); and *Apocalypsis cum Figuris* (1968), drawing on a range of sources including works by Fyodor Dostoevsky and Simone Weil, and the Bible. His architecture-trained collaborator Jerzy Gurawski designed several **scenographic** environments for the Theatre Laboratory – from Faustus's table for his 'last supper' at which the audience sat, to a construction reminiscent of an operating theatre where the spectators peered down on the Constant Prince being tortured. All attempted to draw the spectator deeper into the performance event.

As well as his imaginative directorial and interpretative approaches and his rigorous vocal and physical actor **training** exercises, Grotowski developed several influential concepts expounded in his often quite difficult and abstract writings and statements. Key notions include: the 'poor theatre' that is stripped of all that is extraneous like **lighting and sound** to focus on the actor–audience relationship as an encounter or meeting; the '*via negativa*', whereby actors attempt to 'eradicate their blocks' and remove habits rather than accumulate skills; a 'laboratory' structure for investigating the nature of **performing**; 'holy actors', who somehow transcend their material, 'earthly' presence in 'giving' themselves to the audience; a 'score' or precisely defined set of physical actions, drawing in part from **Konstantin Stanislavsky**'s later work; and the 'total act', a moment of self-sacrifice by individual actors where they offer themselves to the audience with total vulnerability and honesty, to incite the audience to open itself in response. A 'total act' was said by Grotowski and critics to have been achieved by Ryszard Cieślak, Grotowski's central actor, in *The Constant Prince*.

The difficulty of arousing an equivalent reaction in the spectator, however carefully the scenographic arrangement was defined, led Grotowski to develop his work into 'active culture' during his **paratheatre** period in the 1970s, when all participants became actors and there were no observers or spectators. This involved long exploratory workshops led by former actors and new collaborators in rural areas of Poland and later other countries, including France, Australia and the United States. Paratheatre took place beyond formal theatre structures and buildings, and explored natural sites outside the artifice of the constructed theatre space. During martial law in 1982, Grotowski left Poland for the US to continue his work on Theatre of Sources, a search for common or shared principles and techniques in songs and movement from the world's ancient **rituals** and performance-related practices. Like **Peter Brook** in Paris a decade before, his work became increasingly research-based and less public as he focused more closely on the personal processes of the performer in Objective Drama – an attempt to derive objective material from subjective experiences through creating lines of action – and Art as Vehicle, with which he was engaged in Pontedera in Italy when he died.

This last Art as Vehicle phase from 1986 onwards explored ancient vibratory songs and the work of the performer. It was closed to an audience and was therefore considered by Grotowski to be quite distinct from 'art as presentation', which is how he dubbed the theatre work he had left behind decades before, though many have 'witnessed' Art as Vehicle opuses, even if they are not intended overtly for an audience. More than 200 theatre groups have also now been involved in process-based exchanges with Grotowski's 'doers' or 'people of action', as he described his performers in this phase. The 'master' officially handed on his mantle to his student and final collaborator Thomas Richards before he died. His legacy is also disseminated through companies who have perhaps spun off from his investigations. **Eugenio Barba** worked as assistant director to Jerzy Grotowski from 1960 to 1964, and his company Odin Teatret in some ways still continues this Grotowskian tradition. Barba's important collection of early texts in *Towards a Poor Theatre* (1968) helped establish the significance of Grotowski's thinking and practices, which were soon considered fundamental influences on twentieth-century performance, with their specific challenge to those contemplating the wider possibilities of theatre research, the origins of drama, the craft of acting, or potential spaces for performance.

Bibliography

A wealth of texts have been generated by Grotowski in various languages and in response to his work, many of which (in English) are collected in the Schechner and Wolford sourcebook. The other texts relate to specific periods of Grotowski's work: the beginning up to Theatre of Sources (Kumiega), the laboratory period (Barba) and Art as Vehicle (Richards).

Barba, Eugenio (ed.) (1968) *Towards a Poor Theatre*, Holstebro: Odin Teatrets Forlag.
Grotowski Centre, Poland. Online. Available <http://www.grotcenter.art.pl> (accessed 5 February 2005).
Kumiega, Jennifer (1985) *The Theatre of Grotowski*, London: Methuen.
Richards, Thomas (1995) *At Work with Grotowski on Physical Actions*, London: Routledge.
Schechner, Richard and Lisa Wolford (eds) (1997) *The Grotowski Sourcebook*, London: Routledge.

HIJIKATA, TATSUMI (JAPANESE DANCER/CHOREOGRAPHER, 1928–86)

Hijikata created a very dark style of **dance** that was inspired as much by European influences from **Antonin Artaud** and Jean Genet as by Japanese forms like Bunraku **puppetry**. He developed an extensive repertoire of solo as well as collaborative pieces, most notably with Kazuo Ohno, with whom he is credited as being the co-founder of **butoh**. After initial experience in modern dance in Tokyo, Hijikata's first independent work was *Kinjiki* (*Forbidden Colours*, 1959), inspired by the nationalist Yukio Mishima's writing. This is considered (though not unquestioningly) to be one of the pioneering butoh pieces, even though it preceded the actual naming of this form by a year or so. *Kinjiki* involved a chicken's neck being broken during the performance as well as scenes of bestiality and homo-sexuality. Not surprisingly, it created a great stir and the Japanese Dance Association banned Hijikata temporarily from membership. Undeterred, Hijikata relentlessly pursued his exploration of the more painful and suppressed aspects of the human psyche, including sadomasochistic sexuality and homoeroticism in works like *Butoh Genet* (1967). This was a 'dance which crawls towards the bowels of the earth', as he vividly described it. His **direction** of *Admiring La Argentina*, performed by a 71-year-old Ohno in 1977 and inspired by renowned Spanish dancer La Argentina, has become recognized as butoh's signature piece. It also clearly demonstrates the symbiotic potential of these two figures – Hijikata has been described as the 'architect' of butoh in relation to Ohno, who is its soul, with Hijikata's darkness complementing Ohno's lightness. This emphasis on form recalls Hijikata's committed use of extreme physical techniques to transform his body and surpass the habitual, resulting in forceful, often perverse, performance **rituals**. Together they have created a form that has spread well beyond the shores of Japan and which has endured long past the **protest** culture of the 1960s in which it was spawned.

Bibliography

There is little specific in English on Hijikata other than material contained in these general texts on butoh, together with articles like Nanako's and Mikami's detailed book.

Blackwood, Michael (1990) *Butoh: Body on the Edge of Crisis*, New York: Michael Blackwood Productions. Film.

Fraleigh, Sondra (1999) *Dancing into Darkness: Butoh, Zen and Japan*, Pittsburgh: University of Pittsburgh Press.

Mikami, Kayo (1993) *The Body as Vessel: Tatsumi Hijikata – An Approach to the Techniques of Ankoku-Butoh*, Tokyo: ANZ-Do Publications.

Nanoko, Kurihara (2000) 'Hijikata Tatsumi: The Words of Butoh', *The Drama Review* 44:1 (T165): 12–28.

Viala, Jean and Nourit Masson-Sekine (eds) (1988) *Butoh: Shades of Darkness*, Tokyo: Shufunotomo Co. Ltd.

KANTOR, TADEUSZ (POLISH THEATRE DIRECTOR/VISUAL ARTIST, 1915–90)

Kantor was one of the dominant theatre **directors** in what can be called **visual theatre** in the second half of the twentieth century, recognized mostly for work with his company Cricot 2. Developing the theories and practices of **Edward Gordon Craig** with his quest for the *Übermarionette*. Kantor used his actors to create complex visual scenes, most notably in *The Dead Class* (1975) and *Wielopole Wielopole* (1982). Trained primarily as a visual artist, he had a **surreal** and at times catastrophic vision, fostered partly by his experiences of destruction and brutality in the Second World War. Kantor moved from creating **happenings** in the cellars of old buildings in Poland to structured theatre pieces based – in the exemplar performances named above – on his memories of his schooldays and the very different life that existed prewar in his small home town of Wielopole. His work always began with sketches that would be brought to life by his actors, who would sometimes merge with movable props or furniture to create what Kantor called 'bio-objects'.

Like many visual artists, Kantor wrote manifestos at different stages of his working life, most significantly on 'The Theatre of Death' (1975), which developed Craig's belief that the actor could not replicate real life and should rather exploit the deadliness or artifice of representation. His actors, none of whom were professionally trained, consequently moved like mannequins with repetitive actions and deadpan delivery, representing figures from Kantor's depiction of his past. This notion was extended through Kantor's own appearance in his performances, dressed always in a dark suit and **acting** almost as a conductor, occasionally correcting a pose or speeding up the action before returning to his chair stage right. After his death, Cricot 2 briefly toured the piece *Today Is My Birthday*, which Kantor was still rehearsing when he died, placing an empty chair to represent the now absent director. Kantor will be remembered for his interdisciplinary approach, distilled through a very personal, eccentric theatrical vision. He typifies the director as auteur, taking total responsibility for staging and **scenography**, even within the live performance itself.

Bibliography

Kobialka has written extensively on Kantor in English and published a collection of difficult texts by Kantor. Drozdowski provides specific material on *The Dead Class*. The two translations from Polish offer overviews of Kantor's life and work.

Drozdowski, Bohdan (ed.) (1979) *Twentieth Century Polish Theatre*, London: John Calder.
Kobialka, Michal (1993) *A Journey Through Other Spaces: Essays and Manifestos by Tadeusz Kantor*, Berkeley: University of California Press.
Miklaszewski, Krzysztof (2002) *Encounters with Kantor*, George Hyde (ed.), London: Routledge Harwood.
Pleśniarowicz, Krzysztof (1994) *The Dead Memory Machine: Tadeusz Kantor's Theatre of Death*, Krakow: Cricoteka.

LABAN, RUDOLF VON (HUNGARIAN CHOREOGRAPHER/ DANCER/TEACHER/THEORIST, 1879–1958)

Laban was a central figure in twentieth-century **dance**, recognized now mostly for his system of **movement** notation on which he first published in German in 1926. Labanotation, or kinetography, is a process of 'scoring' or annotating movements in **space** and time that has the capacity to define energy or force as well as the weight and direction of movement. This 'script' also provides detail about the flow and speed of each movement. Using ideogrammatic symbols, lines, shadings to denote level, and minimal text, Labanotation enables the detailed reconstruction of dances and has therefore become the dominant mode of passing on choreography by means other than live imitation. To qualify these objective elements of the dance, Laban also articulated eight basic effort actions that describe verbally the qualities of movement. These include pressing, flicking, slashing and thrusting, and range rhythmically from sustained through to sudden. The visual drawing of these in specific dimensions and in relation to certain parts of the body, applied with differing sensations of weight, all build a total picture of the human in motion.

Throughout his life Laban investigated a range of potential applications of such analyses, considering the body as an integrated holistic entity with mental, physical and spiritual impulses and desires, which are all made manifest through motion. His work encompassed theatre, dance, physiotherapy and factory labour, in which he helped workers streamline and make their repetitive actions ergonomic. To teach his dance students how to rediscover their natural predisposition for harmony, balance and flow, he called attention to the rhythms and geometries found in nature and the organic structures found in crystals, for example, or the ease and careful attention to themselves that hunting **animals** demonstrate. Early in his career as a choreographer, Laban worked closely with students such as Mary Wigman and Kurt Jooss, who themselves subsequently became influential dancers and choreographers. They were recognized as part of the *Ausdruckstanz* or Expressionist movement, that influenced, for example, **Pina Bausch** and **butoh**. Laban's reputation was such that he was named principal choreographer for the 1936 **Olympics** in Berlin, though his work was later banned, and after a period of house arrest he sought exile in England. At Dartington Hall in Devon, Jooss became his closest collaborator, followed by former pupils Lisa Ullmann and Jean Newlove. These two championed his pioneering approach globally through the Art of Movement Studio, which Laban founded in Manchester in 1943. Newlove applied Laban's systematic categorization of movement and efforts with actors, notably in Joan Littlewood's Theatre Workshop in London. The effort actions were used to help give physical life to a psychological characterization. Laban's method of recording dance provides an international language of dance notation that through transcription has sustained the life of some performances for many decades and has ensured his place in dance history.

Bibliography

These range from primary sources outlining Laban's key theories and experiences to Newlove's practical guide. All writers are informed by their experience working with, or studying under, Laban.

Laban, Rudolf (1960) *A Life for Dance*, trans. Lisa Ullman, New York: Theatre Arts Books.
—— (1974) *Effort: Economy of Human Movement*, London: MacDonald and Evans.
—— (1975) *The Mastery of Movement*, London: MacDonald and Evans.
—— (1975) *Modern Educational Dance*, London: MacDonald and Evans.
Hodgson, John (2001) *Mastering Movement: The Life and Work of Rudolf Laban*, London: Methuen.

——— and Valerie Preston-Dunlop (1990) *Rudolf Laban: An Introduction to His Life and Work*, Plymouth: Northcote House.

Newlove, Jean (1993) *Laban for Actors and Dancers*, London: Nick Hern Books.

——— and John Dalby (2004) *Laban for All*, London: Nick Hern Books.

LECOQ, JACQUES (FRENCH TEACHER, 1921–99)

Known principally as a teacher rather than a performer or **director**, even though his very early career included directing and teaching, Lecoq has influenced many artists specializing in comic and physically exaggerated styles of performance. His reputation has spread throughout the world mostly through collaborators like Dario Fo and his students rather than through his theories, for he was a reluctant author. His students include Ariane Mnouchkine from France, Julie Taymor from the United States of America, and in Great Britain Steven Berkoff and founder members of Théâtre de Complicité, who met at Lecoq's Paris school, the Ecole Internationale de Théâtre Jacques Lecoq. He founded this in 1956 in a former boxing hall and the school became the hub for his **training** programmes. It is still operative today under the command of his Scottish wife, Fay Lecoq.

Lecoq's and the school's educational programme focuses on encouraging performers to work with simplicity and to use their bodies as the primary source of expression. In broad terms, it begins with finding a state of neutrality through the neutral **mask**, progressing to the exploration of rhythm and **movement** in **space**, before the practical study of **popular theatre** genres such as Greek tragedy, melodrama, mime, clowning, commedia dell'arte and buffoonery, often using choral work and masks. All creativity centres on the actor's ability to **play**. Lecoq also led a separate wing of the school, the Laboratoire d'Etude du Mouvement, which focuses on **scenography**, space and the visual dynamics of performance. Although he published his views on **performing** and performance, his impact has been felt most keenly through the continuing work of his many students, who have become directors and creators of performance in their own right.

Bibliography

Works on Lecoq in all languages are extremely limited and the main translation into English by Bradby was published posthumously. Lecoq's death perhaps spurred the other retrospective analyses, which have endeavoured to emphasize the significance of his teachings.

Bradby, David and Maria M. Delgado (2002) 'Jacques Lecoq and his "Ecole Internationale de Théâtre" in Paris', in *The Paris Jigsaw – Internationalism and the City's Stages*, Manchester and New York: Manchester University Press, pp.83–112.

Chamberlain, Franc and Ralph Yarrow (eds) (2001) *Jacques Lecoq and the British Theatre*, Amsterdam: Harwood.

Ecole Internationale de Théâtre Jacques Lecoq. Online. Available <http://www.ecole-jacqueslecoq.com/> (accessed 21 February 2005).

Lecoq, Jacques with Jean-Gabriel Carasso and Jean-Claude Lallias (2000) *The Moving Body, Teaching Creative Theatre*, trans. David Bradby, foreword by Simon McBurney, London: Methuen.
Murray, Simon (2003) *Jacques Lecoq*, London: Routledge.

LEPAGE, ROBERT (CANADIAN DIRECTOR/DEVISER, 1957–)

Lepage's **directorial** practice emphasizes that theatre is a multidisciplinary artistic activity, created by artists who work not only with words but also with **space**, objects, **lighting and sound**, **movement**, media and time. As a result of this emphasis, his theatre aims to be democratic in its processes of conception and development, and is **scenographically** ambitious in execution.

Lepage trained at the Conservatoire d'Art Dramatique (Quebec City) from 1975 to 1978, and then briefly in Paris with Swiss director Alain Knapp, who stressed the director's role as a multifaceted maker, director, writer and performer. Returning to Quebec, Lepage performed and directed with a number of companies, including the Ligue Nationale d'Improvisation, where he developed his **improvisation** skills, and Théâtre Repère. Here, he learned a version of the RSVP Cycles, a method of collaborative creation devised by choreographer-architect team Anna and Lawrence Halprin in San Francisco in the late 1960s. 'RSVP' stands for 'Resource, Score, Valuaction and Performance'. In **devising** theatre, the resource is a stimulus for the performance – an object, place, piece of music or memory. The score is the material that arises from research, discussion and improvisations – settings, characters, images and events. Valuaction is the process of evaluating, selecting and organizing the collected material, and performance is the testing out in practice of the resulting performance draft. As the acronym 'RSVP' suggests, the method aims to facilitate continuous feedback amongst participating makers and **audiences**. The designation 'Cycles' indicates that the creative process is ongoing, the performance always open to revision.

Lepage's methods show a commitment to the RSVP's principles of creativity, collaboration and process, as well as a development of their terms. For him, a resource provokes not only literal associations but also metaphors and ways of structuring scenic space and dramatic time. In *The Dragons' Trilogy* (1985), the simple resource of a shoebox inspired a chain of associations – a shoe shop, shoes and the characters to wear them – and a row of shoeboxes inverted on the stage floor produced an aerial view of the street where those characters lived. The title of *The Seven Streams of the River Ota* (1994) provided a setting – Hiroshima, where those streams meet – but also a seven-scene structure.

Lepage's use of a collaborative method of composition means that his performances show the influence of many makers: they are frequently multilingual, usually episodic and often generate meaning by accumulating associations rather than telling a linear story. Lepage's dedication to reworking his performances cyclically means they usually evolve over years of public presentation, often taking on extremely different forms, contents and meanings. *Ota*, for example, ran for two hours in 1994, was eight hours long by 1996, and was partially developed into Lepage's third feature film, *Nô*, by 1998. By evolving performance, Lepage creates work that is dynamic and adaptable to changing circumstances of production, and he allows his collaborators to continue working creatively, throughout a show's devising and during its performance.

Lepage's commitment to an organic process of making theatre might suggest the amount of technical, **multimedia** innovation his performance can accommodate is limited. On the contrary, however, he is technically ambitious, exploring the technical potential of theatre as well as the thematic significance of technology for contemporary audiences. In 1994, he founded the production company, Ex Machina, its name indicating his commitment to using technology to create theatrical trickery and innovation. In 1997, in Quebec City, he opened the Caserne Dalhousie, a converted fire station incorporating two well-equipped studio theatre spaces and a range of technical workshops and offices. He now makes all his performance in this laboratory, as well as renting out facilities to other artists.

Lepage's is a **visual theatre** that plays with images and often explores themes visually as well as through text. Justly renowned for its apparently magical ability to perform visual tricks, it transforms **everyday** objects through the subtle alteration of perspective, lighting or a performer's movements: a grand piano becomes a gondola, then a trapdoor (*Tectonic Plates*, 1988); a dinner table becomes a car in a collision (*Geometry of Miracles*, 1997); and the door to a washing machine becomes an aquarium and then the window on a rocket ship, through which the audience looks both out and in (*The Far Side of the Moon*, 2000). Thematically, Lepage's work consistently explores the effects of **intercultural** exchange, the fluidity of identities (national, ethnic and sexual), the cultural significance of historic events (Hiroshima's bombing in *Ota*, the space race in *The Far Side of the Moon*), and the function of art as well as the lives of artists – the eponymous artist of *Vinci* (1986), Jean Cocteau and Miles Davis in *Needles and Opium* (1991) and Frank Lloyd Wright in *Geometry*.

A dedicated multidisciplinary artist, Lepage has directed theatre, opera and feature film – films include *The Confessional* (1995), *Polygraph* (1996) and *Possible Worlds* (2000). One of the leading directors of his generation, he has directed auspicious productions around the world, including Strindberg's *A Dream Play* for Sweden's National Theatre (1995), Shakespeare's *A Midsummer Night's Dream* for Britain's National Theatre (1992) and Michael Nyman's opera version of *The Tempest*, *Noises, Sounds and Sweet Airs*, at the Globe in Tokyo (1994). Some critics suggest that Lepage's peripatetic, organic and **postmodern** style of directing engenders a lack of cultural specificity and a thematic superficiality in his productions. He is certainly aiming to limit his own travel by founding his Caserne Dalhousie, but he remains committed to a collaborative style which, whatever its detractions, continues to produce a theatre rich in opportunities for its makers and rich in visual pleasures for its audiences.

Bibliography

Charest's book is based on interviews with Lepage. Bunzli provides a detailed critical introduction to Lepage's work, the essays collected in Donohoe and Koustas develop this critical context, and Harvie and Dundjerovic focus analysis in relation to postmodernism and film respectively.

Bunzli, James (1999) 'The Geography of Creation: Décalage as Impulse, Process, and Outcome in the Theatre of Robert Lepage', *The Drama Review* 43.1 (T161): 79–103.

Charest, Rémy ([1995] 1997) *Robert Lepage: Connecting Flights*, trans. Wanda Romer Taylor, London: Methuen.

Donohoe, Joseph I. and Jane M. Koustas (eds) (2000) *Theater* sans Frontières: *Essays on the Dramatic Universe of Robert Lepage*, East Lansing: Michigan State University Press.

Dundjerovic, Aleksandar (2003) *The Cinema of Robert Lepage: The Poetics of Memory*, London/New York: Wallflower/Columbia University Press.

Ex Machina. Online. Available <http://www.exmachina.qc.ca/intro.htm> (accessed 10 February 2005).

Harvie, Jennifer (2002) 'Robert Lepage', in *Postmodernism: The Key Figures*, Hans Bertens and Joseph Natoli (eds), Oxford: Blackwell.

Lepage, Robert and Marie Brassard (1997) *Polygraph*, London: Methuen.

—— and Ex Machina (1996) *The Seven Streams of the River Ota*, London: Methuen.

MADRES DE LA PLAZA DE MAYO, LAS (THE MOTHERS OF THE PLAZA DE MAYO, ARGENTINEAN PROTESTORS, ACTIVE 1977–)

Since 1977, these women have protested publicly against the 'disappearance' of their adult children during Argentina's brutal military dictatorship, commonly known as the 'Dirty War' (1976–83). Through their **protests**, the Madres have brought international attention to the human rights violations committed in Argentina during this time, won retribution against some of those who committed the crimes, and pioneered a form of community organization and action that has since been imitated by **feminist** and women's groups around the world.

The Madres' movement began in April 1977, when fourteen women met publicly to demand information. They had encountered each other previously in government offices and courts while searching in vain for their children. Now they gathered in the Plaza de Mayo – the central square in Buenos Aires, facing the presidential palace and in the heart of the capital's financial and political district. Gradually the women began to identify as a group, calling themselves the 'Mothers of the Plaza de Mayo' and wearing white headscarves in order to recognize one another and to be recognized. Within three months, 150 mostly elderly women had joined the Madres. They met weekly to walk slowly, arm in arm, around the Plaza, carrying placards with information about the 'disappeared', wearing their children's photographs on cards around their necks, and sometimes stopping at a microphone to address questions concerning their children to the presidential palace. Like the Chinese who gathered in **Tiananmen Square** in 1989, the Madres occupied and altered a site of state authority in order to challenge the state's claim to that power.

By successfully garnering national and international attention for the 30,000 'disappeared', the Madres' protest threatened the Argentine authorities. In response, the authorities made twelve of the Madres themselves 'disappear' and intermittently banned the women from the Plaza. Despite these circumstances, and now despite the fact the dictatorship has long since ended, the Madres continue to protest, still seeking information, compensation and retribution. They challenge the military's dominance of the public sphere and its 'forgetting' of the Madres' children by presenting an alternative narrative of both the Argentine nation and of gender. In their protests, the Madres remember, record and make visible the names and faces of the 'disappeared' and challenge oppressive patriarchal definitions of motherhood that would have them stay at home and keep silent.

Bibliography

Taylor has written most extensively about this group from a performance studies perspective, especially in her publications of 1997 and 1998. For further resources, see the Madres' Spanish-language website.

Asociación Madres de Plaza de Mayo. Online. Available <http://www.madres.org/> (accessed 9 June 2004).

Taylor, Diana (1997) *Disappearing Acts: Spectacles of Gender and Nationalism in Argentina's 'Dirty War'*, Durham and London: Duke University Press.

—— (1998) 'Making a Spectacle: The Mothers of the Plaza de Mayo', in *Radical Street Performance: An International Anthology*, Jan Cohen-Cruz (ed.), London: Routledge, pp.74–85.

—— (2003) *The Archive and the Repertoire: Performing Cultural Memory in the Americas*, Durham, NC: Duke University Press.

MARKET THEATRE (FOUNDED JOHANNESBURG, SOUTH AFRICA, 1976)

The Market Theatre was founded in the apartheid era by Barney Simon and Mannie Manim and has come to be recognized by many as South Africa's unofficial 'national' theatre as well as a crucible for political critique and engagement. In the wake of the Soweto riots in June 1976, the Market aimed first to produce and host European and African theatre that would raise the consciousness of white South Africans about the inequities of apartheid – inequities which the State tried to mask through social segregation and media control. Second, the Market aimed to produce theatre that would eventually offer black South African artists opportunities for performing in politically meaningful contexts, rather than the commercially driven, white-produced, 'traditional' (exoticizing) musicals they were otherwise often contained within and exploited by (compare with **interculturalism**). Third, it aimed to attract and address both white and black **audiences**, a revolutionary objective in an era when segregation was still legally enforced.

Throughout its first decade and a half, the company focused on producing new South African performances that provided social and political critique, especially of apartheid and its related effects of racial and class discrimination. The predominant production aesthetic was 'poor', evoking the aesthetics, conditions and traditions of black township performance, and seeking – in the traditions of both **Jerzy Grotowski**'s 'poor theatre' and **Peter Brook**'s 'rough theatre' – to foreground the energies of its performers. Performances were sometimes scripted; indeed, the Market has premiered many of the plays of pre-eminent South African playwright Athol Fugard, as well as plays by Zakes Mda and Mbongeni Ngema, among others. But the Market is better known for the workshop style of its most famous productions, including *Born in the RSA* (1985) and *Woza Albert!* (1986). The practice of collectively **devising** productions was developed by Simon following his work with Joan Littlewood at the Theatre Royal in east London in the 1950s and it has, in turn, influenced not only Market productions but contemporary theatre production in South Africa more broadly.

Thanks to its liberal practices, the Market was one of the only South African theatre companies of the apartheid era to bypass other nations' anti-apartheid boycotts and to tour successfully on the international circuit, garnering an international celebrity, which may in turn have protected it from domestic prosecution and allowed it to continue its liberal practices. Nevertheless, and despite its ostensibly liberal politics, the Market has been criticized both during and after apartheid for reinforcing South Africa's deeply entrenched internal imperial relations. Some argue that the Market's commercial priorities reinforce economic apartheid: it accepts private sponsorship and is keen to maintain a wealthy (and therefore mostly white) audience. Others argue the theatre is fundamentally Eurocentric: it emphasizes literary textual production, its audience is predominantly educated and white, it often imports European plays and **directors**, and it relies on bringing black audiences to it, rather than going to them. In the context of South Africa's difficult transition out of apartheid, the Market Theatre illustrates some of the potentials and pitfalls of a history spent balanced precariously on the boundaries of what was and is legal, socially challenging but not overly antagonistic, and economically viable.

Bibliography

Fuchs and Schwartz provide historical information. Solberg includes an interview with Market co-founder, Mannie Manim.

Fuchs, Anne (2002) *Playing the Market: The Market Theatre, Johannesburg*, revised and updated edition, Amsterdam: Rodopi.

Market Theatre. Online. Available <http://www.markettheatre.co.za> (accessed 13 January 2005).

Schwartz, Pat (1988) *The Best of Company: The Story of Johannesburg's Market Theatre*, Craighall, South Africa: Donker.

Solberg, Rolf (1999) *Alternative Theatre in South Africa: Talks with Prime Movers since the 1970s*, Scottsville, South Africa: University of Natal Press.

MEYERHOLD, VSEVOLOD (RUSSIAN THEATRE DIRECTOR/ ACTOR/TEACHER, 1874–1940)

Meyerhold is remembered predominantly for his radically stylized theatre productions and his invention of biomechanics for performer **training**, both of which have helped to displace the dominance of **naturalism** in Western theatre. His style focused on the performer's physicality or plasticity rather than psychological realism or the play text. Meyerhold began by **directing** and **acting** very successfully in some of the earliest productions of Anton Chekhov in Russia, including those directed by **Konstantin Stanislavsky**. Stanislavsky was his teacher, director and mentor, and helped Meyerhold by founding and letting him run the Moscow Art Theatre Studio. Later though – especially after the 1917 Revolution – Meyerhold became convinced that naturalism was an elitist form, so he more doggedly pursued other ways to draw the masses into the theatre. This, he believed, could be done using performance techniques from commedia dell'arte, **circus** and gymnastics, turning the actor into a minstrel or jongleur figure. His biomechanical exercises helped him put into practice this clear vision of a non-naturalistic, **popular theatre**. His belief that the director and actor should construct the **mise en scène** together and that this collaboration was central to the production process itself and should override the director as interpreter of the playwright's text, were at odds with Stanislavsky's own vision. His rejection of naturalism, which he had begun as early as 1903 in experiments with symbolism, finally led to a split from Stanislavsky as patron.

Recent interest in Meyerhold's work, promulgated in part by **Eugenio Barba**, has focused extensively on his biomechanics. Meyerhold **devised** these exercises partly in response to Frederick Winslow Taylor's time and motion studies and his investigation into ergonomic efficiency at work. Similar to **Rudolf von Laban**'s later research into efficiency of **movement** in factories, Taylor attempted to raise workers' output by streamlining their physical labour. Biomechanics also attempted to encourage the performer's awareness of 'excitation', based on his belief that the theatre event comprises a series of physical, visceral interactions that take place between the performer and the **spectator** – the physical action of the former exciting an embodied response in the latter. The twenty or so exercises Meyerhold developed, such as 'Shooting the arrow' or 'The jump on the shoulder', were broken down into their constituent elements as a cycle of actions and responses, testing the performer's reflexes by building muscular strength and dexterity, and refining **spatial** awareness, in particular in relation to other performers. All the exercises begin with the *dactyl*, a short energizing and focusing movement. Biomechanics helped Meyerhold instil, in the spirit of the Revolution, his vision of the theatre as a spectacular event with popular appeal, using precise rhythms and vibrant musicality. He nurtured a great interest in **music and performance** and directed many operas.

Meyerhold's most celebrated and challenging productions were his versions of Vladimir Mayakovsky's *Mystery-Bouffe* (1918) and *The Government Inspector* (1926) by Nikolai Gogol. The latter piece implicitly praised the Revolution in its critique of the bourgeoisie under Tsar Nicholas. His *Magnanimous Cuckold* (1922), the first production to use biomechanics, typified his work with Constructivist sets, reflecting the aspirations of a movement that championed the use of 'real space and real materials'. This ethos carried through into several productions, whose **scenography** included ramps, scaffolding, wheels and ladders that enhanced and dynamized the performers' movement and provided frames for mass choral groupings. Meyerhold also developed a style that he labelled 'grotesque', a combination of the exalted and the base, the comic and the tragic, in an incongruous and exaggerated mix of performance modes, characters and events.

Meyerhold's relations with the Russian authorities were often fraught, and in 1940, a year after his wife had been officially executed and after years of public attacks of his work, he was imprisoned and then shot dead. Ironically, his work was labelled anti-Communist, even though he had strongly supported the Revolution. Meyerhold was officially rehabilitated in 1956 after Stalin was denounced. He is now considered one of the twentieth century's most important directors and has belatedly achieved rightful recognition in the West as well as Russia, following growing interest in stylized and non-text-based theatre, as well as physical methods of performer training. He is celebrated not just for his personal fight for innovation but as much for his realization of a system for preparing the actor for stylized work. Meyerhold demonstrates the artfulness and stamina needed to invent a new theatre performance style, to challenge accepted conventions, and to question the works and thinking of predecessors and mentors.

Bibliography

Braun, Leach and Pitches are all well-recognized English scholars who have written key texts on Meyerhold's life, theories and practice. The Gladkov and Rudnitsky books are important texts amongst an increasing number of translations (from Russian) of books on Meyerhold. The Arts Archives videos focus on biomechanics.

Arts Archives. Online. Available <http://www.arts-archives.org> (accessed 1 November 2004).
Braun, Edward ([1979] 1995) *Meyerhold: A Revolution in Theatre*, revised edition, London: Methuen.
Gladkov, Aleksandr (1997) *Meyerhold Speaks/Meyerhold Rehearses*, Amsterdam: Harwood.
Leach, Robert (1989) *Vsevolod Meyerhold*, Cambridge: Cambridge University Press.
Pitches, Jonathan (2003) *Vsevolod Meyerhold*, London: Routledge.
Rudnitsky, Konstantin (1981) *Meyerhold the Director*, Ann Arbor: Ardis.

ORLAN (FRENCH MULTIMEDIA AND PERFORMANCE ARTIST, 1947–)

Orlan is best known for her series of operation-performances, *The Reincarnation of Saint Orlan* (1990–93), but she has been making **performance art** for much longer – arguably since 1962, when she first 'reincarnated' herself by changing her name to the sexually ambiguous Orlan. Her work is consistently **feminist**, questioning traditional definitions of femininity and challenging the institutions – from art **historiography**, to the Catholic Church, to the plastic surgery industry – that produce and enforce those definitions.

From her earliest work in the 1960s, Orlan, like **Annie Sprinkle**, has challenged cultural taboos that enforce female propriety and domesticity. In an inversion of the conventionally private staining of the honeymoon sheets with blood from the virgin bride's broken hymen, Orlan invited male artists and gallery workers to provide her with sperm, with which she stained the sheets from her trousseau (the domestic linens collected by her mother for when Orlan wed). In *Chiaroscuro Sewing* (1968), she did sloppy embroidery around the stains, confounding the expectation that she should be competent at this traditionally 'feminine' craft.

Since 1971, when she adopted the persona of St Orlan, her work has increasingly made reference to religious iconography and its fetishization of female figures, especially the Madonna (compare with **Guillermo Gómez-Peña**'s *Temple of Confessions*, 1994–97). In *One-Off Striptease with Trousseau Sheets* (1975) she stripped but adopted poses from religious paintings and sculpture, thus combining high and low cultural references, challenging their social esteem as respectively worthy and contemptible, and testing binary definitions of the female as exclusively either virgin or whore. In other **body art** pieces and/or living sculptures, Orlan appeared draped in sheets, black vinyl or white leatherette, testing the sanctity of the religious icon, irreverently portraying the saint as fetish object, and demonstrating that fine art's proclivity to make iconic various parts of a woman's body – the hand, the face, the breast – has literally chopped women up.

Orlan's work explores the female subject of art and religious history not only as object of the gaze but also as economic commodity. Her photo-sculpture *The Kiss of the Artist* (1976) combined the torso of a naked woman (Orlan) with a slot at the throat inviting the audience to insert five francs and with a container at the crotch to catch the money. When money dropped into the container, Orlan would leap out to kiss the person who had paid. In a gesture that *Reincarnation* would enhance, *The Kiss* commented on the art market's economy of commodifying the female nude, partially subverting that economy by making Orlan the beneficiary of the financial transaction.

From 1976 to 1984, Orlan's work concentrated on challenging the male dominance of **space** as well as the dominance of certain masculine art practices. In a series of **site-specific** *Measurings*, she used her own body to take the measure of various environments, offering a female – or gynometric – assessment of male-designed churches, museums and streets, including the rue Victor Hugo. She also responded to Yves Klein's *Anthropométries* (1958–60), paintings in which the fully dressed male artist daubed naked women's bodies in paint and verbally and physically directed their movements on a canvas. After her *Measurings*, Orlan would wash her trousseau sheet costume and preserve the dirty washing water as a relic – a practice of preserving and celebrating the abject residue which she would later develop in her *Reincarnation*.

Orlan continues to make performance art and images that challenge received notions of gender identity and gendered mythologies, frequently recycling – or reincarnating – her own previous work. Her *Self-Hybridizations* (1999), for example, use digital technologies to produce hybrid **intercultural** images that combine Orlan's face with faces from African and pre-Columbian Central American art. In her *Shot at a Movie* series (2001), she makes posters for movies in which she is putatively starring but which do not actually exist. Like her fellow performance artist **Stelarc**, she alters her own body and uses **multimedia** technology to explore and create new mediated and **performative** definitions of identity. The focus of Orlan's work, though, remains firmly on exploring gender and (in particular) femininity.

Bibliography

For critical analysis of Orlan's work, see Augsburg, Auslander, Ince, Kauffman and *Orlan: Carnal Art*; for images, see Buci-Glucksmann, and the Orlans entries. Orlan's website includes detailed information on artwork, biography, bibliography and exhibitions.

Augsburg, Tanya (1998) 'Orlan's Performative Transformations of Subjectivity', in *The Ends of Performance*, Peggy Phelan and Jill Lane (eds), New York: New York University Press, pp.285–314.
Auslander, Philip (1997) *From Acting to Performance: Essays in Modernism and Postmodernism*, London: Routledge.
Buci-Glucksmann, Christine (2000) *Orlan: Triomphe du baroque*, Marseille: Images En Manoeuvres Editions. Includes French and English texts.
Ince, Kate (2000) *Orlan: Millennial Female*, Oxford and New York: Berg.
Kauffman, Linda S. (2002) 'Cutups in Beauty School – and Postscripts, January 2000 and December 2001', in *Interfaces: Women/Autobiography/Image/Performance*, Sidonie Smith and Julia Watson (eds), Ann Arbor: University of Michigan Press, pp.103–31.
Orlan (1996) *This Is My Body . . . This Is My Software*, London: Black Dog.
—— (2004) *Orlan: Carnal Art*, trans. Deke Dusinberre, Paris: Editions Flammarion.
Orlan. Online. Available <http://www.Orlan.net> (accessed 13 January 2005).
ORLAN, Carnal Art (2001), produced and directed by Stephan Oriach, Myriapodus Films.

PHELAN, PEGGY (AMERICAN ACADEMIC/WRITER/ PERFORMER)

In her theoretical and practical explorations of performance, both enacted through writing, Phelan asserts that performance's **liveness** – its fleeting, ephemeral nature

– is psychically, politically and ethically significant. Combining politicized **psychoanalytic**, **feminist** and queer theories, she argues that because performance is ephemeral, it stages loss. Because loss is something everyone has to deal with emotionally and psychologically throughout their lives, examining performance as a staging of loss, absence or trauma can be suggestive, instructive, therapeutic and politically enabling.

In *Unmarked* (1993), she proposes that performance is liminal – between being live and present and immediately over and absent. Because of this liminality, performance is a particularly valuable medium to practise and analyse for those who are themselves made to feel liminal or marginal by dominant culture, whether because of their race, sexuality, gender, politics, ability or class. She challenges the contention that visibility equals power, a logic that informed many marginalized groups' rights advocacy activities in the visibility politics of the 1970s, 1980s, and 1990s. She argues instead that being 'unmarked', a blind spot in the purview of dominant culture, can allow one to evade surveillance and control. It is therefore worthwhile, she suggests, to explore being unmarked – or, as in the case of performance, ephemeral – as a radical aesthetic strategy for empowering liminal subjectivities.

Phelan is an extremely influential practitioner of performance studies. Her work is typical of the field in that it is multidisciplinary, addressing the **performative** politics of media as diverse as theatre, **performance art**, public events and trials, psychoanalytic case histories, acts of grief and mourning, **dance**, and many visual arts, including film, video, photography and painting. Importantly, her work is also distinctive within performance studies, both in content and form. Where **Richard Schechner**, for example, emphasizes anthropology and **ritual**, she focuses on feminism and psychoanalysis. Perhaps more importantly, because she is interested in the performative politics of writing, she has developed performance studies' forms by advocating 'performative writing'. This is a dynamic, hybrid fusion of critical and creative thinking that combines commentary, analysis, story, anecdote, reflection and fantasy and aims to emulate the ephemeral nature of performance (compare with **Hélène Cixous**' practice of *écriture féminine*). For Phelan, performative writing is importantly distinct from more conventional performance criticism, which risks fixing and potentially rendering conservative what might have been elusive and radical in the live event. In *Mourning Sex* (1997), a kind of elegy to loss and the injured body, she argues that performative writing aims to enact the affective force of the performance event, including its sense of loss, and to make performance criticism itself subjective, partial and active in the present, not trying to copy and capture the past.

Phelan's radical and pioneering practice of performance studies has provoked criticism of her own work and crystallized criticism of the field more broadly. The multidisciplinary nature of performance studies that is apparently evidenced by her work, for example, has been accused of neglecting and denigrating theatre and drama as sites of study. Further, performance studies has also been accused of being ahistorical (for example, by David Savran), adopting a renegade attitude to history alongside an emphasis on liveness and the present. In *Liveness* (1999), Philip Auslander specifically takes issue with Phelan's arguments about live performance, arguing against the politically oppositional claims she makes for liveness.

As well as garnering detractors, however, Phelan's work has accumulated many admirers and emulators, its influence arising not only through her writing but also her editing and teaching. With Lynda Hart, she co-edited *Acting Out* (1993), a collection of essays on feminism and performance; and with Jill Lane, she co-edited *The Ends of Performance* (1998), which reflects cogently on the discipline through a selection of essays first delivered at the Performance Studies International conference Phelan organized in New York in 1995 and which led to the establishment of PSI (Performance Studies International), which holds annual conferences. From 1985 she taught in (and later headed) the Department of Performance Studies, co-founded by Schechner at Tisch School of the Arts, New York University. Since 2002, she has been a professor in the Drama Department at Stanford University in California.

Bibliography

Auslander, Philip (1999) *Liveness: Performance in a Mediatized Culture*, London and New York: Routledge.
Hart, Lynda and Peggy Phelan (eds) (1993) *Acting Out: Feminist Performances*, Ann Arbor: University of Michigan Press.
Phelan, Peggy (1993) *Unmarked: The Politics of Performance*, London: Routledge.
—— (1997) *Mourning Sex: Performing Public Memories*, London: Routledge.
—— and Jill Lane (eds) (1998) *The Ends of Performance*, New York: New York University Press.
Reckitt, Helena (ed.), survey by Peggy Phelan (2001) *Art and Feminism*, London: Phaidon.
Savran, David (2001) 'Choices Made and Unmade', *Theater* 31.2: 89–95.

SCHECHNER, RICHARD (AMERICAN ACADEMIC/EDITOR/ WRITER/DIRECTOR, 1934–)

Since the 1960s, Schechner has pioneered an interdisciplinary approach to defin-ing what performance is and does, broadening those definitions and allowing new critical connections to be made across and between them. The approach Schechner advocates – and to a large degree founded – has come to be known as performance studies. It combines knowledge and practices from anthropology, sociology, psychology, art history, folklore and cultural studies, as well as theatre and **dance** studies, to examine a broad range of practices and events, including: religious and social **ritual**, amateur and professional **sport**, games, popular entertainment, performance in **everyday life**, secular public events like **carnivals**, **festivals**, **parades** and political **demonstrations**, as well as conventional theatre performance. One outcome of performance studies' critical innovations is an increased focus on the social, spiritual and political effects of performance, alongside the aesthetic or formal qualities that the study of drama had generally previously emphasized. Another is the international, **intercultural** and generic expansion of Euro-American theatre scholarship to pay greater attention to **Asian performance** forms such as Indian Kathakali and Japanese noh theatre as well as to non-text-based events like Native, Jewish and Indian festivals and rituals (such as the Maori **haka** and the **Yaqui Lent and Easter ceremonies**).

Schechner has practised and promoted performance studies as a **director**, editor, writer and teacher. As the founding director of The Performance Group (New York, 1967–80), Schechner was a primary exponent in the experimental American theatre of the 1960s and 1970s, working especially to enhance theatre's social and spiritual effects as ritual for participating makers and audiences. Using the Performing Garage as a flexible **environmental theatre**, Schechner and The Performance Group sought to increase the interactivity of the performance event by mobilizing both **audiences** and performers and encouraging them to interact directly, as in such productions as ***Dionysus in 69*** (1968–69), *Commune* (1971) and *The Balcony* (1980), all of which Schechner directed. When The Performance Group folded due to difficult internal dynamics, the **Wooster Group** absorbed several of its artists, remained in the Performing Garage, and carried on many of its innovations. Schechner too continues his theatrical experimentation as a freelance director (of, for example, a Chinese-language *Oresteia* in Taiwan, 1995) and as founding artistic director of East Coast Artists (1991–) which has produced a highly physical version of Goethe's *Faust* in *Faust/Gastronome* (1993) and an intercultural *Hamlet* (1999) that eclectically borrowed visual and musical styles from a host of different cultures and periods.

From 1962 to 1969, and again since 1986, Schechner has edited the influential journal *Drama Review* (*TDR*) (formerly *Tulane Drama Review*), first when he taught at Tulane University in New Orleans, and subsequently since his move to the Department of Performance Studies, Tisch School of the Arts, New York University, in 1967. Having accrued the subtitle *The Journal of Performance Studies* in 1986, *TDR* has pioneered research into emerging artists, practices and critical paradigms, including **Jerzy Grotowski**, Fluxus and approaches to understanding performance as ritual, aspects of which were elaborated with his friend **Victor Turner**. As a book editor, Schechner continues to work to expand the discipline; he is Editor of Routledge's Worlds of Performance series. In his numerous publications, Schechner consistently explores the social function of theatre and ritual performance. He published *Performance Studies*, his textbook on the subject, in 2002.

Responses to Schechner's work have not always been positive. Some, like **Rustom Bharucha**, have seen his (and others') incursions into Eastern forms of theatre and ritual as romanticizing and imperialist in ways typical of much intercultural exploration. (In many of his writings, Schechner himself acknowledges this potential problem.) Several of his experiments with The Performance Group have been criticized for the ways they failed to achieve a more democratic performance event. Critics argue that his experiments in using nudity in performance and breaking audience–performer boundaries, for example, were compromised because they did not take adequate precautions to protect performers from exploitative groping by audiences. While there may remain areas where Schechner's practice focuses on one ideological aspect of production at the expense of another, he has nevertheless produced and overseen a radical transformation in the study of theatre and performance and has in many ways forced the field to become more politically accountable.

Bibliography

Schechner, Richard ([1973] 1994) *Environmental Theater*, New York: Applause.
—— ([1977] 1988) *Performance Theory*, London: Routledge.
—— (1983) *Performative Circumstances: From the Avant Garde to Ramlila*, Calcutta: Seagull.
—— (1993) *The Future of Ritual: Writings on Culture and Performance*, London: Routledge.
—— (2002) *Performance Studies: An Introduction*, London: Routledge.
—— and Willa Appel (eds) (1990) *By Means of Performance: Intercultural Studies of Theatre and Ritual*, Cambridge: Cambridge University Press.
—— and Lisa Wolford (eds) (1997) *The Grotowski Sourcebook*, London: Routledge.

SISTREN THEATRE COLLECTIVE (WOMEN'S THEATRE COLLECTIVE, FOUNDED KINGSTON, JAMAICA, 1977)

Taking as its name the female counterpart of the word 'brethren', Sistren is a theatre collective founded by working-class women with artistic director Honor Ford-Smith. Since its beginnings, it has aimed to advance **audience** awareness about issues affecting Caribbean women especially through the combined effects of racial, sexual and class oppression (see **feminism**). Initially, Sistren worked almost wholly through the medium of theatre, but by 1982 it had expanded to run a programme of drama-based workshops with both urban and rural community groups, was producing silk-screened textiles, had popularized Jamaican research on women and was publishing a quarterly magazine. Across its activities, it aimed to empower its participants and audiences by analysing and commenting on gender roles in Jamaican society, organizing itself as an autonomous collective, and taking performance, education and other opportunities to a wide variety of audiences in Jamaica, the Caribbean region and beyond. Sistren's activist practices also included bringing together women of different races and classes and participating in campaigns criticizing Jamaica's debt and violence against women.

Sistren's performance work was both particular to Jamaica in its use of specific Jamaican stories, oral histories, languages, **rituals** and aspects of **carnival**, for example – and typically postcolonial, in its reclamation of indigenous stories, languages and performance practices. Sistren's performances were collectively **devised** using games and **improvisation** to combine participants' own stories with other research materials, especially interviews. Its shows included features typical of a community-based **popular theatre** of political advocacy, combining song, stories and monologues, and dealing consistently with social issues. They were also, however, very particular to their specific contexts, using Jamaican Creole, stories from Jamaican popular culture and history, traditional and current popular songs, and addressing Caribbean women's history and experiences, both domestic and public.

Sistren has produced over a dozen plays. One recurring thematic concern has been with women's experiences as labourers. *Downpression Get a Blow*, Sistren's first show, devised for performance at Jamaica's 1977 Workers' Week celebrations, dealt with the unionization of women in the garment industry; *Domesticks* (1981–83) focused on women's abuse as domestic servants; and the documentary film *Sweet Sugar Rage* (1985) looked at women in the Jamaican sugar industry. The company explored Caribbean women's history in *Nana Yah* (1980), about a seventeenth-century Maroon warrior woman who fought the British, and in *QPH* (1981), a memorial to more than a hundred women who died in a fire in the Kingston Alms House in 1980. Women's relationships were the focus of several shows, including *Bellywoman Bangarang* (1978), about women's sexuality and mothering, *Muffet Inna All a We* (1985), a reggae musical partly about global capitalism in which three women try to enter a dancehall DJ competition, and *Buss Out* (1989), which investigated questions of colour and shade and women's interclass relations.

Sistren have demonstrated theatre's community-building potential in tours throughout the Caribbean (including to rural Jamaica) and to the USA, Canada and Europe. The company's work, like that of **Augusto Boal**, demonstrates the potential of theatre and performance to build skills and confidence and to empower communities that may otherwise be marginalized by economics, gender and geography. The trajectory of the company's history – from relatively modest beginnings, through quick and extensive expansion, to reduction in the 1990s – points to the ways many collectives (like **Bread and Puppet Theatre**) established in the 1960s and 1970s in a climate of democratic 'grassroots' empowerment, political **protest** and political possibility flourished in the 1980s, but thereafter retrenched as political conditions changed.

Bibliography

The collective's work is described in Sistren's 1983 article and in introductions to the published plays. *Lionheart Gal* is a Sistren project that documented Jamaican women's lives. Ford-Smith's article analyses in detail the interlinked political, financial and historical conditions for the collective's decline.

Ford-Smith, Honor (1997) 'Ring Ding in a Tight Corner: Sistren, Collective Democracy, and the Organization of Cultural Production', in *Feminist Genealogies, Colonial Legacies, Democratic Futures*, M. Jacqui Alexander and Chandra Talpade Mohanty (eds), London: Routledge, pp.213–58, 390–92.

Sistren Theatre Collective (1983) 'Women's Theatre in Jamaica', *Grassroots Development* 7.2. Reprinted in Charles David Kleymeyer (ed.) (1994) *Cultural Expression and*

Grassroots Development: Cases from Latin America and the Caribbean, Boulder and London: Lynne Rienner, pp.71–82.

—— (2001) Introduction and *Bellywoman Bangarang*, in *Contemporary Drama of the Caribbean*, Erika J. Waters and David Edgecombe (eds), Kingshill, St Croix: The Caribbean Writer, pp.77–131.

—— (2001) Introduction and *QPH*, in *Postcolonial Plays: An Anthology*, Helen Gilbert (ed.), London: Routledge, pp.153–78.

—— with Honor Ford-Smith (1986) *Lionheart Gal: Life Stories of Jamaican Women*, London: The Women's Press.

SOYINKA, WOLE (NIGERIAN WRITER/ACADEMIC/POET/ ESSAYIST/NOVELIST/EDITOR/SOCIAL COMMENTATOR, 1934–)

A prolific writer and winner of the Nobel prize for literature in 1986, Soyinka is best known for his playwriting. His oeuvre of over twenty plays includes *The Swamp Dwellers* (1958), *Madmen and Specialists* (1970) and *Death and the King's Horseman* (1976). Throughout his writings, he has observed and offered critiques of his changing Nigerian culture and its history of colonial and post-colonial oppression. His commitment to speaking out against social injustice in this context is indisputable; indeed, it was 'rewarded' by detention by the Federal Military Government from 1967 to 1969 during the Nigerian Civil War and has since, at times, required him to live in exile for his own safety.

However, some critics from both Africa and the West have debated whether Soyinka chooses the most appropriate methods for speaking out. Some post-colonial African writers have argued against using colonial languages (for example, English and French), colonial myths and colonial literary structures and symbols, in favour of using, respecting and celebrating indigenous African ones. Soyinka considers this approach atavistic, calling its proponents 'Neo-Tarzanists', and advocates an **intercultural** strategy of combining colonial and indigenous languages, myths, symbols and structures. His own work is particularly well-known for its exploration and comparison of classical Greek dramatic form and Yoruba myth. While some Western critics have complained that this approach is discordant, Soyinka has pursued it to create a drama which he sees as not only internationally accessible, but – through the English language – accessible within his own multilingual and multicultural country as well. Thus, he pioneers a new dramaturgy that acknowledges the hybridity of post-colonial cultural expression and experience like his own. Born and educated in both Christian and Yoruba traditions in Nigeria, Soyinka completed a BA at the University of Leeds and worked at the Royal Court Theatre, London, from 1957 to 1959.

Soyinka's writing strategies – and responses to them – demonstrate some of the issues at stake in post-colonial cultural practice. He continues to speak out about political corruption in Nigeria and has been particularly fierce in his condemnation of the 1995 execution of fellow Nigerian playwright Ken Saro-Wiwa. He has himself received a death sentence in 1997 and has since lived in exile.

Bibliography

Jeyifo includes a full list of Soyinka's books to 1999, a chronology of his life, and numerous interviews. *Art, Dialogue and Outrage* collects some of Soyinka's critical writing.

Jeyifo, Biodun (ed.) (2001) *Conversations with Wole Soyinka*, Jackson: University Press of Mississippi.
Soyinka, Wole (1984) *Six Plays*, London: Methuen.
—— (1988) *Art, Dialogue and Outrage: Essays on Literature and Culture*, London: Methuen.
—— (1999) *Plays 2*, London: Methuen.

SPLIT BRITCHES (LESBIAN AND FEMINIST THEATRE COMPANY, FOUNDED NEW YORK, 1980)

Since its inaugural performance – *Split Britches*, in New York in 1980 – the eponymous company has performed throughout the USA and Europe, particularly the UK, and has become the most influential (mostly) lesbian performance group of its time. The company's central members are Lois Weaver, Peggy Shaw and Deb Margolin, although they often work in collaboration with other groups, solo and sometimes in pairs (especially Weaver and Shaw).

Split Britches have pioneered organizational and aesthetic models for lesbian and **feminist** theatre and **performance art**, and provided some of the most important performance material for the growing feminist critical discourse on theatre throughout the 1980s and into the 1990s. They founded a theatre **festival** called WOW (Women's One World) in 1980 and the WOW Café in New York in 1982. These provided a festival and then a **space** for women's performance, as well as a home for New York's lesbian and feminist communities and, in the analysis of critic Jill Dolan, a site for specifically feminist **spectatorship**. Aesthetically, they developed a **postmodern** style to articulate postmodernity's split subjectivity and to interrogate the patriarchal and heterosexist assumptions of much dominant theatre and culture. As performers, they play both themselves and characters, often blurring the distinction between the two and drawing attention to the **performativity** of identity. Their shows are typically satirical and episodic and combine lip-synching (familiar from gay and drag cabaret), self-conscious butch–femme role-playing, and sequences of popular song and **movement**. The shows present generically unconventional, **camp** approaches to canonical texts, including a vaudeville *Beauty and the Beast* (1982), a *Little Women* (1988) and a comic *Streetcar Named Desire* in *Belle Reprieve* (with Bloolips, 1991). The plays explore issues of economics (*Upwardly Mobile Home*, 1984), personal relationships (*Anniversary Waltz*, 1989), sex roles (*Lust and Comfort*, with Gay Sweatshop, 1995) and class and gender violence (*Lesbians Who Kill*, 1992). Split Britches' shows are irreverent in their humorous and playful subversion of both canonical texts and elitist theatre-making practices and they resolutely retain a rough theatre style – sometimes by force of economic circumstance, certainly, but also to interrogate the economics of theatre and patriarchal capitalism and, through a **Brechtian** aesthetic, to defamiliarize the myths of gender and culture they present.

Bibliography

Case collects the company's plays, Dolan examines their work in detail, and Jenkins provides an introduction, including a brief interview with Split Britches' members.

Case, Sue-Ellen (ed.) (1996) *Split Britches: Lesbian Practice/Feminist Performance*, London: Routledge.

Dolan, Jill (1988) *The Feminist Spectator as Critic*, Ann Arbor: University of Michigan Press.

Jenkins, Linda Walsh (1987) 'Split Britches', in *Women in American Theatre*, revised and expanded edition, Helen Krich Chinoy and Linda Walsh Jenkins, New York: Theatre Communications Group.

SPRINKLE, ANNIE (AMERICAN PERFORMANCE ARTIST/ SEXUAL ACTIVIST/WRITER/PHOTOGRAPHER, 1954–)

A former prostitute and hardcore porn film star and **director**, since the early 1980s Sprinkle has been making films, videos, and live performances that are, to use her term, 'post-porn' – that is, critically and playfully self-reflexive about pornography. Her live performances are autobiographical **multimedia** hybrid **performance art/body art** 'herstories', detailing her transition from prostitute to porn actress to sexual activist. They include *Post-Porn Modernist* and *Post-Post-Porn Modernist* (1990–95), *Hardcore from the Heart* (1996–7) and *Annie Sprinkle's Herstory of Porn, from Reel to Real* (1997 and continuing). These performances critically acknowledge that women are vulnerable to exploitation within the sex industry, for example by abusive clients or film directors. But they also actively celebrate porn's potential for exploring and expressing sexuality (especially safer sex practices in an age of AIDS), and female sexuality in particular, which Sprinkle believes is violently oppressed within the sex-negative culture of the West.

Sprinkle's work has been a challenge and an inspiration to **feminism**. For some feminists, her work has the negative effect of both objectifying the female body and essentializing female identity by locating it in its biological contexts rather than the social ones, which feminism might then act to change. For others, however, her work has several positive effects. Sprinkle's body may be an object in her shows, but she is also a subject: she is self-authoring and self-pleasuring; she addresses her **audiences** directly; she returns their gaze; and she actively invites them to explore her body beyond the limits that porn normally adopts in order to preserve the female body as a strictly sexual object. In 'A Public Cervix Announcement', a scene in *Post-Porn Modernist* (and viewable in part on Sprinkle's website), Sprinkle inserted a speculum into her vagina and invited audience members to come forward and view her cervix. Where much Anglo-American academic feminism of the late 1980s and 1990s concentrated on language and discourse (see, for example, **Judith Butler** and **Peggy Phelan**), Sprinkle's work reasserts the body as an important site of (and for) feminist campaigning without arguing that a single body necessarily houses a unified identity. For many critics, this irreverence towards feminist pieties is typical of the **postmodernism** of Sprinkle's shows. Other recognizably postmodern features include the shows' pastiche of non-linear scenes, the ambiguity of their ironic and celebratory attitudes towards pornography, and their acknowledgement of Sprinkle's own split subjectivity as commodity and seller, as object and subject, and as unresolved into a unified sexuality (with past sexual partners including men, women and transsexuals, Sprinkle refers to herself as metamorphosexual).

Debates about the effects of her work aside, Sprinkle's motivations are clear. She aims to help women to explore and express their sexuality, whether through conventional or alternative sexual practices, including 'ecstasy breathing' and erotic meditation, and she campaigns to spread safer sex practices, especially within the sex industry. She completed a PhD at the Institute for the Advanced Study of Human Sexuality in San Francisco with a dissertation entitled 'Providing Educational Opportunities for Adult Industry Workers', and she continues to offer sex workshops, to write and publish, and to perform internationally.

Bibliography

Sprinkle's websites and books offer detailed information on, and images of, her work.
Annie Sprinkle. Online. Available <http://www.anniesprinkle.org/> (accessed 21 January 2005).
Post-Porn Modernist. Online. Available <http://www.bobsart.org/sprinkle/menu. html> (accessed 11 January 2005).
Schneider, Rebecca (1997) *The Explicit Body in Performance*, London: Routledge.
Sprinkle, Annie (1998) *Annie Sprinkle, Post-Porn Modernist: My Twenty-Five Years as a Multimedia Whore*, revised and updated edition, San Francisco: Cleis Press.
—— (2001) *Hardcore from the Heart: The Pleasures, Profits and Politics of Sex in Performance: Annie Sprinkle: Solo*, ed. Gabrielle Cody, London: Continuum.

STANISLAVSKY, KONSTANTIN (RUSSIAN THEATRE DIRECTOR/ACTOR/TEACHER, 1863–1938)

With his insights into the processes of **acting** and **directing**, Stanislavsky forged a definitive position in the development of twentieth-century theatre, laying the groundwork for many innovators. With Vladimir Nemirovich-Danchenko, he founded the Moscow Art Theatre in 1897, through which he developed and documented a system of acting as a way of creating believable roles on stage. This process depends on the concept of the actor seeming to transform into another being before the **spectator**, who observes from 'behind' (or literally in front of) the fourth wall. Like **naturalism**, these notions of verisimilitude and believability were innovative at the time. They were a reaction to the star system and the Romantic drama that existed before Stanislavsky, which highlighted individual actors and their melodramatic techniques while simultaneously marginalizing the text and other cast members.

The acting process of recreating a fictional character outlined by Stanislavsky begins with the self. The actor has to search in his or her subconscious, through a technique called emotion memory for a personal experience equivalent to that which the character must depict on stage. The actor uses the 'magic if' to suspend disbelief and to ask what he or she would do in such a situation. Beyond the self, Stanislavsky's meticulous attention to text gives the actor a method of dissecting and compartmentalizing text into units and objectives. Actors must find their character's own aim, desire or objective for each unit, to ascertain what he or she wants at any given moment. This segmentation must then be reconstituted and overridden by the character's total desire or superobjective, that is the principal aim or desire in his or her fictional life, ultimately providing the performer with a consistent through-line. Alongside these very specific skills, the actor has to understand the character's tempo-rhythms (the rhythm of actions and thoughts) and search for an organic fluidity in all his or her reconstructed behaviour. This sense of truthfulness to **everyday life** has to pervade the actors' interactions, their speaking of text (including the unspoken subtext which the actor has to assiduously ascertain and imagine), and their physical actions. Stanislavsky envisaged the actor as a naturally creative, imaginative being rather than a director's sop or physical acrobat, though he also stressed that actors must train the body as much as the mind through gymnastics, fencing and other physical elements of **training**.

Stanislavsky researched, questioned and documented his own processes through the fictional actor/student Tortsov, who appears in his writings as a willing, though questioning, subject. Stanislavsky's discoveries are partly significant, if at times confusing, for his later admission and redress of previous failings and limitations, exacerbated no doubt by the longevity of his working life and the radical changes in Russian society and culture during this time. Stanislavsky's ideas evolved to place more emphasis on the actor's physical actions rather than on his or her emotional life, a system known as the Method of Physical Actions, or MOPA for short, though he never completed research into this to his satisfaction. What was important for him in this emphasis was that actions can be fixed, whereas emotions are temperamental and unreliable. Stanislavsky also recognized the introversion on stage that his psychological processes were creating in his actors. The work of **Jerzy Grotowski** (who cited Stanislavsky as his 'master'), as well as a recent general growing interest in physical approaches to **performing** led by exponents like **Eugenio Barba**, have all confirmed the significance of this shift in Stanislavsky's later years.

As a director, Stanislavsky was the central proponent in the new movement of naturalism in the theatre. In spite of their disagreements, he championed Anton Chekhov's writing, acting in and directing several of the première productions of his major plays like *The Seagull* (1897) and *The Cherry Orchard* (1904). Chekhov cursed Stanislavsky's tendency to fill the stage with overdetailed **scenography**, both visual and aural, rather than relying on the stripped-back symbolism he desired. But Stanislavsky's meticulous explanation of the performance processes required for naturalistic acting and the success and ambition of his productions still command immense respect, however much questioning there has been of naturalism itself. His techniques are taught in acting schools throughout the world (most notably the State Institute GITIS in Moscow) and used widely in **rehearsals**, though only in a few places are they followed through with such detail and over such time scales of a year or more, as Stanislavsky proposed and practised. His writings and exercises continue to be utilized extensively, if somewhat randomly, with scant regard for their value as a total system. His work provided a systematic base for students such as Evgeny Vakhtangov and **Vsevolod Meyerhold** to depart from, and for Lee Strasberg to develop (though many would say misconstrue) into the Method via students of Stanislavsky like Richard Boleslavsky, who went to work in the United States of America.

Stanislavsky weathered the great changes in Russian society in the first two decades of the twentieth century and was in the State's and Stalin's favour until his death, however much Meyerhold and others decried his work as elitist and out of touch. At the other end of the twentieth century, Perestroika in the Soviet Union has meant a further revision and embellishment of Stanislavsky's theories. This has encouraged new translations of his writings to replace Elizabeth Hapgood's 1950s versions, which have been shown to be partial and highly selective. These are still awaited, but testify to the ongoing significance and continued re-evaluation of Stanislavsky's achievements.

Bibliography

There is a vast amount of published material on Stanislavsky by recognized authorities like Benedetti. Merlin has usefully updated thinking by drawing on her own work as an actor in Britain and Russia. The Gorchakov and Toporkov translations provide illuminating insights into Stanislavsky's methods of work.

Benedetti, Jean (1982) *Stanislavski: An Introduction*, London: Methuen.

Carnicke, Sharon M. (1998) *Stanislavsky in Focus*, Amsterdam: Harwood.

Gorchakov, Nikolai M. (1954) *Stanislavski Directs*, trans. Miriam Goldina, New York: Grosset and Dunlap.

Merlin, Bella (2001) *Beyond Stanislavski: The Psycho-Physical Approach to Actor Training*, London: Nick Hern Books.

—— (2003) *Konstantin Stanislavsky*, London: Routledge.

Stanislavski, Konstantin (1924) *My Life in Art*, trans. J. J. Robbins, London: Geoffrey Bles.

—— (1968) *An Actor Prepares*, London: Methuen. First published in 1937.

—— (1968) *Building a Character*, London: Methuen. First published in 1950.

—— (1981) *Creating a Role*, London: Methuen. First published in 1957.

Toporkov, Vasily (1979) *Stanislavski in Rehearsal: The Final Years*, trans. Christine Edwards, New York: Theatre Arts Books.

STELARC (AUSTRALIAN PERFORMANCE ARTIST, 1946–)

Stelarc (or Stelios Arcadiou, as he was formerly known) has extensively explored notions of what it is to be human, most often through solo performance works. This has led him to state that the body is redundant and needs to be replaced or at least enhanced by technological developments. In practice he has demonstrated this shift towards artificial intelligence, cyborgs, robots and advanced prosthetics through performance projects that include the attachment of a robotic arm to his body to make a third hand, and the connection of his body to the **internet**. For some of the internet-based performances (for example, *Muscle Stimulator System*, 1994), Stelarc uses Stimbod software that makes electrical impulses activate him. His involuntary **movements** – the disjointed jumpy **dance** of his wired-up limbs – are caused by electrical charges stimulating selected muscles, programmed directly either by **spectators** present at his events or by those thousands of kilometres away, moving him electronically via the internet. His image is then relayed on to the internet through a 'live' website, creating a dynamic cycle of Stelarc's reactions and spectators' stimuli. Stelarc has also worked with external machinery and robots, 'dancing' with an industrial robot of the kind found in car factories (various projects between 1991 and 1994). His and the robot's movements were programmed to modify each other's patterns in a random interactive sequence.

In his various writings, many of his statements may seem hyperbolic but they perhaps anticipate the not-too-distant reality of extensive medical and technological enhancement of the human body, reflected also in the performance work of **Orlan**. The irony is that Stelarc's **performance art** practice began with very simple mechanisms, though with comparable danger – he famously suspended himself on meat hooks above a New York street as part of his body suspension work (1976–88). As well as showing **body art** performances and pictures from these on the internet, including his 'stomach sculptures' or images filmed by an internal probe, he presents live work in numerous galleries and non-theatre **spaces** and has extensively explored both the interior and exterior dimensions of the body. Through these events he continues to test and question the parameters of acceptable exploitation of the human form in a typically **postmodern** way. However serious the issues and the potential consequences of his practice, it is inflected with a **playful** sensibility. He appeals to the spectators' voyeurism, opening himself up to their direct intervention and whim as well as to life-threatening danger, be it from meat hooks or power surges.

Bibliography

Writings about Stelarc are mostly found in collections like these below, which deal generally with technology and human interactions. The Marsh text concerns the earlier period of Stelarc's work. Stelarc's website is an excellent primary source.

Geary, James (2002) *The Body Electric: An Anatomy of the New Bionic Senses*, London: Weidenfeld and Nicolson.

Hungate, Claire, Ian Farr and Sholto Ramsay (eds) (1996) *Totally Wired: Science, Technology and the Human Form*, London: Institute of Contemporary Arts.

Marsh, Anne (1993) *Body and Self: Performance Art in Australia 1969–92*, Melbourne: Oxford University Press.

Murphie, Andrew (1998) 'Negotiating Presence: Performance and the New Technologies', in *Culture, Technology and Creativity in the Late Twentieth Century*, Philip Hayward (ed.), London: John Libbery, pp.209–26.

Stelarc. Online. Available <http://www.stelarc.va.com.au> (accessed 1 November 2004).

SUZUKI, TADASHI (JAPANESE THEATRE DIRECTOR/ THEORIST, 1939–)

Suzuki has a composite identity as **director**, trainer, designer of theatre **spaces**, **intercultural** theorist and practitioner, and writer. He has directed a large number of performances, many of which have attracted acclaim around the world, especially *The Trojan Women* (1977), with Kayoko Shiraishi in the lead role, and *The Bacchae* (1978). His creation and theorization of his **training** system – the Suzuki method – is perhaps his most notable contribution to twentieth-century performance. It has transformed comprehension of the performer's vocation and what performing is, and is now taught in several universities and drama schools in North America, as well as through regular training sessions in London and Australia. As well as working regularly with SCOT, the Suzuki Company of Toga, Suzuki has also directed productions with just Australian and American actors, as well as with Japanese and American actors combined in a production of *Dionysus* (1992), performed in both English and Japanese. Through such projects and as an Asian director he has made a significant and original contribution to intercultural debates, initially through his book *The Way of Acting* (1986), a translation of one of the twelve books he has published in Japanese. As part of his cross-cultural vision, he collaborated with American director Anne Bogart, with whom he co-founded SITI, the Saratoga International Theatre Institute (1992). Though now separate from Suzuki, Bogart's group is today one of the USA's leading experimental companies, who still use his training method.

Suzuki has developed a range of performance work, from intimate classical pieces to outdoor celebratory spectacles with fireworks. One dominant form has been collages of European texts, creating surprising conjunctions and juxtapositions. This integration of multiple Eastern and Western sources applies to the **music** and **scenography** he employs, as well as the spaces he has developed. For an outdoor theatre in the village of Toga he mixed ancient Greek theatre architecture with elements from a noh stage, for example. In his performances, extracts of texts by Samuel Beckett and Anton Chekhov sit alongside contemporary Japanese pop songs. His is an eclectic **postmodern** directorial style that is rooted in his strict training method, centred on the 'grammar of the feet'.

Derived in part from the traditional Japanese forms of noh and kabuki, this 'grammar' uses ways of walking and **movements** centred on the lower half of the body to challenge and ground the performer. It tests the performer's stamina and concentration as well as physical flexibility, muscular strength and spatial sensitivity, generating what Suzuki calls '**animal** energy' in the performer. Suzuki believes actors need to rediscover the body's potential, which has been neglected in the name of progress and civilization. The theatre should return to non-electricity-dependent resources, as in premodern forms such as noh or the Elizabethan stage. Suzuki has followed this idea through in locating his practice outside of the metropolis of Tokyo. From 1976 he was based in the tiny village of Toga in the remote Japanese alps, where he founded Japan's first international theatre **festival** in 1982. The Toga Arts Park contains a mixture of theatre spaces, including a noh-like farmhouse theatre and an outdoor amphi-theatre overlooking a lake. Crucially, it has also provided a 'home' for SCOT. In the 1990s, his empire expanded, when (with architectural collaborator Arata Isozaki) he oversaw the building and management of a theatre in a newly built arts centre in the city of Mito, and then developed a multi-million-pound arts park in hills outside the city of Shizuoka, an hour from Tokyo. Suzuki continues to tour the world, since the late 1990s under the auspices of the Theatre **Olympics** Festival, which he co-founded. He has energized and experimented with contemporary Japanese theatre as much as he has challenged the dominance of **naturalist** and psychologically based **acting** processes in the West.

Bibliography

Only one of Suzuki's many books has been published in English. Both Allain and Carruthers and Takahashi introduce all aspects of Suzuki's work.

Allain, Paul (2002) *The Art of Stillness: The Theatre Practice of Tadashi Suzuki*, London: Methuen.
Carruthers, Ian and Yasunari Takahashi (2004) *The Theatre of Suzuki Tadashi*, Cambridge: Cambridge University Press.
Shizuoka Performing Arts Center. Online. Available <http://www.spac.or.jp> (accessed 21 February 2005).
Suzuki, Tadashi (1986) *The Way of Acting*, New York: Theatre Communications Group.

TURNER, VICTOR (BRITISH ANTHROPOLOGIST/THEORIST/ TEACHER, 1920–83)

Turner embraced connections between anthropology and performance, most notably through his collaboration and friendship with **Richard Schechner**. After his initial fieldwork with the Ndembu tribe of Central Africa, he researched the nature of symbols, **play**, pilgrimages and the dramatic properties inherent in social **rituals** in various contexts, both tribal and industrial. Building on the pioneering ideas of anthropologist Arnold van Gennep, who attempted to classify the liminal structure of rituals, Turner further defined a distinction between the liminal and liminoid. He saw the former term as an essential element of play or rituals, denoting how participants enter into a 'betwixt-and-between' field of behaviour outside social rules of **space** and time, where symbols might suggest links to the sacred. The liminal is familiar to tribal societies where rituals do not tend to have a subversive agenda, but rather endorse the status quo. The liminoid refers to more complex modes of play found in modern societies, in which people might choose to participate or not, and which often have transgressive potential. One example Turner gives is radical performance, a connection that brought him into contact with theatre-makers like Schechner.

Turner's thinking has offered anthropological models to reflect on performance but has also reversed this process using dramatic forms and practices both to analyse social behaviour and to perform ethnographic research. For example, he analysed the features that dramaturgical structures in classical drama have in common with ritualized social practices, or 'social dramas' as he called them, and he 'staged' rituals with his students in order to elucidate their understanding of how and why rites of passage mark important moments in life. He and his wife and collaborator Edith called this practice 'performing ethnography'.

Turner continually broadened the scope of anthropological studies and theories, partly through contact with experimental performance in America, a country in which he spent most of his working life. Before his death he wrote 'Body, Brain and Culture' (1983), in response to growing interest in brain-mapping and attempts to explain consciousness. This explored the idea that there might in fact be a biologically determined desire or need for the kind of play that is found in rituals, which exists outside cultural constructs of games and socialization. Controversially, this questioned much anthropological theory, including the premises of most of his life's research. It is a line of enquiry disputed by theorists like **Judith Butler** who have emphasized the importance of cultural constructions of identity and behaviour over and above biologically determined givens. Turner's new avenue of research was tentative and unfinished, but its fundamental principles were explored in subsequent writings by Schechner and in the practice of **Jerzy Grotowski**, who investigated the possible existence of universal behaviour that is not culturally determined. Through his research, Turner built a bridge between studies of everyday life and performance.

Bibliography

This lists the books by Turner that are most relevant to theatre and performance. Schechner's texts articulate some of the connections between their ideas.

Schechner, Richard (1985) *Between Theater and Anthropology*, Philadelphia: University of Pennsylvania Press.
—— (1993) *The Future of Ritual: Writings on Culture and Performance*, London: Routledge.
Turner, Victor (1969) *The Ritual Process*, Chicago: Aldine.
—— (1974) *Drama, Fields and Metaphors: Symbolic Action in Human Society*, Ithaca, NY: Cornell University Press.

—— (1982) *From Ritual to Theatre: The Human Seriousness of Play*, New York: Performing Arts Journal Press.
—— (1986) *The Anthropology of Performance*, New York: PAJ Publications.

WILSON, ROBERT (AMERICAN DIRECTOR/SCENOGRAPHER/ PERFORMER/WRITER/VISUAL ARTIST, 1941–)

For his revolutionary work in creating a **theatre of images** – which explores and promotes the visual potentials of **space**, **light**, objects, figures, costumes and **movement** – Robert Wilson is one of the most important **directors** of the twentieth century. Throughout a prolific and celebrated international career, he has challenged conventional theatre practice, especially its emphasis on **naturalistic** representational idioms, de-emphasizing the text in the theatre event and concentrating instead on the formal properties of time, space, movement and **sound**.

Wilson's concern with form typically means that his shows appear stylistically **surreal**, moving without apparent psychological motivation from image to image. Trained in painting and architecture, he often begins work on his productions by drawing his shows in black-and-white storyboards that feature starkly minimalist, abstract landscapes. The storyboards are translated into usually very large proscenium arch stagings, with action – or near-static images or shapes of light – filling the vertical plane. In *A Letter for Queen Victoria* (1974), the visual composition of the stage was inspired by an envelope, with the horizontal and vertical planes providing a rectangular shape and diagonal lines of light, and with costume and performer movement sometimes cohering to suggest the envelope's flap. Wilson's sets are pictorial, architectural and often abstract, resisting naturalism's 'real life' and offering instead what may appear to be dream, fantasy or meditation.

Wilson experiments also with the formal properties of time, exploring what aesthetic, emotional and psychological effects can be produced by drawing action out, or by juxtaposing slow and quick movements. Action is often performed repetitively, in a non-linear structure, in a style Wilson has described as 'politely mannered', or over great lengths of time. *The Life and Times of Joseph Stalin* (1973) was twelve hours in duration, and *KA MOUNTain and GUARDenia Terrace* (Iran, 1972) took seven days to perform. He experiments, too, with sound. Frequent repetition of words in his productions focuses attention on their formal properties – length and sound – rather than their meanings. For Wilson, the crucial feature of an opera is not sound but action.

Wilson's theatre is innovative, in terms not only of what it is but also of how it is made. His renown as an auteur director suggests that, because his shows are firmly imprinted with his signature style, his mode of direction must be autocratic. Certainly, his ways of working can be repetitive, mechanical, demanding, unfamiliar and uncomfortable for many performers, asking them, for example, to adopt positions in the stage picture rather than to build a character or find a motivation. But, given that Wilson's sets of rules can be seen as simply different from other, more conventional, sets of rules, it is perhaps not surprising that many performers have found Wilson's style of directing productively challenging.

Arguments for seeing Wilson's auteurism as autocratic are also undermined by the fact that he is a keen collaborator. Early in his career he co-created scripts for silent operas with Raymond Andrews, a deaf-mute boy (*Deafman Glance*, 1971), and scripts that explored fractured language with Christopher Knowles, a boy who had been born with brain damage (*A Letter for Queen Victoria*). (Wilson himself overcame a teenage speech impediment through work with a dancer, Mrs Byrd Hoffman, after whom he named his first theatre company, The Byrd Hoffman School of Byrds, in 1968.) Subsequent writer-collaborators include Susan Sontag (*Alice in Bed*, 1993), William S. Burroughs (*The Black Rider: The Casting of the Magic Bullets*, 1991) and the German playwright Heiner Müller, who co-authored the German section of Wilson's multinational epic *the CIVIL warS: a tree is best measured when it is down* (1983–84). Music collaborators include **Laurie Anderson** (*Alcestis*, 1986), opera singer Jessye Norman (*Great Day in the Morning*, 1982), and Philip Glass, with whom Wilson and another frequent collaborator, choreographer Lucinda Childs, produced *Einstein on the Beach* (1976).

Although Wilson's work has maintained a striking aesthetic consistency throughout his career, it has also made a number of sizeable shifts. After **devising** silent operas and plays that deconstructed language, he began to produce more literary plays that were still elliptical and lyrical (*the CIVIL warS*), and then more classical plays and operas. In this later period, he has directed and designed many plays by modernists, such as Henrik Ibsen (*When We Dead Awaken*, 1991), Gertrude Stein (*Doctor Faustus Lights the Lights*, 1992) and August Strindberg (*A Dream Play*, 1998). He has also designed and directed numerous operas, including Wagner's *Parsifal* (Hamburg, 1991) and *Lohengrin* (Zürich, 1991, New York, 1998) and Puccini's *Madame Butterfly* (Paris, 1993–97). As well as directing and designing, Wilson frequently performs, as in *Hamlet: A Monologue*, 1995. He also makes a variety of other forms of visual art, including sculpture, painting, drawing and **installation** (for example, *H.G.*, London, 1995).

Wilson's work has frequently been criticized for being elitist, both aesthetically and financially. His innovations and expansions in physical and temporal scale have indeed had implications for the financial scope of his work, usually making it very expensive to produce. For much of his career, this condition has resulted in his work being produced more frequently in European countries with relatively high levels of state subsidy to the theatre (especially Germany) than in Wilson's native USA, not to mention any non-Western contexts. In his defence, Wilson frequently uses amateur performers in his productions, so that in this respect at least participation can be seen as not elitist (unless one considers him to be exploiting these amateurs). Wilson's theatre may certainly not be without fault, but in a theatre industry dominated by **realism** his formalism is startling, provocative and welcome. His theatre demonstrates the potentially awesome effects that can be produced by experimenting in epic scales of time and space and by prioritizing the making of images over the speaking of text.

Bibliography

Brecht, Donker, Holmberg and Shyer all provide sustained description and analysis of Wilson's work.

Brecht, Stefan (1978) *The Theatre of Visions: Robert Wilson*, Frankfurt am Main: Suhrkamp Verlag.

Donker, Janny (1985) *The President of Paradise: A Traveller's Account of Robert Wilson's* the CIVIL warS, Amsterdam: International Theatre Bookshop.

Holmberg, Arthur (1997) *The Theatre of Robert Wilson*, Cambridge: Cambridge University Press.

Robert Wilson. Online. Available <http://www.robertwilson.com/> (accessed 25 February 2005).

Shyer, Laurence (1989) *Robert Wilson and His Collaborators*, New York: Theatre Communications Group.

Simmer, Bill (1976) 'Theatre and Therapy: Robert Wilson', *TDR: The Drama Review* 20.1 (T69): 99–110. Partially reprinted in Rebecca Schneider and Gabrielle Cody (eds) (2002) *Re:Direction: A Theoretical and Practical Guide*, London: Routledge, pp.147–56.

Wilson, Robert ([1977] 1996) *A Letter for Queen Victoria* in *The Theatre of Images*, ed. Bonnie Marranca (ed.), Baltimore: Johns Hopkins University Press. Originally published by Drama Book Specialists.

WOOSTER GROUP (PERFORMANCE GROUP, FOUNDED NEW YORK, 1975)

The Wooster Group has pioneered politically engaged **postmodern** performance to a degree and with a longevity unmatched in American experimental performance from the last quarter of the twentieth century. Made up of a small core ensemble of artists, some of the Group's original members, including **director** Elizabeth LeCompte and performer Spalding Gray, were working with **Richard Schechner**'s The Performance Group when they splintered to form their own company in 1975. This new group developed many of Schechner's practices – including strategies for collectively **devising** and eclectically composing their work – while dropping others, particularly his emphasis on **ritual** and his promotion of the director as a kind of guru. Based in the Performing Garage in SoHo, New York City, the company's main members have included LeCompte, Willem Dafoe, Kate Valk, Jim Clayburgh, Peyton Smith, and Ron Vawter and Spalding Gray (who died in 1994 and 2004, respectively). The company has won many awards (including, for LeCompte, a National Endowment for the Arts Distinguished Artist's Fellowship for Lifetime Achievement) and has toured widely in the USA, Europe, Asia, South America and Canada, influencing many other theatre-makers.

The Wooster Group's work is aesthetically pioneering and politically radical and pivots around combining old and new texts and practices to interrogate the cultural power of both. In content, the Group's productions typically collage elements from classic modern plays (usually from the American repertoire) with diverse samplings from popular culture, including material which is culturally taboo. *Route 1 & 9 (The Last Act)* (1981) combined Thornton Wilder's *Our Town* with pornography and a Pigmeat Markham comic routine from the 1960s performed by the company in blackface. *LSD (. . . Just the High Points . . .)* (1984) combined Arthur Miller's *The Crucible* with accounts of Timothy Leary's experiments with LSD. Juxtapositions like these produce new resonances in both sources of material, often working to deconstruct the assumed elitism of the 'classic' texts and to expose some of the prejudices – about race, gender, and age for example – on which they rely. In form, the company is exploring and experimenting with a host of theatre languages available to it alongside dramatic text, including **dance**, **scenography** and the **multimedia** potentials of video and **lighting and sound** design. Sets are often organized around tiered metal grids, with on-stage video playback and microphones, and with tables facing audiences for the performers' presentation of material. These sets and the presentational style they facilitate have acquired a signature status and spawned numerous imitative table plays – for example, Forced Entertainment's *Speak Bitterness* (1994) and *The Travels* (2002). Stylistically, the productions are again eclectic, intercutting documentary-style presentation with **naturalistic** scenes (which are often, however, estranged through video or microphone mediation) and sequences of flamboyant theatricality often involving dance (for example, the shoe dance at the end of *LSD*).

The political engagement of the Wooster Group's work operates on multiple fronts. The work deconstructs received high cultural artefacts, especially classic plays, and queries popular assumptions about what theatre should do and be. While acknowledging the power and seduction of naturalism's illusionistic performance, the Group's work also challenges its cultural dominance and perceived truth through a number of alienation techniques – for example, showing the actor putting drops in his eyes to simulate tears, and replaying a monologue, first as emotive **realism** and a second time accelerated and ridiculous (both in *LSD*). Finally, it provokes debate about the responsibilities of both producing and consuming culture by explicitly including controversial material, the most spectacular example being the blackface in *Route 1 & 9*, for which the company temporarily lost a major portion of its public funding.

A pioneer in postmodern American performance, the Wooster Group celebrates performance's pleasures (the actor's **presence**, classic texts' literary achievement, the thrill of dance), interrogates its prejudices, explores the new forms it might take and remains committed to democratic methods of devising. The Group continues to make challenging productions, including *Brace Up!* (1991), which combined Chekhov's *The Three Sisters* with Japanese theatre forms and on-stage video capture and playback, and *House/Lights* (1998), based on Gertrude Stein's

Dr Faustus Lights the Lights (1939) and the 1964 softcore bondage film *Olga's House of Shame*. In its exploration of new media, it has also made several videos, including *White Homeland Commando* (1992).

Bibliography

Savran provides detailed descriptions and analysis of many productions up to the late 1980s, while Shank describes and analyses work through the 1990s. Callens collects new essays on both the Group and other companies and directors it has influenced, including The Builders Association and Richard Maxwell. Auslander's books analyse the Group's work, especially *LSD*. Giesekam considers the Group's work in the context of postmodernism.

Auslander, Philip (1992) *Presence and Resistance: Postmodernism and Cultural Politics in Contemporary American Performance*, Ann Arbor: University of Michigan Press.
—— (1997) *From Acting to Performance: Essays in Modernism and Postmodernism*, London: Routledge.
Callens, Johan (ed.) (2004) *The Wooster Group and Its Traditions*, Brussels: Peter Lang.
Giesekam, Greg (2002) 'The Wooster Group', *Postmodernism: The Key Figures*, Hans Bertens and Joseph Natoli (eds), Oxford: Blackwell.
Savran, David (1988) *Breaking the Rules: The Wooster Group*, New York: Theatre Communications Group.
Shank, Theodore (2002) *Beyond the Boundaries: American Alternative Theatre*, revised and updated edition, Ann Arbor: University of Michigan Press.
The Wooster Group, Online. Available <http://www.thewoostergroup.org/> (accessed 25 February 2005).

ZEAMI, MOTOKIYO (JAPANESE NOH ACTOR/THEORIST/ PLAYWRIGHT, 1363–1443)

Zeami is one of the founders of noh theatre who wrote approximately 100 of the extant 240 noh plays. His insights, and those of his father (Kanami Kiyotsugu), into the practices and concepts of this ancient form provide one of the fullest and earliest analyses of **performing** and performance, and are equivalent perhaps to Bharata-muni's *Natyasastra* from India and to a lesser extent Aristotle's *Poetics*. Zeami's treatises categorized principles like Grace (*yugen*) and the Flower (*hana* – the spiritual quality and **presence** a performer can acquire with maturity, insight and practice), as well as more pragmatic notions like 'reading the **audience**'. His work offers not only invaluable historical information but vital instruction to the contemporary performer, even though he does not fit within the temporal parameters of this book.

Zeami's writings have also influenced several European artists, including **Edward Gordon Craig**, **Eugenio Barba** and **Jerzy Grotowski**, some directly and others more obliquely. Several Japanese experimental theatre practitioners, like **Tadashi Suzuki**, returned to his work keenly in the 1960s, reacting against *shingeki*, the Japanese version of Western **realism**, and in order to return to the source of Japanese theatre. European and **Asian performance** practitioners have been attracted to several aspects of his work: the long apprenticeship of decades rather than years which he proposes; his combination of pragmatism (for example, how to structure events in the day-long noh **festivals**) and spirituality; his technical advice to the performer on sustaining energy and focus on stage; and the structured methodological approach of a performer moving through different 'levels', which peak in 'The art of the flower of peerless charm'. Zeami also defined performing as a 'way' of being, a principle shared by theatre **directors** and martial artists alike, and evident in groups that range from The Living Theatre to Poland's Gardzienice Theatre Association.

Bibliography

This is the main translation of Zeami's treatises in English.

Zeami, Motokiyo (1984) *On the Art of the No Drama – The Major Treatises of Zeami*, trans. J. Thomas Rimer and Yamazaki Masakazu, New Jersey: University of Princeton Press.

Part II
EVENTS

EVENTS

4′ 33″ (BLACK MOUNTAIN COLLEGE, NORTH CAROLINA; 'COMPOSED' BY JOHN CAGE; 1952)

Conceived by **John Cage**, *4′ 33″* (four minutes and thirty-three seconds) constructed the absence of **music**. This timed period of silence invited the **audience** to listen not to the piano playing of concert pianist David Tudor but instead to incidental **sounds** – their own breathing, coughs or the rustling of programmes. Tudor began *4′ 33″* by lifting the lid of a grand piano. He ended by replacing the lid. Between these two clearly defined actions he moved his arms three times, breaking the whole composition into three movements, in both the literal sense of the word and in terms of a musical score. The elements of chance, non-intentionality and naturally occurring sounds which made up *4′ 33″* were features that also appeared in many of Cage's later works. The piece's significance lay in its insistence that auditors or spectators must find their own meanings in the performance rather than respond to the expressive ideas of the artists. Through this seemingly simple decision, Cage defined the process of creativity as an essentially democratic one. He was undermining his status as a composer who intentionally constructs sounds to affect the spectator. But he was also playfully negating Tudor's role as a virtuoso musician, as the piece prevented both artists from demonstrating their talents.

Not surprisingly, *4′ 33″*'s first audience was deeply provoked and the piece generated avid debate. It was an early example of, and inspiration for, the kind of provocative practices that became widespread in the 1960s, initially known as **happenings** and then **performance art**. These all questioned the audience's role as passive observers and tried to make them somehow the object of the performance. *4′ 33″* still stands up as a conceptually challenging event, continuing to fuel debates about the nature of art. In summer 2002, it was the centre of a copyright dispute when composer Mike Batt was accused by Cage's estate of plagiarism when he included a piece called 'A Minute's Silence' on his album *Classical Graffiti*. Batt settled out of court. In January 2004, the piece was played for the first time in Britain by a full orchestra in a season of Cage's works titled 'John Cage Uncaged', and transmitted on the radio. These examples and the interest that surrounded both events indicate how much the piece still lies firmly within the public consciousness and how it still functions as a paradigm of the extreme nature of some creative explorations.

Bibliography

Understandably, none of these texts gives much detail about the performance, but rather they follow questions and issues it provoked. Kaye places the work in a broader context of the history of postmodern performance.

Cage, John (1967) *A Year from Monday: New Lectures and Writings*, Middletown, CN: Wesleyan University Press.
—— (1968) *Silence: Lectures and Writings*, London: Calder and Boyars.
Kahn, Douglas (1999) 'The Impossible Inaudible', in *Noise, Water, Meat: A History of Sound in the Arts*, Cambridge MA: MIT Press, pp.155–99.
Kaye, Nick (1994) *Postmodernism and Performance*, London: Macmillan.
Kostelanetz, Richard (ed.) (1993) *Writings About John Cage*, Ann Arbor: University of Michigan Press.

BALINESE DANCE-THEATRE (THE DUTCH PAVILION, PARIS COLONIAL EXPOSITION; DIRECTED BY COKORDA RAKA SUKAWATI; 1931)

This **dance**-theatre presentation has come to epitomize the infiltration of **Asian performance** into Western theatre, shaping its practices and theories alike and taking it inexorably on a path towards **interculturalism**. This performance was not, however, by any means the first appearance of Asian performing arts in the West. W. B. Yeats, for example, had already seen Japanese theatre in Europe and had been working with a Japanese dancer, Mr Ito, when he wrote his noh-inspired *Four Plays for Dancers*, published in 1920. But the fact that **Antonin Artaud** saw this particular performance which inspired his essay 'On the Balinese Theatre' in *The Theatre and Its Double* (1938) has thrust this specific event irrevocably into the limelight.

Presented in a mock-temple setting, the presentation included short modernized extracts from a myriad of Balinese forms – Balinese dance-theatre includes the popular Barong dance, the sacred Wali dance and the warrior dance Baris, all of which have centuries-long genealogies. The irony in Artaud's analysis and the subsequent significance this has accrued is that he misunderstood what he was watching and its context, investing in the performance the spirituality and history he desired for his own theatre. He misinterpreted the performers' codified hand gestures as abstract 'hieroglyphics', and he emphatically imbued the rather artificial event with a mysticism that the performers did not themselves intend to convey. Rather than being an authentic enactment of a Balinese sacred dance, the performance was pragmatically devised to entertain paying visitors to the exposition. Nevertheless, the Balinese dance-theatre's gamelan **music** and striking physicality helped Artaud envisage a total theatre, much as **Bertold Brecht**'s meeting with Chinese performer Mei Lan Fang four years later supported the development of his theory of alienation. We can also use Artaud's essay to gauge Western theatre artists' growing preoccupation and frustration with the limitations of **naturalist** mimesis.

Balinese **ritual** performance in its own domestic context has also become known through anthropologist Margaret Mead's film footage, which shows performers in trance piercing themselves with the long thin ceremonial knives known as *kris*. The ethnographic film *Trance and Dance in Bali* (1952) is based on fieldwork conducted in Bali from 1936 to 1938 by Mead and her husband Gregory Bateson, with cinematographer Jane Belo. The access such documentaries and their earlier album *Balinese Character: A Photographic Analysis* (1942) give to sacred ritual practices has led to deeper analyses of trance states in several investigations of **acting**. Within a wide spectrum of approaches to acting, the total absorption of those in trance stands at the other end from the detachment espoused by Brecht. Such analyses also emphasize the differences between what the **spectator** and the performer perceive even on a biological level, with the trance-dancer insensitive to the pain that spectators might assume he feels.

Artaud's limited perception during a time of still intense imperialism differs greatly from the later detailed anthropological surveys produced by Belo and Mead, and shows how understanding moved on. Hindsight has helped us understand the necessity of mutual insight into the 'other's' position and context in cross-cultural projects. The exoticizing contained within his essay – perhaps inevitable, given the falsifying nature of the exposition – reminds us of the impositions and assumptions potentially implicit in intercultural projects. Current examinations of Asian performance practices by outsider onlookers must now have a more sophisticated sense of alternative perspectives, thanks in part to the knowledge Artaud and anthropological studies and documents such as Mead's have bestowed.

Bibliography

The two essays given look at the specific misunderstandings in Artaud's writing and the implications of this, while Schechner looks at the relationship between theatre and anthropology in general, including discussions of trance and Balinese performance.

Artaud, Antonin (1970) *The Theatre and Its Double*, London: Calder and Boyars.
Belo, Jane (1960) *Trance in Bali*, New York: Columbia University Press.
Savarese, Nicola (2001) 'Antonin Artaud Sees Balinese Theatre at the Paris Colonial Exposition', *The Drama Review* 45.3 (T171): 55–77.
Schechner, Richard (1985) *Between Theater and Anthropology*, Philadelphia: University of Pennsylvania Press.
Winet, Evan (1998) 'Great Reckonings in a Simulated City: Artaud's Misunderstanding of Balinese Theatre', in *Crosscurrents in the Drama – East and West*, Stanley Vincent Longman (ed.), Alabama: University of Alabama Press and Southeastern Theatre Conference, pp.98–107.

CABARET VOLTAIRE (ZURICH, SWITZERLAND; PERFORMED BY VARIOUS ARTISTS; 5 FEBRUARY 1916)

The first night of the Cabaret Voltaire saw the birth of a challenging movement called **Dada** that has influenced much performance experimentation since, especially **performance art** and **happenings**. In the neutral country of Switzerland during the First World War, the events' destructive and irrational drives chimed with the nihilism of the surrounding mass slaughter. Dada's appeal also lay in the fact that it cut across artistic boundaries with participants drawn from literature, **music**, theatre and the plastic arts. Consequently, its impact has also traversed disciplines. **Antonin Artaud** and **Tadeusz Kantor** are just two amongst many theatre artists who were clearly inspired by the **surrealist** movement into which it evolved.

The word 'dada' itself, selected when plucked randomly from a dictionary, means a horse or a hobbyhorse in French or 'yes, yes' in Russian and indicates the movement's attempt to deny all significance, to resist categorization and, ultimately, to destroy art. The nature of the first Cabaret Voltaire performance at No. 1 Spiegelgasse was eclectic, including shouted poems, folk songs, the display of paintings, the recitation of manifestos, drumming and short sketches. Nightly themed performances ensued (initially these were country-specific based on materials from Russia, France and Switzerland), with both solo and collaborative work, most of it provocative. Performers **played** with words and reduced them to **sounds** in order to displace their functionality. With the exception of the highly skilled cabaret performer Emmy Hennings, performances were rough and ready, denying virtuosity, professionalism or dramaturgical organization. The simultaneous reading of poems and nonsense texts accompanied by cacophonic noise, **masks** and absurd costumes led to riotous **audience** responses. Such interaction became commonplace and was even encouraged. As this animation and the audience's hunger for scandal grew, so did the performers experiment more wildly, striving to keep breaking their own rules.

The Cabaret Voltaire closed after five months. It had had some popular success, but its influence went well beyond these events alone. The Dada movement that the Cabaret spawned has provided a constant reminder of the ability, and perhaps indeed the necessity, of art to disturb the public and their expectations, and continually to move beyond the parameters which it establishes.

Bibliography

There is a wealth of material on Dadaism, but these texts place it in relation to the evolution of performance and its beginnings at the Cabaret Voltaire.

Esslin, Martin (1961) *Theatre of the Absurd*, New York: Doubleday.

Goldberg, RoseLee (1988) *Performance Art: From Futurism to the Present*, revised and expanded edition, London: Thames and Hudson.

Melzer, Annabelle Henkin ([1976] 1994) *Dada and Surrealist Performance*, Baltimore: Johns Hopkins University Press.

CHERRY ORCHARD, THE (MOSCOW, RUSSIA, MOSCOW ART THEATRE [MAT]; DIRECTED BY KONSTANTIN STANISLAVSKY, WRITTEN BY ANTON CHEKHOV; 17 JANUARY 1904)

At the beginning of the twentieth century this production cemented the place of **naturalism** as a dominant and successful form, even though it had its detractors. These included **Vsevolod Meyerhold** and Chekhov himself, who saw *The Cherry Orchard* as comic and symbolic rather than the tragic slice of life for which **Konstantin Stanislavsky** strove. With designer Viktor Simov, Stanislavsky loaded his production of the play with **sound** effects such as frogs and corncrakes and numerous **scenographic** elements, like a mound of hay, whereas in the text Chekhov had stipulated the vast emptiness of the steppe. Chekhov's desire for minimalist symbolism clashed head-on with Stanislavsky's own love of stage technology and conspicuous detail. In spite of such conflicts during the process, the **audience** responded positively to this verisimilitude at *The Cherry Orchard's* première, timed to coincide with an ailing Chekhov's birthday. The play acted as an epitaph to the vanishing life of the gentry in the early years of the new century and signalled the changes sweeping through Russia before the imminent revolutions. This change was embodied in the character Lopakhin, who surprises even himself by buying the orchard in order then to chop it down and exploit the land commercially. The end of Act 4 resonates to the sound of axes and the orchard's destruction. The play became the longest-running Chekhov piece in the MAT's repertoire and has subsequently become one of Chekhov's most produced works, the focus of its social critique shifting for each epoch and culture that produces it. The MAT production was soon followed by Chekhov's death, closing the debates that had raged between himself and Stanislavsky as to the timbre of his plays. However, these differences continued in the tensions between Stanislavsky and Meyerhold regarding their divergent approaches to **directing**.

Though numerous other plays and productions could supplant *The Cherry Orchard* as a paradigm of early twentieth-century naturalist theatre, it has become emblematic of such work. The play has proved versatile enough to allow diverse approaches like **Peter Brook**'s stripped-back 1981 production at his Théâtre Les Bouffes du Nord, Paris, or Giorgio Strehler's rather more poetic 1974 rendition. The naturalist detail of its première was often emulated, though, and as a result its over-complex detail has reinforced both skewed notions of what naturalism is and how Chekhov might stereotypically be interpreted (with white dust sheets, dull lassitude and bubbling samovars). This production of *The Cherry Orchard* reminds us how canonized theatre so easily starts to reproduce not so much **everyday life** but in fact itself alone.

Bibliography

The play and its production have spawned numerous analyses, such as the ones by Edward Braun (in the Allain/Gottlieb collection) and Rayfield. Senelick and Benedetti place this production in the context of Stanislavsky's numerous other works.

Benedetti, Jean (1982) *Stanislavski: An Introduction*, London: Methuen.

Gottlieb, Vera and Paul Allain (eds) (2000) *The Cambridge Companion to Chekhov*, Cambridge: Cambridge University Press.

Rayfield, Donald (1994) *The Cherry Orchard: Catastrophe and Comedy*, New York: Twayne Publishers.

Senelick, Laurence (1997) *The Chekhov Theatre – A Century of the Plays in Performance*, Cambridge: Cambridge University Press.

CONSTANT PRINCE, THE (WROCŁAW, POLAND: THE LABORATORY THEATRE, DIRECTED BY JERZY GROTOWSKI; 1965)

The Constant Prince was a central performance in **Jerzy Grotowski**'s oeuvre as well as in world theatre of the twentieth century. Most remarkable was the actor Ryszard Cieślak's portrayal of the eponymous Prince, which epitomized Grotowski's approach to **acting**. Critics considered that Cieślak had achieved a 'total act' and, while they struggled to describe what this meant in practice, they agreed unanimously that he had somehow transcended both the role and his material presence, becoming what Grotowski defined as a 'holy actor'. Cieślak recalled **Antonin Artaud**'s vision of the martyred actor, 'burning alive at the stake but still signalling to the audience through the flames', communicating even in his death throes.

The production's playtext, which is delivered at great speed in an incantatory way, had a complex cross-cultural evolution. The nineteenth-century Polish Romantic playwright Juliusz Słowacki had written a version of Pedro Calderón de la Barca's play *El Principe Constante* (1629) from the golden age of Spanish drama, which Grotowski further drastically cut. As well as this pared-down text, in keeping with the principles of 'poor theatre' Grotowski used few props and simple costuming and had **scenographer** and architect Jerzy Gurawski construct a striking scenic arrangement for this piece. Gurawski had invented models of staging for several of the Laboratory Theatre's previous productions, each time altering the perspective and position of the spectator. In *The Constant Prince*, the actors performed in a pit surrounded by wooden walls, reminiscent of a bullring or operating theatre. Seated on benches, the spectators had to lean forward over the barriers to look down on the action. They were thus meant to become suppliant witnesses of, and voyeuristic participants in, the Prince's torture and subsequent martyrdom at the hands of his captors.

On one level, Cieślak's role symbolized a Poland which has been 'crucified' (or invaded and occupied) several times in its history. The piece used Christian imagery such as the pietà with a dead Jesus lying across his mother Mary's lap. But the role was also a deeply personal exploration. Months of private work with Grotowski plumbing Cieślak's memories of his first feelings of love as a teenager led to the precise physical and vocal sequence of actions or 'score' that was meant to contain and control the performer's emotions. Cieślak's 'self-penetration', as Grotowski described it, helped generate the piece's acclaim on an international tour. Critics testified that *The Constant Prince* went beyond specific Polish referencing through its central archetype of the martyr and through Cieślak's 'gift' of vulnerability before the audience.

The Constant Prince is recorded minimally in a poor-quality film shot from a fixed position with a single camera with minimal lighting, for which the sound was recorded two years after the performance in another country. The near-perfect match between sound and action shows the absolute precision of the actors' scores, even with this two-year gap. It is hard to discern a lot in the film, but in spite of this it affirms Grotowski's vision of performance as an encounter between spectator and actor that attempts to change all participants on a deep, personal level as they remove the **masks** and habits inculcated in daily interaction. The basic premises of Grotowski's performances in this period – the small audiences of under a hundred people, the efficacy of communicating through Jungian archetypes, as well as the actors' profound and almost destabilizing work on themselves – have been repeatedly questioned. Few can deny, however, the enormous impact the piece had aesthetically, or its many imitators, as well as the debates about theatre's function, the need for craft and discipline, and the ethics of the director–actor relationship that it subsequently spawned.

Bibliography

The following texts contain short accounts of this performance from various perspectives: the director's, the critics' and the scholars'. All these books relate this piece to Grotowski's other works, though with focuses on different periods. The film is available privately and contains subtitles in several languages.

Barba, Eugenio (ed.) (1968) *Towards a Poor Theatre*, Holstebro: Odin Teatrets Forlag.
Kumiega, Jennifer (1985) *The Theatre of Grotowski*, London: Methuen.
Schechner, Richard and Lisa Wolford (eds) (1997) *The Grotowski Sourcebook*, London: Routledge.

COYOTE: I LIKE AMERICA AND AMERICA LIKES ME
(RENÉ BLOCK GALLERY, NEW YORK; 'ACTION' PERFORMED BY JOSEPH BEUYS AND A COYOTE; 1974)

Joseph Beuys's temporary cohabitation with a coyote broke down boundaries between **everyday life** and art in a compelling way, furthering his belief that everyone (even a coyote, perhaps) can be an artist or present art. Beuys had not been alone in integrating **animals** into performance but here the interaction was sustained and was unavowedly central to the piece. For a week, before an intrigued public in the René Block Gallery in New York, the German artist shared a small cage with the animal, with not much more than a pile of straw, a large sheet of felt and numerous copies of the *Wall Street Journal*, which the coyote enjoyed tearing up and urinated on. Beuys followed its every move and attempted to communicate with the animal constantly.

Like many of his pieces, *Coyote: I Like America and America Likes Me* explored the indeterminate crossover between **ritual**, daily behaviour and performance. Beuys called these events 'Actions', though they shared many properties with **happenings**, and were even briefly connected to the very socially aware fluxus movement (1962–65). His works gained their gravity from their social critique as well as allusions to religious symbolism. He described his role as being akin to a shaman figure. Politically, he operated in left-wing and ecological groups, an engagement that fed directly into his art and that, in one event (*Kukai/Akopee-nein/Brown cross/Fat corners/Model fat corners*, 1964), led him to being attacked on stage by right-wing demonstrators. The performance with the coyote, for example, questioned the status of the United States' native population. With the protagonist of the coyote and a simple repeated sequence of structured moments of interaction, Beuys invoked the close contact to nature with which Native Americans live. Traditionally, for them, the coyote is a powerful totemic animal, whereas for contemporary Americans its status has been downgraded to little more than a pest. The piece's challenge to America lay in Beuys's allusion to this discrepancy.

Beuys's inspiration for his events, sculptures and **installations** derived in part from his personal experience during the Second World War, when his aeroplane was shot down over the Crimea and he was kept alive by Tartars, who wrapped him in felt and rubbed animal fat on to him to keep him warm (a claim that some have queried). From a visual arts background (for twelve years, Beuys was Professor of Sculpture in Düsseldorf – before being dismissed in 1972 for his controversial views), the striking sculptural and physical **presence** of his works was usually animated by his own interactions, be it with the wild coyote, a dead hare with whom he was privately discussing his own artworks (*How to Explain Pictures to a Dead Hare*, 1965) or a cardboard box in which he spent a whole day (*Twenty Four Hours*, 1965). His 'social sculptures' and Actions influenced and excited many, perhaps most surprisingly the Glaswegian ex-gangster prisoner/author Jimmy Boyle, with whom Beuys began a series of dialogues as a result of the coyote event. In November 2002, Flemish actor Benjamin Verdonck staged an anti-war piece during the buildup to the Iraq war, spending three days in a cage with a pig named 'Coyote: I Like America and America Likes Me'. Although Beuys died in 1986, works like Verdonck's perpetuate his quirky but politically engaged practice and attest to his enduring impact.

Bibliography

These books are a mixture of essays, interviews, statements and visual information, providing helpful ways into Beuys's often difficult to grasp visual and performed artworks.

Bower, Alain (1996) *The Essential Joseph Beuys*, Lothar Schirmer (ed.), London: Thames and Hudson.

Tisdall, Caroline (1976) *Joseph Beuys: Coyote*, Munich: Shirmer Mosel.

—— (1979) *Joseph Beuys*, London: Thames and Hudson.

DEAD CLASS, THE (CRACOW, POLAND; CRICOT 2, DIRECTED BY TADEUSZ KANTOR; 1975)

Polish **director Tadeusz Kantor**'s production of *The Dead Class* was a master-piece of **visual theatre**. Exploring notions articulated in his manifesto on 'The Theatre of Death', Kantor **played** with the staging of personal childhood memories, images of lifelessness and the replication of real life inherent in **performing**. The piece draws on a range of sources but was based loosely on a framework developed by the Polish Jewish writer, artist and teacher Bruno Schulz in his short story 'The Old Age Pensioner' (1934). On the verge of dying, an old man returns to his former school and gradually regresses to become a schoolboy before he is swept away into the sky by the wind and disappears. The performance also contained fragments from Polish writer Witold Gombrowicz's novel *Ferdydurke* (1937), an imaginative homage to idle youth. The novel's narrative sometimes focuses on (and thereby 'enlarges') parts of the body, a sort of textual zoom-in. Kantor's actors replicated this device gesturally, through face-pulling, for example. Excerpts of text were also lifted from Stanislaw Ignacy Witkiewicz's *Tumor Brainiowicz* (1920), an absurdist piece by the eccentric Polish writer, artist, photographer and philosopher, whose difficult and **surreal** plays Kantor frequently and successfully staged. Finally, *The Dead Class* also drew on Kantor's own experience, or rather the memories of his childhood days. Kantor aptly described himself as a 'text-mincer', as this wide-ranging collection of sources and stimuli demonstrates.

The Dead Class's haunting macabre images were reminiscent of the sketches of hollow-eyed dome-headed figures that accompany Schulz's stories. The **scenography** consisted of an archetypal pre-Second World War schoolroom with desks, where the uniformed children (played by adult performers) were straddled by mannequins strapped to their backs. At times these figures even replaced them, propped up at their desks – they were omnipresent as shadows that cannot be forgotten or erased. The unusual collection of characters included the Old Man with a Bike, who was represented semi-literally by a wheel tied to an old man's body – one of Kantor's 'bio-objects' as he described them. All action was overseen and orchestrated by the on-stage black-suited figure of Kantor himself, whose looming **presence** and critical eye focused moments through gestures of encouragement or admonishment. His participatory presence clearly framed the **mise en scène** as a representation of his own experience, and made the **audience** aware of his ongoing role as director and creator of that experience – a practice common to all Cricot 2 productions.

The impact of the piece was sustained by several years of international touring as well as its presentation in other media. Textual transcripts of the performance exist, as well as grotesque, humorous photographs and the vivid sketches with which Kantor's creative process always began. Polish filmmaker Andrzej Wajda made a film as a response to the piece, shot in a Cracow cellar as well as outdoors where the characters become liberated from the schoolroom and their mannequin selves, in a departure from Kantor's original performance. Théâtre de Complicité's *Street of Crocodiles* (1992, UK), directed by Simon McBurney and based on another story by Schulz, was visually and thematically inspired by *The Dead Class* and Kantor's work, a testament to the long-lasting impact Kantor has had.

Bibliography

Apart from videos of the performance and Wajda's film, none of which are commercially available, the best access to this piece is through the Drozdowski book. This includes a transcript of the performance text as well as reflections on the piece and its characters by Kantor. More indirect analyses and visual information are available in the other texts below.

Drozdowski, Bohdan (ed.) (1979) *Twentieth Century Polish Theatre*, London: John Calder.

Kobialka, Michal (1993) *A Journey Through Other Spaces: Essays and Manifestos by Tadeusz Kantor*, Berkeley: University of California Press.

Miklaszewski, Krzysztof (2002) *Encounters with Kantor*, George Hyde (ed.), London: Routledge.

DIONYSUS IN 69 (NEW YORK; THE PERFORMANCE GROUP; 1968–69)

Based on Euripides' *The Bacchae*, *Dionysus in 69* was **devised** by The Performance Group and its **director**, **Richard Schechner**, and performed in a purpose-built **environmental** set at the Performing Garage in SoHo, New York, for over a year from 1968 to 1969. It demonstrates some of the innovative performance methods Schechner and The Performance Group helped to pioneer in the late 1960s and early 1970s, as well as some of those methods' advantages and problems.

Schechner and his collaborators wanted to make theatre that produced more meaningful communication and a stronger sense of democratic community for its makers and **audiences** than they felt was produced by conventional text-based Western theatre. They wanted a theatre that performed a **ritual** function, making all participants feel they were building a community. Schechner and The Performance Group therefore adopted innovative approaches to text, performance practices and **scenography**. Written texts provided a starting point for performance rather than an authoritative blueprint. *Dionysus in 69* used *The Bacchae*'s characters, story and some text, though not where The Performance Group's performers felt they could portray material more effectively by other means, especially by speaking as themselves, and through highly physicalized, non-**realist movement** sequences. Dionysus's birth ritual, for example, began with the actor playing Dionysus telling the audience a little about his own birth, and was performed with five male performers lying on the floor, five women standing, straddling them, and Dionysus being passed – or 'birthed' – through the resulting canal. The performers did the scene in minimal costumes for the first several months of the show, but in a bid to make it more sexually expressive and ritualistic they later performed it naked. The Performance Group created its shows in ways that aimed to be democratic, devising *Dionysus in 69* over many months of workshops and **rehearsals** and continuing to alter the show throughout its run. Scenography for The Performance Group's productions transformed the entire **space** of the Performing Garage, literally enveloping audiences in the show and facilitating a degree of audience–performer interaction that The Performance Group felt was qualitatively better than what conventional, proscenium-arch theatre allowed. Performer movement in *Dionysus in 69*'s multi-level set was designed to be circular, thereby producing a sense of inclusion and intimacy. The audience was invited to sit and move where it liked in designated audience areas. But they were also asked to join in the performance, for example in a **dancing** scene, a caressing scene (sometimes also performed naked), and the concluding **parade** from the theatre out on to Wooster Street. For many, *Dionysus in 69* produced a sense of democratic community-building and challenged taboos of self- and group expression, especially sexual expression.

Despite its apparently altruistic aims and egalitarian effects, however, *Dionysus in 69*, Schechner and The Performance Group were sometimes criticized for being precisely the opposite – undemocratic and exploitative. As long as Schechner directed the show, the company was inevitably organized at least partially hier-archically. For example, when a student group in the audience executed a premeditated kidnapping of the performer playing Pentheus part way through one performance, Schechner made an executive decision about whether or not – and how – to continue the show. His decision was subsequently hotly debated amongst the company. Further, while the show idealized community, there was disagreement within the company. One of the chief points of debate concerned opportunities for audience contact, especially during scenes performed naked. While the nudity may have served director Schechner's thematic aims, it nevertheless left the performers – especially the women – vulnerable to actual groping on stage. Like the Living Theatre's ***Paradise Now*** (1968), *Dionysus in 69*'s bold exploration of methods for democratizing performance encountered and exposed some of the possibilities and hazards of that ambition.

Bibliography

De Palma *et al.*'s film is a split-screen documentary of The Performance Group's production, showing both performers and audiences. The Performance Group's book documents the show's development through text and images. Schechner articulates his arguments about environmental theatre and describes this show. Shank provides summary description and analysis. Shephard performed in the show and offers a personal account.

Dionysus (1970) film directed by Brian de Palma, Robert Fiore and Bruce Joel Rubin, USA: Performance Group Stage Productions and Sigma III Group.
Performance Group, The (1970) *Dionysus in 69*, Richard Schechner (ed.), New York: Farrar, Strauss and Giroux.

Schechner, Richard ([1973] 1994) *Environmental Theater*, New York: Applause Books.
Shank, Theodore (2002) *Beyond the Boundaries: American Alternative Theatre*, revised and updated edition, Ann Arbor: University of Michigan Press.
Shephard, William Hunter (1991) *The Dionysus Group*, New York: P. Lang.

EINSTEIN ON THE BEACH (AVIGNON FESTIVAL, FRANCE; DIRECTED BY ROBERT WILSON, MUSIC BY PHILIP GLASS, VOCAL TEXTS BY ASSORTED CONTRIBUTORS, CHOREOGRAPHY BY ANDREW DE GROAT AND LUCINDA CHILDS; 1976)

Robert Wilson and Philip Glass's opera *Einstein on the Beach* marks a shift in the development of Wilson's work and indicates the scale of his achievement as an innovator of **visual theatre** for the twentieth and twenty-first centuries. Like *A Letter for Queen Victoria* (1974), it shows Wilson moving away from his visually complicated 'silent operas' towards a **scenography** that is more architecturally controlled and into an exploration of the theatrical power of language and speech – even when they are nonsensical. In a broader context, since its première in 1976, *Einstein* has shown how theatre can be non-linear and multidisciplinary – not prioritizing narrative sense and text, as most **naturalist** theatre and opera does, but fracturing narrative and exploring the aural qualities of speech as well as the equally important features of image, **space**, **light**, non-vocal **sound**, and **movement**.

Einstein on the Beach combines a mathematically precise structure with allusive, dreamlike content – Wilson's familiar trademarks. It is composed of nine episodes over four acts spanning five hours. Three images – a train, a courtroom and a space machine hovering over a field – appear first in pairs and, finally, all together in a trio. Wilson's signature knee-plays (literally, joints between scenes) provide a prologue and interludes. Architectural precision is central to the design, too, as horizontal, vertical and diagonal lines of objects, movement and light dominate the visual field, and most performers wear the Einstein 'uniform' of shirt, braces, trousers and tennis shoes. This precision is reiterated in Glass's sound score, which features insistent patterned thematic repetition.

The allusiveness of the performance is in its images and texts. The three recurring images are relatively banal and can form logical narrative links to Einstein's lifetime, which stretched from the age of the steam locomotive to the brink of the age of space travel. But the enactment of these images is illogical and dreamlike. In the courtroom, for example, an elderly black male judge delivers a monologue about romance in Paris or women's liberation, and **dancer** Lucinda Childs sways on a bed reciting a disjointed monologue written by Wilson's collaborator, Christopher Knowles, who was born with brain damage. Meanwhile, the chorus sings patterns of numbers – a 'text' introduced in rehearsals by Glass as a placeholder for the libretto he had not yet written, but adopted for performance by Wilson, who loved both its order and its arbitrariness.

As in much of Wilson's work from the mid-1970s to the mid-1980s, speech and song do not tell a linear story; rather, they enhance mood, compel **audiences** to think or daydream associatively, and refer obliquely to the opera's subject – Einstein and his mathematics. Other aspects of staging, too, compel audience engagement with the apparently irrational as well as the apparently rational, and with scenic and aural elements of theatre. As in most of Wilson's work, *Einstein* presents images that slowly transform before us, it is collaborative, and it combines elements of high and popular culture, juxtaposing Einstein's mathematics and his tennis shoes. It also indicates the European appeal of Wilson's work and the support he has found there: it received funding from the French government and was initially produced at the Avignon **Festival**. Its various remountings in 1984, 1988 and 1992, and the design changes these incorporated, show the evolution of his aesthetic towards an ever more architectural, elegant and refined theatre of images style as demonstrated in, for example, his *Dream Play* (1998).

Perhaps most significant is the opera's distinctive formality, in both its composition and its relationship to the audience. Wilson's theatre almost never addresses the audience directly, unlike much American theatre of the same period, for example that of **Richard Schechner**'s Performance Group. Wilson was, and continues to be, interested in altering audiences' ways of seeing and hearing, rather than trying to revise ways of literally interacting with the audience. His advice to audiences going to see *Einstein* was, 'Go like you would to a museum, like you would look at a painting . . . You just enjoy the scenery, the architectural arrangements in time and space, the music, the feelings they all evoke. Listen to the pictures' (quoted in Shyer).

Bibliography

Obenhaus' documentary film of the 1984 revival includes excerpts from the production and interviews with Wilson and Glass. All sources describe and analyse the opera.

Brecht, Stefan (1978) *The Theatre of Visions: Robert Wilson*, Frankfurt am Main: Suhrkamp Verlag.
Einstein on the Beach: The Changing Image of Opera (1985) film directed by Mark Obenhaus, USA, produced by the Brooklyn Academy of Music.
Holmberg, Arthur (1997) *The Theatre of Robert Wilson*, Cambridge: Cambridge University Press.
Shank, Theodore (2002) *Beyond the Boundaries: American Alternative Theatre*, revised and updated edition, Ann Arbor: University of Michigan Press.
Shyer, Laurence (1989) *Robert Wilson and His Collaborators*, New York: Theatre Communications Group.
Wilson, Robert, Einstein on the Beach. Online. Available <http://www.robertwilson.com/common/featuredworks/eob2.html> (accessed 28 January 2005).

GOVERNMENT INSPECTOR, THE (SOHN THEATRE, MOSCOW; WRITTEN BY NIKOLAI GOGOL, DIRECTED BY VSEVOLOD MEYERHOLD; 9 DECEMBER 1926)

Vsevolod Meyerhold's production of Gogol's 1836 play demonstrated his view of the **director** as interpreter and orchestrator of both the **mise en scène** and the text with a confidence that caused shockwaves in Russian theatre. By placing the onus of interpretation on himself as auteur rather than on the writer, Meyerhold was tampering with sacred cows – in this case, classical Russian material from the mid-nineteenth century. Critics balked at his heavily altered adaptation of the play, which he divided into fifteen episodes and interpolated with lines from other works by Gogol, such as his *Petersburg Stories*. They also questioned his tragicomic pantomime style, a major departure from the reverential **realism** with which such works had been treated previously, by the likes of **Konstantin Stanislavsky** and Vladimir Nemirovich-Danchenko. In spite of criticism that verged on abuse and which helped generate animosities that later culminated in Meyerhold's officially sanctioned assassination, the production heralded a new path of experimentation with the classics in Russian theatre. Even with these detractors, the piece stayed in the company's repertoire until 1938.

Although in **rehearsal** Meyerhold initially asked his actors for clearly defined characters with biographies consistent with **naturalist** approaches, he soon pushed them towards caricature and the grotesque, asking them to find repeated habitual gestures, defined postures, idiosyncratic **movements** and a specific rhythm for their characters. By such means they caricatured petty officialdom and Tsar Nicholas's bourgeois society and affectations. Elaborate stage business departed from the text and choreographed sequences sublimated the individual in carefully composed *tableaux vivants*. Meyerhold focused on the ensemble rather than the individual with several interpolated and additional choral scenes, like that of young officer-suitors strumming imaginary guitars. By now his cast were highly trained in biomechanics and were working with assured synchronicity and discipline. The actors' movement was enhanced by exaggerated costumes and kinetic **scenography**, with sets that moved on trucks and that kept the action of this four-hour version flowing. Orchestral **music**, some of it original and some by nineteenth-century Russian composers, heightened their gestural, rhythmical **acting** in a style that Meyerhold intended to be consonant with Gogol's satirical vision.

Meyerhold's uncompromising combination and exploitation of all elements of the theatre was ahead of its time. The production has since come to be considered an influential precursor of physical and **visual theatre**, an early example of successful theatrical stylization. While this might also be claimed for Meyerhold's earlier productions, like *The Magnanimous Cuckold* (1922), written by Belgian author Fernand Crommelynck, *The Government Inspector* is significant because of the text's esteemed place in Russian culture and Meyerhold's willingness to go beyond accepted interpretations and practices with such hallowed material, however great the risk.

Bibliography

Both book authors are respected experts on Meyerhold. The Worrall article gives details about this particular production.

Braun, Edward ([1979] 1995) *Meyerhold: A Revolution in Theatre*, revised edition, London: Eyre Methuen.
Leach, Robert (1989) *Vsevolod Meyerhold*, Cambridge: Cambridge University Press.
Worrall, Nick (1972) 'Meyerhold Directs Gogol's *Government Inspector*', *Theatre Quarterly* 2.7: 75–95.

GULF WAR (IRAQ AND KUWAIT; 1990–91)

Battles are often described as taking place in the 'theatre of war', which denotes the arena where the operations happen and suggests the dramatic nature of wars. In arguing that the Gulf War did not actually happen (his original short 1991 treatise stated this in its title, 'La Guerre du Golfe n'a pas eu lieu', an intentional reference to Jean Giraudoux's 1935 play *La Guerre de Troie n'aura pas lieu*), French philosopher and bête noire Jean Baudrillard was not directly referring to this metaphor. Nor was he being literal. Rather, he was developing his idea of 'simulacrum' and the hyperreal. His notion of simulation, developed especially in his book *Simulacra and Simulations* (1985), suggests how in a **postmodern** world life is intensively theatricalized and mediated, so we lose sight of what reality is. There are copies without originals and these merge as mass-produced items become replications, all equivalent to each other. As such, the very idea of 'an original' ceases to exist. Disneyland is considered by Baudrillard to be the archetypal simulated place, positioned as a fantasy, but in fact (for Baudrillard) as 'real' as much of America itself. This raises serious ethical issues of responsibility. Where does responsibility lie and how does one take it if the actual event itself is a simulacra and no 'truth' can be determined? In relation to performance it also demonstrates how the idea of **presence** is questionable if our reality is in fact merely constructed.

Extending this concept to actual events, Baudrillard has consistently questioned how we know whether or not events such as the Gulf War, which began when Iraq invaded Kuwait in 1990, are actually taking place or not. His earlier writings focused on Vietnam (proverbially the first television war) and Cold War conflicts such as a supposedly 'staged' massacre in Timisoara, Romania, in December 1989. For the public, the source of information about these events is often uncertain, but through the intervention of the media they swiftly become endorsed as exciting history-forming spectacles. News is frequently presented by reporters in hotels at a safe distance from the front or site of action, underlining the lack of reality that pervades the media representation of such loss of life and violence. The sense of hyperrealism in the Gulf was further enforced by the theatre of war: a non-specific area of desert sand between Iraq and Kuwait, with few identifiable landmarks. In his controversial essay, Baudrillard was also referring to the fact that Iraq inevitably faced defeat at the hands of America's disproportionate counterattack under the codename Desert Storm, with sophisticated high-tech weapons and 'smart-bombs'. Several of these had cameras attached to their noses that relayed their explosion, producing a new sense of technical involvement in the war while simultaneously maintaining the viewers' distance from it. There really was no contest and the actual war was short-lived compared to its much more protracted buildup and anticipation – the 'war of words'. Baudrillard questioned what relation the events we see on television have to the actual war (for example, the pictures of charred bodies in tanks on the 'turkey shoot' road to Basra, as the Iraqis' escape route from Kuwait was described), when they potentially become a simulacrum or hyperreal. Furthermore, he asked how we can then respond politically to such a constructed absence when the 'reality' is so elusive.

Published as a very short book Baudrillard's essay received much criticism and misunderstanding but it adds a useful dimension to the field of performance studies that has long interrogated the intentional reproduction and artifice of forms like **naturalism**. Though this is distinct from simulation as Baudrillard sees it (the live human performer is always original, for example), such ideas question the political purpose and social context of much theatre. How does performance move beyond simulation to create a psychophysical reaction as **Antonin Artaud** espoused, or a political relevance as **Bertold Brecht** sought, and how does it keep abreast with the ever-increasing sophistication of contemporary media? Live performance, with its comparatively limited technology and budgets, can easily lose ground to media which operate on quite another scale of representation, with wider distribution and wider social impact, and which can more easily simulate reality, as films or theme parks sometimes appear to do.

Bibliography

Baudrillard's writings are dense and difficult, as this sample demonstrates. British group Blast Theory created a game/performance, *Desert Rain* (1999–2003), inspired by Baudrillard's text, which Giannachi briefly describes.

Baudrillard, Jean (1985) *Simulacra and Simulations*, New York: Sémiotext(e).
—— (1988) *Selected Writings*, Mark Poster (ed.), Cambridge: Polity Press.
—— (1995) *The Gulf War Did Not Take Place*, trans. and introduction Paul Patton, Sydney: Power Publications.
Giannachi, Gabriella (2004) *Virtual Theatres: An Introduction*, London: Routledge.

HAKA (TRADITIONAL MAORI DANCE)

Haka is the generic name for the **dance** of the Maori, natives of Aotearoa/New Zealand, but it is probably best known internationally through the particular haka performed before matches by the New Zealand national rugby team, the All Blacks. This haka is known as the 'Ka mata, Ka mata' (the opening words of the chant, translatable as 'I die! I die!') or the 'Te Rauparaha' (after the Maori chief who is credited with having composed it in around 1820). Its chant speaks of the threat of imminent death and then the triumph of survival. Its dance portrays strength, control and determination and involves the whole body and face in a range of quick, alert, disciplined and powerful movements, including stomping, jumping, slapping the legs, quivering the arms, chanting, and grimacing with the eyes wide open and the tongue stretched out of the mouth. It was first performed internationally in 1888 by the New Zealand Native Team, a rugby team made up predominantly of Maoris. Even today, it is an All Black player of Maori descent who initiates its performance before a match. Like many **rituals**, the haka warms up and focuses its performers, strengthening their sense of community and poten- tially alienating those who watch and cannot perform it – notably, the opposing team.

The All Blacks' 'Ka mata, Ka mata' haka performs Aotearoan/New Zealand national identity, more actively and distinctively than the conventional act that precedes many **sports** events – passively standing for a national anthem. However, it raises important issues about **intercultural** crossover and appropriation. The Maori were historically colonized by European settlers, or pakeha. Read negatively, the haka's adoption as a performance of New Zealand national identity can be seen as an appropriation of the historically and culturally specific tradi- tions of a colonized people to signify a bit of ethnic colour for their colonizers. Read more positively, this adoption credits the Maori with founding the culture of Aotearoa/New Zealand, demonstrates the strength of that culture and articulates the pre- and post-colonial hybridity of contemporary Aotearoan/New Zealand identity. More broadly, the haka demonstrates how identity is produced through all kinds of **performative** acts, including – and even especially – those that take place in mass popular culture.

Bibliography

All the sources provide history and description of the haka (or direct links to this information). *Haka!* is a page on a site dedicated to New Zealand rugby and is the most detailed.

Haka! Online. Available <http://www.haka.co.nz/haka.php> (accessed 21 January 2005).
'*The Haka: In the Beginning*', *New Zealand Rugby Museum*. Online. Available <http://www.rugbymuseum.co.nz/asp/container_pages/normal_menu/rmArticle.asp?IDID=137> (accessed 21 January 2005).
Karetu, Timoti (1993) *Haka! The Dance of a Noble People*, Auckland: Reed.
New Zealand Rugby Union. Online. Available <http://www.nzrugby.com/> (accessed 21 January 2005).

HOLOCAUST MEMORIALS AND MUSEUMS (WORLDWIDE; POST-1945)

The horror of the Holocaust produced a crisis in practices of representation and **performative** acts of memorialization. Memory had previously been widely conceived as objectively knowable, recoverable, and so possible to memorialize in static and solemn monuments, be they statues, poems or museums. **Postmodern** thinking, especially from the 1970s onwards, questioned this model of memory, suggesting it risked displacing the horrific event with an aesthetic representation, replacing social acts of remembrance with inert placebos, and thereby actually sanctioning forgetting, instead of stimulating, remembrance. These problems of memorialization were particularly urgent as people struggled to decide what to do with sites like the death camps at Auschwitz. Preserve them as memorials to the dead and reminders to the living? Or obliterate them as atrocities? Facing such critical decisions, postmodern thinking reconceived memory as subjective, multiple and possibly unknowable – although it acknowledged that remembering is both an emotional urge for individuals and an ethical responsibility for societies. Postmodern culture has not stopped producing memorials but has attempted to make them possess other responsibilities and presumptions that acknowledge the radical mutability of memory; that stimulate active engagement and remembering in **audiences**; that provoke audiences to take responsibility for preventing past horrors from being repeated; and continue to question if, how and when it is even possible to represent traumatic memories.

An influential example of this kind of postmodern counter-monument is conceptual artists Jochen and Esther Gerz's *Monument Against Fascism, War, and Violence – and for Peace and Human Rights*, which was erected in Hamburg in 1986. Aiming neither to pay tribute to fascism nor to immobilize spectators in the face of it, the *Monument* was designed to be interactive, changing and ultimately itself only a memory – or, rather, multiple memories. The *Monument*'s 12m-high pillar was covered in soft lead with steel-pointed pens attached near its base. Multilingual signs invited spectators to write on it and to commit to remain vigilant. In a series of seven ceremonies, the pillar was gradually lowered into the ground so that the whole of its surface could be written on. It was finally interred in 1993, its site marked with a stone, thereafter evoking silence and absence. This example demonstrates counter-monuments' potential interactivity, performativity and dynamic production of meaning in concert with their participant audiences.

The United States Holocaust Memorial Museum in Washington, DC, designed by James Ingo Freed and opened in 1993, uses other strategies to act as an appropriately awe-inspiring memorial, while it resists being inappropriately celebratory or even definitive. It deliberately combines seemingly contradictory elements – granite and brick, a tower and a hexagon, grand and prosaic entrances – in order to acknowledge its role as necessarily monumental and simultaneously democratic. These dual meanings were deemed vital as a response not only to the Holocaust but also to the museum's location in the US state capital (see study by Patraka).

Probably the most famous museum of this kind is the Jewish Museum in Berlin, designed by Daniel Libeskind and opened in 1999. Libeskind sought to evoke the very *absence* of the Jews in post-Holocaust Berlin by incorporating into his building a number of voids – empty **spaces** that span several floors, interrupt the spaces of the rest of the building, and can be looked into and sometimes entered. As Berlin's Jews experienced profound displacement, this building produces a strong sense of disorientation through its asymmetries and contrasts. Its structure is a zigzag; its windows are rarely horizontal or vertical and appear like slashes in the building's façade; its surfaces contrast shiny zinc and dull concrete; and its garden contains a square area of forty-nine rough, inclined rectilinear concrete columns atop which willow oaks grow, their curving branches intertwining. While Libeskind's building may appear to prioritize chaos and absence, it nevertheless incorporates many elements of order and **presence**: its heterogeneity validates the heterogeneity of the architecture surrounding it; and the apparently random lines of its windows actually 'connect' the addresses of great figures in Berlin's Jewish cultural history. Furthermore, the building is not just about the past; its grounds are accessible to the public and provide access to a playground. The building explores and manifests the traumas and evacuations of Berlin's Jewish past but suggests also Jewish achievement and endurance, inviting its visitors to witness all of these aspects of Jewish history in Germany.

Many other communities worldwide who have experienced massive loss and trauma must also face, in different ways, the issues of commemoration addressed by these Holocaust and Jewish memorials. This is as true of **las Madres de la Plaza de Mayo**, who witnessed Argentina's 'disappearances' of the 1970s and 1980s, as it is of the citizens of New York after the events of 11 September 2001, for whom how or whether to mark Ground Zero is a haunting question. Such issues must be addressed in different media as well. Jeannette Malkin, for example, examines how twentieth-century drama has worked to produce a kind of counter-memorial theatre.

Bibliography

Young provides extensive information and analysis of memorials. His article, Schneider's book, and two articles in *Performance Research*'s special issue focus on the Jewish Museum, Berlin. Malkin analyses the work of memory in postmodern theatre, while Patraka looks closely at both theatre and performance.

Malkin, Jeanette R. (1999) *Memory-Theater and Postmodern Drama*, Ann Arbor: University of Michigan Press.
Heathfield, Adrian and Andrew Quick (eds) (2000) 'On Memory', a special issue of *Performance Research* 5.3. London: Routledge.
Patraka, Vivian M. (1999) *Spectacular Suffering: Theatre, Fascism, and the Holocaust*, Bloomington: Indiana University Press.
Schneider, Bernhard (1999) *Daniel Libeskind: Jewish Museum Berlin: Between the Lines*, trans. John Gabriel, Munich: Prestel Verlag.
Young, James E. (ed.) (1994) *The Art of Memory: Holocaust Memorials in History*, Munich: Prestel-Verlag.
—— (2001) 'Daniel Libeskind's Jewish Museum in Berlin: The Uncanny Arts of Memorial Architecture' in *Visual Culture and the Holocaust*, Barbie Selizer (ed.), London: The Athlone Press, pp.179–97.

LADY DIANA'S FUNERAL (WESTMINSTER ABBEY, LONDON, ENGLAND; 6 SEPTEMBER 1997)

The significance of the Princess of Wales's funeral was not only the scale of the event but also the way that the media involved the public in a spectacle, both live and mediated through the **internet**, television and newspapers. In death, some people like James Dean and Marilyn Monroe have achieved semi-mythological status, the display of their deaths and funerals significantly contributing to this phenomenon. The spectacle of both Diana's death in Paris on 31 August (shown in countless photos of the crash-site and a twisted Mercedes), and her funeral, was exacerbated by the frenetic media interest that they fuelled. Ironically, her accidental death was caused by the fact that her chauffeur was travelling at speed to escape the camera lenses of the paparazzi, the often devious and illicit photographers of the rich and famous. The media paid little heed to this and exploited the funeral in a similarly obsessive vein. American global news network CNN stated that the 'World watches as Britain bids farewell to Diana', almost as though she was somehow still alive and could herself wave goodbye.

The media's construction of Diana's funeral as a global event was no doubt encouraged by her own exploitation of the media during her lifetime, as in her self-crowning as the 'Queen of Hearts', and the celebrated televised interview with British journalist Martin Bashir with its gesture of wiping a tear, which critics saw as a cleverly crafted act to gain sympathy. Even before the funeral took place, the British nation was reported to be united by its shock and sorrow, brought together in one grieving mass. These emotions were enacted by the 'performing' public as they brought flowers to Kensington Palace, where the Princess had lived. Visitors created a visual backdrop of flowers to the mourning that soon became a rotting mass of vegetation and which thereby remembered the biological actuality of death. As even more people came to see those already camped out along the Mall and around Kensington Palace, the mourners themselves augmented the spectacle. Comparisons of Diana to the Madonna and other religious connotations surfaced with the offering of candles, iconographic portraits and flowers. The cortège and funeral itself, with its elaborate sequence of hymns, tributes, a one-minute silence 'observed by the nation', readings and songs – notably an adapted version of 'Candle in the Wind' by pop star Elton John – was televised, with videos of it sold subsequently. Not only did the fairy-tale figure of Diana seem to live on through such films and in headlines like CNN's, but the legend was perpetuated further through condolence books, memorial statues and gardens, such as the one opened in Paris on Valentine's Day 2001.

Public participation in the mourning was rapidly followed by journalists' and then academic analyses of the event (termed 'Diana studies') and what it indicated about Britain's psyche. French philosopher Jean Baudrillard penned a short tongue-in-cheek poem called 'Lament for Lady Di', and theorists and commentators such as Homi K. Bhabha were drawn into the discussions. Speculation and rumours ran rife about the death, fuelled by the fact that Diana's then-partner Dodi Fayed was an Arab. This all cultivated the already-extant notion of the Royal Family as a glorified soap opera, while simultaneously shoring up the myth of Diana.

After her death, Diana's dresses and accessories sold for hundreds of thousands of pounds, totemic costumes of a being that in her afterlife seemed to become as much a media-generated character as a real person. Lady Diana's funeral is just another example of how a local event becomes global spectacle when it is constructed by the vast resources of the world's media. It also shows the extensive aftermath of emotions, analysis and discussion that performance events on this scale sometimes generate – it reportedly attracted more media coverage than the outbreak of the Second World War! The fact that, even though the live events were shown so extensively on television, thousands of people still felt the need to visit the palace in person or sign condolence books says much about the value placed on **liveness** and actual participation, however vicarious, in such events.

Bibliography

Steinberg and Kear bring together a range of new material, whereas Merck collects previously published essays and more populist material, including the piece by Bhabha and Baudrillard's poem, as well as a few cartoons and photographs. Thomas provides a more distant reappraisal of what he calls the 'Diana Event' and its complex public interfaces.

CNN News. Online. Available <http://www.cnn.com/WORLD/97/08/diana/mourns/funeral> (accessed 13 November 2004).
Merck, Mandy (ed.) (1998) *After Diana: Irreverent Elegies*, London: Verso.
Steinberg, Deborah Lynn and Adrian Kear (eds) (1999) *Mourning Diana – Nation, Culture and the Performance of Grief*, London: Routledge.
Thomas, James (2002) *Diana's Mourning: A People's History*, Cardiff: University of Wales Press.

MAHABHARATA, THE (PARIS AND TOURING; CENTRE INTERNATIONAL DE CRÉATIONS THÉÂTRALES [CICT], DIRECTED BY PETER BROOK; 1985–1988)

The Mahabharata has at least a twofold significance for twentieth- and twenty-first-century theatre. It epitomizes many of the methods and aims of its highly influential **director**, **Peter Brook**, and it has provoked and sustained some of the most hotly contested debates around the risks and potentials of **intercultural** theatre from the late 1980s onwards.

The source for Brook's performance text originated in India in the third or fourth century AD and is known there simply as 'the Epic'. At more than 100,000 stanzas in length, it is the world's longest narrative poem. For many Indians it provides a foundational account of Indian – especially Hindu – cultures. Following extensive research in India and Europe, Brook's collaborator, writer Jean-Claude Carrière, adapted this epic into a nine-hour playtext which Brook's cast subsequently rehearsed and developed for nine months. The French-language *Mahabharata* premièred at the Avignon **Festival** in 1985, toured Europe, was adapted into

English, and toured to six countries on four continents from 1987 to 1988. It was finally adapted into a three-hour film and then a six-hour television version that was broadcast worldwide in 1989.

For Brook, *The Mahabharata* offered a monumental opportunity to explore theatre as a vehicle for communication. He argued that, although 'the Epic' text may be Indian, it 'carries echoes for all mankind' (Brook, quoted in Williams 1991: 44); it is Indian and it is universal. This liberal humanist attitude influenced not only his selection of text, but also his decisions about **scenography**, **music**, performance styles and casting. He did not want design and music to attempt to be authentically Indian but rather to give 'a flavour' of India. Consequently, set design, for example, was minimal, using performance spaces largely as the company found them, but adding some accents of warm colour as well as the real elements of fire, water and earth. A firm believer in the universal power of storytelling, Brook staged *The Mahabharata* as a series of stories, sometimes narrated by a teller to a young boy and sometimes represented by performers. The action flowed easily between these modes of performance and acknowledged the communicative power of both speech and **movement**. Brook cast thirty performers and five musicians from eighteen countries, including France, Greece, India, Indonesia, Italy, Japan, Poland, Senegal, Trinidad and Vietnam. He cast this range partly because he believed the performers could each bring differences – of culture, language and performance skills – but centrally because he believed those differences would nevertheless be universally understood by his **audiences**. *The Mahabharata* is probably Brook's most ambitious show to date, but it is nevertheless typical of his work. It aimed for direct communication, eschewed elaborate design and performance styles, was rehearsed by a multicultural company over many months, celebrated the power of myth and demonstrated his conviction that cultural difference is not a barrier to communication.

This last point is the one that has caused major disputes. Brook advocates an understanding of communication as potentially universal. His most virulent critics, led by **Rustom Bharucha**, argue that, rather than communicating the meanings of 'the Epic', Brook desecrated them, largely by trivializing them. By decontextualizing 'the Epic' and leaving out the core section of the *Bhagavad Gita*, Brook removed 'the Epic' from the specific contexts in which its mythology, vocabulary, social and religious references could be understood. By condensing it into a linear narrative, he disregarded the cultural significance of its many stories, its forms and its modes of expression. Brook's aim to evoke merely 'a flavour' of India might have been an attempt at modesty, but for Bharucha and others it was irresponsible, rendering a complex culture superficial. Some have extended these arguments to a critique of Brook's casting as well, arguing that he homogenizes his performers' different skills, styles and cultural identities to produce a fluid but bland multicultural sameness. Brook has defended himself against these accusations by reiterating both his commitment to universal communication and his belief that universalism is more important than cultural difference. Other critics, keen to defend Brook's *Mahabharata* as a powerful performance that does not appropriate

Indian culture irresponsibly, but eager also to credit the significance of cultural difference, have posed a third argument. Recognizing the numerous diversities brought to *The Mahabharata*, they argue that it is multi-voiced or polyphonic rather than homogenized, that it allows interaction rather than assimilation, and that it produces new, hybrid, syncretic cultures rather than desecrating old ones. Debates around *The Mahabharata* may have lessened, but they continue to influence intercultural performance-making and critical debate.

Bibliography

Brook articulates his aims in the foreword to the play. Williams collects an excellent range of critical and documentary material. Chaudhuri summarizes critical debate succinctly.

Bharucha, Rustom (1993) *Theatre and the World: Performance and the Politics of Culture*, London: Routledge.
Carrière, Jean-Claude (1987) *The Mahabharata*, trans. and foreword by Peter Brook, London: Methuen.
Chaudhuri, Una (1998) 'Working out (of) Place: Peter Brook's *Mahabharata* and the Problematics of Intercultural Performance', in *Staging Resistance: Essays on Political Theatre*, Jeanne Colleran and Jenny S. Spencer (eds), Ann Arbor: University of Michigan Press, pp.77–97.
Mahabharata, The (1989), directed by Peter Brook, screenplay by Jean-Claude Carrière, COL.
Williams, David (ed.) (1991) *Peter Brook and* The Mahabharata. London: Routledge.

MOTHER COURAGE AND HER CHILDREN (DEUTSCHES THEATER, BERLIN, GERMANY; DIRECTED BY BERTOLD BRECHT AND ERICH ENGEL; 1949)

Although not the première, this performance of one of **Bertold Brecht**'s central full-length plays is recognized as a model of what he championed for the theatre. The play was written in 1938 just before and in anticipation of the Second World War, and premièred in 1941 at the Zurich Schauspielhaus, **directed** by Leopold Lindtberg. Brecht, though, had no direct involvement in this production, as he was then in exile from Germany in Finland. The image from the 1949 production, which Brecht co-directed, of his wife Helene Weigel as Mother Courage dragging her wooden cart across the stage has become an iconic image of twentieth-century theatre, and a role that has become inseparable from the actress. The performance was also significant in that it led to the foundation of the Berliner Ensemble, a hugely influential theatre company that was based initially in Socialist-administered East Berlin, but which still operates today in a reunited country. Core members of the 1949 production's cast went on to develop pivotal roles in this ensemble. In addition, the piece cemented Brecht's position as a director of repute as well as a writer.

The play centres on the characters of the title, showing how the economics of war and the quest for survival in precarious times can corrupt, displacing the mother's natural instinctive protection of her children. The reference to the mother's 'courage' is partly ironic, but also indicates her stoicism and ability to keep her head above water economically in the face of the adversity war brings. Accompanied by her mute daughter Kattrin on the fringes of battle, Mother Courage scavenges what she can as the spoils of war, but even this is meagre. The performance plays out the economic and theatrical concerns of Brecht in his later period of work, embodied in techniques such as *Gestus* and through the disruptive placing of the dialectical songs. Scenes such as that in which the mute Kattrin is shot – unable to shout, she is conspicuously drumming on a barn roof in order to alert the townspeople of Halle to the advance of soldiers – are a good example of Brecht's plays' emotional power, belying the mistaken conviction that his works lack feeling.

Although the Berlin production was a huge success both in a partitioned Germany and internationally on tour and stayed in repertoire for more than ten years, the play has never proved an easy piece to produce, with its embedded Brechtian techniques, complex central role and large cast. Many Western actresses – including Diana Rigg, Anne Bancroft, Judi Dench and Glenda Jackson – have struggled with the role of Courage. Brecht and Engel's production is preserved in its 'original' form in a 1960 film as well as in a model book (one of the series of *Modellbücher*). This text assiduously documents the production through photos and a written commentary that gives details of the **mise en scène**, including blocking and **scenography**. This document initially led to some failed imitations, which were against the spirit of the model books – these were meant to give guidance only and not encourage replication. Other directors have experimented more boldly, including **Richard Schechner** in a 1975 version that ran successfully off-Broadway. The play has been produced consistently and has been studied across the world, providing a recurrent critique of the personal and social devastation wreaked by war and proving an enduring testimony to Brecht's ideology and artistic vision.

Bibliography

Willett is the most recognized English-language Brecht scholar. Numerous other writers, including Eddershaw, have analysed the play and its many productions.

Brecht, Bertold (1970–present) *Collected Plays*, 10 vols, vol. 5, part 2 *Mother Courage and Her Children*, ed. and trans. John Willett and Ralph Mannheim, London: Eyre Methuen.
Eddershaw, Margaret (1996) *Performing Brecht*, London: Routledge.
Willett, John (ed.) (1964) *Brecht on Theatre*, London: Methuen.
—— (1964) *The Theatre of Bertolt Brecht*, London: Methuen.

OLYMPICS (WORLDWIDE; EVERY FOUR YEARS 1896–)

Though primarily a competitive **sporting** event, the Olympics have become recognized as extravagant displays of cultural identity for nations' self-promotion. They do not always make economic sense. Countries usually run the events at a great loss, though the 1984 Los Angeles Olympics was an exception and made a huge profit. However, an implicit sense of enduring tradition and a legendary history – the Olympiads were sporting displays held in ancient Greece – lend the event authority and weight, even though in their modern form the first Olympics were held in Athens as recently as 1896. Now the Olympics take place every four years, with summer and winter events staggered, providing both the host and the guest countries with the opportunity to create spectacles that frame their sports-people as heroes. The winning of individual medals has been subsumed by obsession with the total tally, evident in the nationalistic rivalry between the United Soviet Socialist Republic (USSR) and America during the Cold War, and now between Russia, the US and China. The Olympics are a clear example of the potential seriousness of human **play**, when individual commitment becomes symbolic of national prowess.

The sporting performances are circumscribed and embellished by theatrical devices, especially in the televised opening ceremony, which increasingly comprises the following to an extravagant level: fireworks, pyrotechnics and the eternal Olympic torch; flagwaving; music and especially national anthems; choreographed **dance** displays and **parades** using national teams; and elaborate **masks** and costuming. These events are **directed** by high-profile artistic teams, which in 1992 in Spain included experimental Catalonian theatre group La Fura dels Baus. Critics lament the lack of focus on the sports themselves that the mediatization and interest in spectacle has brought, with its inevitable prurience about off-track relationships and rivalries, drugs scandals (as in Athens in 2004), and the creation and promotion of celebrity sporting personalities.

The most renowned example of a host country attempting to manipulate the Olympics to its own ends was in 1936 in Adolf Hitler's Nazi Germany. The performance of German national achievement and Aryan racial supremacy was, however, upstaged by the brilliance of black American athlete Jesse Owens, who quashed the Nazis' aspirations. Owens won four gold medals and broke several records to become 'the fastest man on earth' at that time. The event can also be hijacked for other ends, its importance guaranteeing mass publicity – in the 1972 Munich Olympics, eleven Israelis were killed in a terrorist attack. The organized exploitation of the global stage for national promotion inevitably generates counter-**demonstrations** and counter-actions, though not usually as bloody as the Munich attack.

The Olympics' theatrical nature has instigated a corresponding artistic event, the Theatre Olympics. This international festival, run by a committee of major world directors and theatre artists including **Tadashi Suzuki**, **Robert Wilson** and **Wole Soyinka**, has so far taken place in Greece, Japan and Moscow. Exploiting the global repute of the Olympics, the theatre has at last attempted to reverse the mirror and create artistic events in sport's likeness.

Bibliography

MacAloon's text is one of the few pieces that places the Olympics directly in relation to theatre and performance. A wealth of information can be accessed through the official Olympics website.

Fura Dels Baus, La. Online. Available <http://www.lafura.com> (accessed 1 November 2004).

MacAloon, John J. (1984) 'Olympic Games and the Theory of Spectacle', in *Rite, Drama, Festival, Spectacle: Rehearsals toward a Theory of Cultural Performance*, Philadelphia: Institute for the Study of Human Issues, pp.241–80.

Olympics, The. Online. Available <http://www.olympics.org> (accessed 13 July 2003).

PARADISE NOW (AVIGNON FESTIVAL, FRANCE; THE LIVING THEATRE, DIRECTED BY JULIAN BECK AND JUDITH MALINA; 1968)

Like The Performance Group's *Dionysus in 69* (1968–69), *Paradise Now* epitomizes the radical, political and collective creations of 1960s experimental theatre groups. Adopting **ritualistic** patterns, the piece was structured in eight sections or rungs of a ladder. Each section had an 'Action' sequence which depended on the voluntary participation of **spectators**. Only through this close interaction with the audience could all the participants – that is, actors *and* audience – progress towards spiritual and political enlightenment and the piece's final positive vision of an equal, open society (or Paradise). This process had to begin 'now', as the title indicated and as the symbolic action on the streets at the end of the performance demonstrated. In this way, theatre could intervene directly in **everyday life**, in order to change life's rules and conventions, and could become truly 'living'.

Throughout their many productions, the Living Theatre tested and pushed at the boundaries of legal and theatrical possibilities. As a highly politicized artistic group attempting to practise what they preached, the Living Theatre collective promoted non-violent revolution in both their lifestyle and their performances. *Paradise Now* was created through much discussion and individual improvisational input. Further synthesizing life and art, the company attempted to use theatre as a tool to change the audience's awareness of social, political and cultural restrictions. One notorious Action section – Rung Four, 'The Exorcism of Violence and the Sexual Revolution' – invited the audience to take off most of their clothes (which the actors had already done) and sit with their genitals in contact with a partner. Public sexual acts were of course illegal, even if this did not prevent everyone from refraining. Trust exercises (such as leaping into the group members' linked arms) had become a hallmark of the Living Theatre's **training**, and in *Paradise Now* they even solicited audience members to commit physically to their ideals and 'make the big leap' through such devices. The carefully structured piece was a collage of statements, shouted slogans, exercises and tableaux that vocally and physically stretched the body and tested the audience's responsibilities and the parameters of their participation.

When they first showed *Paradise Now*, the Living Theatre collective had become tax exiles from the United States in 1964 and so were based in Europe. Here they had achieved almost mythical status and gathered a large following that travelled with them, at times numbering in the hundreds. In the wake of Paris's mass **protests and demonstrations** in May 1968, the première of *Paradise Now* at the Avignon Festival added fuel to the fire. In the final stages of the performance the company rallied their audience to meet on the streets and so begin the process of revolution. Fearful of unrest, the Festival authorities asked the group to present another work instead, but the group refused, railing against this censorship. On their return to the United States to tour *Paradise Now* after its French première, the group faced similar difficulties, including arrest. Frustrated by the restrictions inherent in the theatre **spaces** and administrative structures of Europe and America, the group split into cells, with one led by the anarchist couple Julian Beck and Judith Malina (the group's leaders, if they can be so described) moving to Brazil in 1970. Shifting the focus of their work outside theatre buildings and institutional structures, they could then be open to audiences not dominated by the middle class, as had been the case in their performances in the United States and Europe. On the streets of Latin America, the Living Theatre pursued their search for paradise on earth with the poor and oppressed people who perhaps had the greatest need for it. They continue this mission today, touring to **festivals** and leading community-based projects, though without Beck (who died in 1985). The group has gone further than most to embody **Antonin Artaud**'s vision of a total, transformative theatre.

Bibliography

Shank places Malina and Beck's own accounts in their book in a broader context of American experimental performance, while Tytell provides an easy introduction to their work and lives.

Malina, Judith and Julian Beck (1971) *Paradise Now: Collective Creation of The Living Theatre*, New York: Vintage Books.
Shank, Theodore (2002) *Beyond the Boundaries: American Alternative Theatre*, revised and updated edition, Ann Arbor: University of Michigan Press.
Tytell, John (1997) *The Living Theatre: Art, Outrage and Exile*, London: Methuen.

RAVES (LATE 1980S–PRESENT)

Raves share with experimental performing arts some transgressive properties and, like much performance, they operate liminally outside daily parameters of **space**, time and economics. In practice, raves use theatrical devices like sophisticated

lighting and sound and the role of the DJ can be compared to a stage **director-cum-producer**. Terminology and concepts from within performance studies have therefore often been used to describe such events, in analogies to **rituals**, for example. The participants' sense of communal empathy or 'communitas' – a term coined by **Victor Turner** – is generated by drug-taking and highly energetic **dance movement** in close proximity to others, compounded by music that runs at 120 beats per minute or faster. Under these conditions, individuals often lose self-consciousness and inhibitions, transported to levels of heightened, pleasurable tactile awareness. The trance-like state the dancers enter into can be compared to that of a shaman, as they undergo a physically demanding process of trans-formation and transportation, immersing themselves in the vibrating sound, the dense crowd and the apparently pulsating space in order to reach an intense liberating experience. The shaman, however, typically uses such states to heal, reassure or predict. Similarities pertain more to process than outcome, but such comparisons are intriguing.

Historically, raves evolved out of acid-house parties in the late 1980s in England. They often take place in temporarily abandoned or empty structures such as railway arches, warehouses or even fields. Their **site-specific** and one-off nature – designed in part to eschew potential judicial restrictions – is enabled by modern technology such as cars for transportation, as well as mobile phones, faxes and the internet for last-minute and fleeting advertising. This use of technology is also crucial within the **multimedia** events themselves, since they usually employ intricate other-worldly visual effects and films, and powerful sound systems with which the DJs project their 'composed' music. The DJ's role is to anticipate and respond to the **audience** mood, whipping them into a state of ecstatic dancing through impromptu mixing, scratching and the careful selection of tracks. With the provision of free tickets, the politics of raves are meant to be democratic and inclusive. This can be on a vast scale and raves frequently rally tens of thousands of people. Fatboy Slim's Party on the Beach at Brighton, England, in July 2002, shocked the authorities with an unanticipated attendance of approximately 250,000 people, ten times the number expected. The media thrive on such events, further fuelling popular interest in them as well as attendance. Yet raves may also be considered conservative in that they provide only a short-lived escape from social jurisdiction and the pressures of work. While they evade the law and attempt to operate outside its authority, they are not a platform for the dissemination of political thinking or strategies other than claiming and enacting the right to have fun and party. Debates about the transgressive nature and potential of such events circulate more commonly around **carnivals** like that in Notting Hill, West London.

The ethos and spirit of raves have looped back into theatre in the work of groups such as Argentina's De La Guarda, whose performance *Villa Villa* (1995) uses loud and fast pounding music, a standing, tightly compacted audience and physical contact between actors and selected spectators. The group's performances are aimed at the kind of young people who might well attend raves. In such works the thin boundary between a lived-in participatory event and a lived-in spectacle is blurred, nowhere more so than when in *Villa Villa* a performer sweeps an audience member off her feet and up into the air on a bungee rope, a 'high' perhaps equivalent to that gained from drug use or 'Hi-NRG' dancing.

Bibliography

As well as being considered in sociological studies – like the edited collection by St John and music-centred books like Frith's – raves are often referred to in passing in texts like Broadhurst's, which is interested in the fringes of performance practices. Rietveld's book is based on her doctoral study.

Broadhurst, Sue (1999) *Liminal Acts*, London: Cassell.
Frith, Simon (1998) *Performing Rites: Evaluating Popular Music*, Oxford: Oxford University Press.
Rietveld, Hillegonda C. (1998) *This is Our House: House Music, Cultural Spaces and Technologies*, Aldershot: Ashgate Publishing Company.
St John, Graham (2004) *Rave Culture and Religion*, London: Routledge.

REINCARNATION OF SAINT ORLAN, THE (SERIES OF OPERATION-PERFORMANCES; ORLAN; 1990–93)

In a series of nine surgical operations, French **feminist performance artist Orlan** altered her face to incorporate features from famous works of art, including the forehead of Leonardo's Mona Lisa and the chin of Botticelli's Venus. Orlan was not trying to make herself into a static image of ideal beauty. Rather, through pastiche, parody and **camp** performance, she questioned who produces ideals of female beauty – pointing the finger at male artists and a male-dominated medical establishment. Further, she staged identity as something that is not inert and biologically given, but is continuously socially produced – or **performative** – and therefore contestable.

Orlan's *Reincarnation* challenged the medical objectification of women's bodies by taking control of the operating theatres where her *Reincarnation* took place, in a gesture similar to Roberto Sifuentes and **Guillermo Gómez-Peña**'s occupation of bourgeois art galleries in their *Temple of Confessions* (1994–97). Orlan decorated the theatres, hired designers (including Paco Rabanne and Issey Miyake) to costume the participants (surgeons included), and remained conscious throughout the operation-performances. During the events, she **directed** action, read excerpts from texts on **psychoanalysis**, philosophy, feminism and performance (by, for example, **Antonin Artaud**), and responded to faxed queries from **audiences** watching via electronic link-up in art galleries around the world. By introducing intertextual references, Orlan invited her audience to understand her work as a commentary on ideas of beauty, self-fashioning, the Theatre of Cruelty, and boundaries – of the body, of propriety and of performance practice. By interacting with her audience, she challenged the conventional separation of audience and performer and – like fellow **body artists Marina Abramović** and **Stelarc**

– compelled her audiences to take responsibility for what they witnessed. By using **multimedia** to perform and transmit her work, Orlan challenged the assumption that the meaning of the biological body is transparently available.

Orlan documented her recovery from the operations with daily photographs and other relics, including videos of the surgical procedures, blood finger paintings and mounted samples of extracted bodily tissue. These relics challenged her audience to consider what distinguishes the sacred relic from the profane. They made flesh the problems of documenting **liveness** and the ephemeral performance event, while revealing the post-operative physical trauma that cosmetic surgical practice conventionally hides. Irreverently, Orlan inserted her self-*Reincarnation* into a long history of religious and spiritual art, collapsing the historical distance between archaic relics and her **postmodern** present, and challenging the grand narratives of Catholicism and art history.

Reincarnation's first four operations took place in 1990, the fifth in 1991, and the sixth to the ninth in 1993. Orlan subsequently discussed the possibility of completing *Reincarnation* with an operation to extend the bridge of her nose to her forehead, but eventually decided to stop the surgery because it became both too risky and too expensive. She then considered concluding her *Reincarnation* by asking an advertising agency to rename her – or, more accurately, to rebrand her, creating a new identity and passport. This conclusion would reiterate Orlan's ongoing critique of – and engagement with – the consumerism of the art market. It would also reinforce *Reincarnation*'s proposition that the body and identity are socially produced.

In what she calls her 'carnal art', Orlan is intentionally non-conformist, questioning what the body, the face and identity are, and who defines and controls them, throughout art history as well as in our contemporary, technologically advanced culture.

Bibliography

Ince's book is well illustrated, as well as analytically thorough and insightful. For more sources of information, see the Orlan entry in Part I.

Ince, Kate (2000) *Orlan: Millennial Female*, Oxford and New York: Berg.
Orlan. Online. Available <http://www.Orlan.net> (accessed 13 January 2005).

ROUTE 1 & 9 (THE LAST ACT) (NEW YORK; THE WOOSTER GROUP; 1981)

Route 1 & 9 is typical of the **Wooster Group**'s work in that it experimented with form and combined radically different source materials in order to explore and challenge cultural assumptions about art, performance practices and American society. As the first part of a trilogy, it both returned to and raised ongoing company practices and concerns. Almost all of the Group's work has successfully provoked debate, but this can be seen as their most controversial piece, its blackface performance and sexually explicit video attracting accusations of racism and sexism and leading to a withdrawal of a significant portion of their state funding.

The main sources for *Route 1 & 9* are Thornton Wilder's classic American play, *Our Town* (first produced in 1938), and vaudeville routines performed in the 1960s in blackface by African-American entertainer Dewey 'Sweet Papa Pigmeat' Markham. *Our Town* is a close study of a handful of characters in the small town of Grover's Corners in early twentieth-century New Hampshire. Grover's Corners is fictional, but the 'Our' of the title invites **audiences** to see the town as typically American and the play as containing universal truths about life and death. *Route 1 & 9* disrupted *Our Town*'s universalizing fantasy of a white, middle-class, puritan American idyll by introducing the racial and cultural difference Wilder's play omitted. It first proposed an alternative version of the United States by shifting the suggested location from *Our Town*'s imaginary, idealized, pastoral New Hampshire town to an actual urban environment of heavy industry, traffic and commerce: Route 1 and 9, a 50km-long stretch of highway flanked by petrol stations, malls, restaurants and industrial plants in New Jersey. It further challenged *Our Town*'s white-washed, **realist** version of American culture by embedding Wilder's play in sections of performance that were non-realist and came from non-white **acting** traditions. These included sequences where white actors in blackface emulated Pigmeat Markham's scatological comic routines from the 1960s and phoned out of the theatre trying – often unsuccessfully – to get uptown Harlem restaurants to deliver downtown to the Performing Garage in SoHo, across a social divide marked by class and ethnicity. Other non-realist sections of performance included a parodic opening video 'lesson' on how to understand *Our Town*, a mid-show high-energy **dance**, and a concluding set of videos showing a road trip from Manhattan to Route 1 and 9 and a couple trying out a variety of sexual positions in what appears to be a pornographic film in the making. Using video playback and extreme close-up reminiscent of soap opera, *Route 1 & 9* presented sections of *Our Town* but always using alienation techniques that are typical of the Wooster Group's efforts to deconstruct realism's claim to portray 'the truth'.

The Wooster Group's **director**, Elizabeth LeCompte, has argued that in *Route 1 & 9* she aimed to confront not the audience but difficult source material, which the audience must then witness. However, many audiences – including critics and state-funding representatives – found the show's use of blackface and extreme racial stereotyping not critical but offensive, so much so that the New York State Council on the Arts (NYSCA) rescinded the Group's funding by forty per cent the following year. The Group held public forums to discuss the show's alleged racism and appealed the NYSCA's decision, but the appeal was not upheld. Perhaps what was most successful about *Route 1 & 9* was its provocation to debate issues around who has the right to represent whom, what new forms political theatre might take, and how to **devise** a deconstructive, provocative, but engaging form of **multimedia postmodern** performance. These debates continue, often in direct relation to the Wooster Group's work.

Bibliography

Savran excellently documents and analyses much of the Group's work to the mid-1980s. Auslander's books include useful analyses of this piece and another in the trilogy, *LSD (. . . Just the High Points . . .)* (1984).

Auslander, Philip (1992) *Presence and Resistance: Postmodernism and Cultural Politics in Contemporary American Performance*, Ann Arbor: University of Michigan Press.
—— (1997) *From Acting to Performance: Essays in Modernism and Postmodernism*, London: Routledge.
Savran, David (1986) *Breaking the Rules: The Wooster Group*, New York: Theatre Communications Group.
—— (1991) 'Revolution . . . History . . . Theater: The Politics of the Wooster Group's Second Trilogy', in *The Performance of Power: Theatrical Discourse and Politics*, Sue-Ellen Case and Janelle Reinelt (eds), Iowa City: University of Iowa Press, pp.41–55.

SPORTS

Sports events run parallel to theatrical performance, providing inspiration, theoretical analogies, and serving as spectacles in themselves. The **Olympics** are the grandest example of theatricalized sport, the event framed by spectacular opening and closing ceremonies, **parades** and the dramatic stagings of the awarding of medals accompanied by national anthems. The very idea of performance is embedded in sports and especially in the word '**play**'. But, while most performance playing is ultimately for entertainment, sports have more serious outcomes and are highly competitive. There is subsequently a lot more at stake in sport than there is in performance, and events like the Olympics put national pride and confidence on the line. Sports also have much greater public inclusion than the theatre, and the public's emotional investment in sports is extensive. Sports stars are as celebrated today as Hollywood actors, their off-pitch activities attracting as much interest as their games. Spain's bullfighting brings this relationship between sports, ceremony, **ritual** and **everyday life** into even sharper focus, more so than other potentially fatal sports such as boxing and motor-car racing. Bullfighting involves elegant costuming and a flamboyant red cloth, as well as the sophisticated '**dances**' of the toreadors. These decorative performance elements do not, however, hide the fact that this ritual-like event frequently ends in bloodshed or death, of both the bull and occasionally the bullfighter.

The more gentle race against time is one of sport's primary aims, embodied in landmark moments such as the achievement of the four-minute mile or the smashing of the ten-second 100m. With their emphasis on physical achievement, the need for **training** is central to sports. Sports-like training principles and practices have crossed over into the performing arts, recognizable in **Vsevolod Meyerhold**'s functional biomechanics, in some highly athletic approaches to dance like Eurocrash, and in actor training methods such as that of **Tadashi Suzuki**, which is based partly on martial arts, which many people practise as sports. In martial arts, the two fields of sport and art are even more integrated, for they demand a way of life, or at least a psychophysical approach. As the rewards for sporting success have grown, so has greater significance been attributed by sports psychologists and coaches to sportspeople's lifestyles and their mental conditioning. David Beckham's performance for England in Euro 2004 is a case in point – the football player's domestic life was seen to be impacting negatively on his play.

In spite of advances in technique, psychological analyses and training, much in sport still depends on what might be called '**improvisation**' – performances and sports both have unpredictable outcomes. This element of chance is what gives it its excitement and generates sport's massive popularity. And, as in the theatre, **spectators** can affect the outcome of events (consider the difference it makes to a football team's performance whether it is playing away or at home). Unlike most theatre, however, sports carry no message as such, even if they use complicated systems and codes or rules which the spectator must know how to read. This is what separates them so clearly from theatrical performance, even if many of their processes are shared.

The popularity and the aesthetics of sport have inspired many theatre practitioners, especially **Bertold Brecht**. He advocated that the boxing ring is a useful model for the theatre and that spectators should approach the theatre as though a boxing match – critically detached, with pleasure, and smoking. Italian comic performer Dario Fo has presented several satirical performances (like *Mistero Buffo*) in vast sports stadia in Italy in order to reach a large and predominantly working-class audience. Appropriating the aesthetics rather than the political and inclusive dimension of sport, the **Wooster Group** played badminton to signify battles in their piece *To You, the Birdie! (Phèdre)* (2002), based on Racine's *Phaedra*. British choreographer and dancer Shobhana Jeyasingh's *Raid* (1995) investigated the boundaries between dance and sport, and specifically an Indian street game called Kabbadi. But the cross-fertilizations are not just practical. **Richard Schechner** is one theorist who has investigated similarities between sport and performance on a theoretical level, revealing the difficulties in classifying such activities. There are many examples of the convergence of sport and performance in both practice and theory.

Bibliography

Brecht's views are posited in his 1926 chapter, an article originally written for newspaper publication. Social psychologist Russell has a detailed section on social influences on sports performance that includes analysis of crowds. Schechner's 'Event–Time–Space Chart' in *By Means of Performance* lists sports as a specific category and provides a useful introduction to comparative analyses.

Brecht, Bertold ([1926] 1964) 'Emphasis on Sport', *TDR: The Drama Review* 16.1 (T53): 3–15. Reprinted in John Willett (ed. and trans.) *Brecht on Theatre*, London: Methuen, pp.6–9.

Russell, Gordon W. (1993) *The Social Psychology of Sport*, New York: Springer-Verlag.
Schechner, Richard (2002) *Performance Studies*, London: Routledge.
—— and Willa Appel (eds) (1990) *By Means of Performance: Intercultural Studies of Theatre and Ritual*, Cambridge: Cambridge University Press.
Willett, John (ed.) (1964) *Brecht on Theatre*, London: Methuen.

TEMPLE OF CONFESSIONS, THE (TOURED USA; GUILLERMO GÓMEZ-PEÑA AND ROBERTO SIFUENTES; 1994–97)

This performance-**installation** by **Gómez-Peña** and Sifuentes is representative of their innovative work as **performance artists** and activists, and indicates how their **intercultural** agendas have tested the artistic and social potentials of interactive performance.

The Temple of Confessions opened in Arizona in 1994 and toured the USA until 1997, visiting a range of venues, from art galleries, to a convent, to city **festivals**. It was composed of three areas, the Chapel of Desires, the Chapel of Fears, and a sort of mortuary chamber in the middle. In 'living dioramas' in the two Chapels, Sifuentes and Gómez-Peña posed in Plexiglas boxes as 'living saints' with hybrid identities composed mostly of what they saw as 'Anglo' fantasies of Mexicans. Sifuentes was covered in tattoos and fake bulletholes, evoking fantasies of youths of colour as simultaneously sexually attractive and threatening. Gómez-Peña wore a clichéd 'Tex Mex' outfit festooned with souvenirs and talismans, evoking fantasies of Mexican culture as being in touch with some sort of pagan wisdom. (Effigies replaced Sifuentes and Gómez-Peña in the installation after they had appeared live for three days.) A body bag marked 'INS' (Immigration and Nationality Service) implicated American bureaucracy as potentially violent in its relationship to other cultures. The installation's ironic undercutting of an authentic spirituality was further enhanced by velvet paintings of other hybrid saints, small tables covered with votive candles and icons, and two live **dancers** dressed as nuns who used their veils to clean the Plexiglas boxes and visitors' shoes. **Audiences** were invited to confess their intercultural fears and desires, whether orally (at two prayer benches with microphones placed before Sifuentes and Gómez-Peña), in written statements to be placed in an urn at the installation, or over the phone to a toll-free number. Recorded confessions were subsequently played back in the installations soundscape, further encouraging audiences to confess.

Sifuentes and Gómez-Peña challenged dominant cultural assumptions and the public's interest in confessional behaviour, by both displacing and reanimating them in disturbing ways. Where artists like **Orlan** have occupied galleries to criticize how they display and objectify women, Sifuentes and Gómez-Peña did the same here to interrogate how forms of dominant culture objectify other cultures. By making the performance a semi-**ritualized** opportunity for audience confession, Sifuentes and Gómez-Peña extended the limits of audience–performer interaction developed in many different ways by other theatre-makers (for example,

Richard Schechner, **Eugenio Barba**, **Peter Brook** and **Jerzy Grotowski**). Specifically, they wanted to compel audiences to explore their complicity as cultural tourists in producing the clichéd images Sifuentes and Gómez-Peña inhabited. At the end of its tour, Sifuentes and Gómez-Peña created an online version of *Temple*, using the **internet** to extend *Temple*'s interactive reach still further into time and cyberspace.

Bibliography

The Temple of Confessions publication includes an audio CD; its website is still under construction in 2005.

Gómez-Peña, Guillermo (2000) *Dangerous Border Crossers: The Artist Talks Back*, London: Routledge.
—— and Robert Sifuentes (1997) *The Temple of Confessions: Mexican Beasts and Living Saints*, New York: powerHouse.
Temple of Confessions, The. Online. Available <http://www.echonyc.com/~confess/> (accessed 21 January 2005).

Tiananmen Square demonstrations (Beijing, China, April–June 1989)

In what is reportedly the largest public square in the world, a mass popular **demonstration** and sit-in turned into a massacre. The significance in recalling this event is not only its symbolism on a political and social level, representing how mass movements can emerge to threaten the authorities, but also how **performative** such occasions become. They utilize theatrical elements such as costumes, props and non-daily modes of behaviour – in Beijing, for example, there was music, **dancing**, chanted slogans and the parading of a home-made statue of a 'Goddess of Democracy and Freedom'. When participants actively seek out and exploit the mass media in order to spread the message about what is happening, the ensuing sense of being observed, both locally and even globally, and therefore of per-forming, deeply informs these protests. Inevitably, then, there is a fine line which is often crossed between such events and more artistic **happenings** that might be primarily motivated by aesthetic concerns. Reversing this equation, happenings might also accrue or utilize political connotations and implications, a premise which many groups, including **Bread and Puppet Theatre**, have explored.

Events such as those in Tiananmen Square frequently manipulate and subvert the dominant modes of representation and the symbols that public **spaces** possess. This square is first and foremost a site for May Day military parades, where thousands of soldiers march past Communist Party officials with rows of tanks and other weapons, and where the State's authority is celebrated. All is ordered and tightly structured in space and time to foster the appearance of control, overlooked by giant placards of Mao Tse-tung, whose mausoleum is in the square. It is a performance of state power directed at the nation, its 'enemies' and the global media. Such images were exploited continuously in the Cold War by the opposing sides. The 1989 uprising, which had many other forms but was most manifest in this square in Beijing, was a performance of another kind, with few rules and another cast, led by **carnivalesque** subversive **play**. The third 'act' of this large-scale 'production', when hundreds were killed as the authorities cleared out the protesters in order to re-establish the square's place within the regime's construction of authority, was a tragic denouement. It is this slaughter which makes the two-month sequence of events so unforgettable.

There are countless examples of such **performative** mobilizations of people throughout the world and throughout history. The Tiananmen Square protests took place only months before the fall of the Berlin Wall in November of the same year, for example. Tiananmen demonstrators also used some of the same tactics of spatial occupation as the protests of Argentina's **las Madres de la Plaza de Mayo**. Tiananmen Square stands out because of its scale, its closing violence, and the surprise it generated by happening in what was largely perceived abroad as a nation of passive conformists. Such moments have helped shape the field of performance studies and broadened the scope of what its analytical terrain might be. Performance theorists and especially **Richard Schechner** have argued how loose the boundaries are between consciously staged events and those which become theatricalized incidentally through being observed or mediatized. They also reveal how frequently devices used in performance are adopted in **everyday life** to heighten demands, draw focus, or simply as inevitable elements of public celebrations and community gatherings, when the fluid rules of play displace the rigid structures of government.

Bibliography

The theatrical dimension of these protests has been analysed in these short pieces – one end of the wide spectrum that is political theatre.

Esherick, Joseph W. and Jeffrey N. Wasserstrom (1990) 'Acting Out Democracy: Political Theatre in Modern China', *Journal of Asian Studies* 49.4: 835–56.
Kershaw, Baz (1999) 'Fighting in the Streets: Performance, Protest and Politics', in *The Radical in Performance: Between Brecht and Baudrillard*, London: Routledge, pp.89–125
Schechner, Richard (1993) 'The Street Is the Stage', in *The Future of Ritual*, London: Routledge, pp.45–93.

TRIO A (JUDSON CHURCH, NEW YORK; CHOREOGRAPHED BY YVONNE RAINER; 1966)

Although only just over four minutes long, *Trio A* – or *The Mind is a Muscle, Part 1* as it was originally called – opened up the parameters of **dance** and performance in general, and helped to define what has been labelled **postmodern** dance. In practical terms, the piece attempted to flatten crescendos and phrasing, working against the natural rhythms of breathing and climactic cycles which usually exist in dance as buildup, culmination and then release. *Trio A* explored a pared-down minimalist aesthetic, without **music**, costume, reference to an **audience** or intentional interaction with other dancers, even though the work was made for three people (hence its later name). Its vocabulary was daily or 'actual', as Rainer saw it, rather than extraordinary, with deceptively simple turns of the torso or a controlled sinking to the floor, and a mode of engagement in the **movements** that was low-key and apparently effortless. *Trio A* tried to de-emphasize dance technique, in part by replacing phrasing with continuous flow. Ironically, great skill was needed to suppress the performer's tendency to utilize climaxes and instead create a consistent, even rhythm and application of energy. This mastery and effort was made as invisible as possible, focusing attention instead on the movements as tasks rather than on the dancers, their abilities and their interpretations.

Trio A was part of the Judson Dance Theatre group's experiments in a community centre in Manhattan, New York, at a time of artistic ferment, being temporally close to such pieces as **Richard Schechner**'s Performance Group's *Dionysus in 69* (1968–69) and the Living Theatre's *Paradise Now* (1968). The Judson group's explorations shifted emphasis away from virtuosity towards an absence of technique and **everyday** movement under an umbrella notion of the dancer utilizing a 'democratic body', as dance critic and theorist Sally Banes described it, referring to these attempts to break out of dance's apparent elitism and incorporate different kinds of dance and dancers. One group member was Steve Paxton, who later created the discipline of Contact **Improvisation** and who choreographed pieces based on walking. Although many works have played a similarly influential role in dance experimentation at that time, *Trio A*'s impact has been endorsed by Rainer's own lucid analysis of the performance in a 1968 article, as well as through the existence of a short silent black-and-white film recording. This shows the piece firstly in its entirety and then focuses on detailed movements of parts of the body to highlight the craft of abnegation and suppression. Banes has described *Trio A* as a paradigm of postmodern dance which questions all previous rules, even though it draws on a modernist interest in minimalism, evident in Rainer's reference to minimalist sculptures in her analysis. The piece exemplifies the difficulty of categorizing creative works within historical and theoretical boundaries and the complexity of defining what postmodernism is.

Bibliography

Banes contextualizes this piece within the larger body of the Judson group's work, whereas Kaye relates it to postmodern performance of all kinds from this important period of artistic activity. A short film of the work is unfortunately not widely available.

Banes, Sally (1981) *Democracy's Body: Judson Dance Theatre 1962–1964*, Ann Arbor: UMI Research Press.
Kaye, Nick (1994) *Postmodernism and Performance*, London: Macmillan.

Rainer, Yvonne (1974) 'A Quasi Survey of Some "Minimalist" Tendencies in the Quantitatively Minimal Dance Activity Midst the Plethora, or an Analysis of *Trio A*', in *Work, 1961–73*, New York: New York University Press.

UBU ROI (THÉÂTRE DE L'OEUVRE, PARIS; WRITTEN BY ALFRED JARRY, DIRECTED BY AURÉLIEN LUGNÉ-POE; 1896)

Alfred Jarry (1873–1907) was not only an inspiration for the **surrealist** movement but can also be considered the progenitor of much experimental performance in the twentieth century. *Ubu Roi*, the first of a trilogy of Ubu plays that Jarry began writing at the age of 15, achieved a central role in twentieth-century theatre in spite of Jarry's short, self-destructive life (he died aged 34). Its première was a landmark that heralded the beginning of modern performance, which offered an uncompromising alternative to **naturalist** or illusionist theatre.

The première of *Ubu Roi* immediately erupted into uproarious tumult amongst the 2,500 **audience** members, when the absurd pot-bellied, **masked** figure of Ubu opened the play with his first word, 'merdre', a corruption of the French word for 'shit'. The audience were provoked by the scatological puns, the eccentric visual **scenography** (in Scene 3, King Ubu brandishes a toilet brush) and the childish content. The previous night's public dress rehearsal for 1,000 people had been equally tumultuous. The scandal among a wildly animated public was fuelled by the press response, much to Jarry's evident enjoyment: he was mocking the illusionistic devices of naturalism with its attempted verisimilitude and psychologically motivated characters, but he was also launching a broader attack on the values of bourgeois society enshrined in naturalism. The **playful puppet**-like characters with cardboard horse-heads stemmed in part from Jarry's youthful games, the central character based on a school physics teacher. But *Ubu Roi* was also sophisticated – for example, in its parody of Shakespeare, when the stupid king is urged by his wife Ma Ubu to kill King Wenceslas, just as Macbeth is spurred on to assassinate Duncan. Such derision and absurdity were picked up by the **Dadaists** and the surrealists and later in the Theatre of the Absurd, whose dark and often grotesque comedy borrowed much from Jarry's exaggerated characterization and zany dialogue.

As Jarry continued to write new Ubu material, notably *Ubu Cuckolded* and *Ubu Enchained*, as they are known in English, the play was performed in Paris again in 1898, this time with marionettes as it had originally been envisioned. Anticipating **Vsevolod Meyerhold**, the roots of Jarry's imaginative vision were clearly in **visual theatre** and **popular theatre** forms and figures, such as those from commedia dell' arte and clowning, both of which are licensed to lampoon society. Jarry took this buffoonery and mockery one step further when he began to dress like and adopt the manner of Père Ubu, as his art and **everyday life** merged. Events surrounding the performance became as much part of the spectacle as the staging of the play. The Ubu plays themselves are rarely performed – not surprisingly, given the provocative nature of the material and the difficulty it gives translators and

directors. Yet the first performances and the play itself still possess an almost mythological status.

Bibliography

Braun and Esslin deal briefly with this performance as part of their overviews of the evolution of directing and the absurd. Shattuck focuses on Jarry as both person and artist in relation to his fellow Frenchmen and the political, social and artistic background.

Braun, Edward (1982) *The Director and the Stage: From Naturalism to Grotowski*, London: Methuen.
Esslin, Martin (1961) *Theatre of the Absurd*, New York: Doubleday.
Jarry, Alfred (1968) *The Ubu Plays*, London: Methuen and Co.
Shattuck, Roger (1959) *The Banquet Years: The Arts in France 1885–1918: Alfred Jarry, Henri Rousseau, Erik Satie, Guillaume Apollinaire*, London: Faber and Faber.

WAITING FOR GODOT (THÉÂTRE DE BABYLONE, PARIS; DIRECTED BY ROGER BLIN, WRITTEN BY SAMUEL BECKETT; 5 JANUARY 1953)

Like **Bertold Brecht**'s *Mother Courage* (1949), *Waiting for Godot* has become a globally recognized signature piece of twentieth-century theatre, its significance embodied in the distilled image of a stunted tree and two tramps on a bare stage. The play by Irish author Samuel Beckett was written at the end of 1948 and in January 1949, and was informed by the loss and violence of the Second World War, which goes some way towards accounting for its bleak mood. It is a simple story that involves a child, a tree and four adult characters, waiting for the enigmatic figure of Godot. Yet this simplicity belies a deep complexity in the material, which has seen the play continually evolve and cross cultural borders through its many translations. Its atmosphere of desperate anticipation and existential questioning is wide open to interpretation, for thematically it never posits *what* the meaning of life might actually be – it simply depicts the rather pathetic search for meaning.

The play's cross-cultural transferability also stems from the fact that it is set in a non-**space** of an almost empty stage and is not rooted in a specific epoch. This metaphorical and suggestive nature has helped give the text its longevity and value. It is also stylistically open in terms of its genre. The Japanese première in 1960 incited several Japanese writers to experiment with minimalism and absurdity, exploring the difficult balance between tragedy and comedy that Beckett's play treads so delicately. It has achieved acclaim in a multitude of contexts – from its successful reception in the San Quentin prison in California in 1957, to Susan Sontag's production in a besieged Sarajevo in 1993. The plot-confounding play has a distinct human dimension that allows it to operate on what might be considered a universal level. Godot is not only shorthand for a Christian God, as many critics have suggested, but can equally be Clinton stalling on making a decision to save a bombed city, or (for a convict) Godot is long-awaited parole.

The play's style, with its rhythmical, poetic nature and anti-plot was startlingly original when written, and even now proves difficult to play. It has its roots in **popular theatre** and especially clowning and music-hall vaudeville tradition, but its philosophical disposition runs much deeper than these forms might suggest. Beckett's own production as **director** in 1975, at the Schiller Theatre, Berlin, was long awaited, to see how the writer would present the elusive material. The production was much faster and lighter than anticipated, and influenced numerous productions afterwards. The necessity for directors to adhere strictly to the stage directions, demanded formerly by Beckett and now by his estate, has meant that few have been able to make radical experiments with the material. But the difficulty also lies in the play's strict rhythm and pattern, which does not lend itself to edits, cuts or radical interpretations. In spite of this seeming restriction, productions vary extensively in their mood, pace and in the balance between comedy and darkness, such is the text's richness.

Waiting for Godot is considered a landmark piece of experimental twentieth-century theatre writing. The play clearly continued the investigations of the **Dadaists** and **Antonin Artaud** some thirty years before, but it also looked ahead, and was the foundation of the artistic movement that Martin Esslin defined as the Theatre of the Absurd. Wherever and whenever it is played, it still attracts good ticket sales and fervent critical and academic interest.

Bibliography

These are just a few of the numerous analyses of Beckett's work in general and this play in particular. Esslin demonstrates the play's important position in the evolution of the absurd, while Bradby gives detailed accounts of the play and various key productions. States' short essay examines the play and its structure more theoretically.

Bradby, David (2001) *Waiting for Godot*, Cambridge: Cambridge University Press.
Esslin, Martin (1961) *Theatre of the Absurd*, New York: Doubleday.
States, Bert O. (1978) *The Shape of Paradox: An Essay on* Waiting for Godot, Berkeley: University of California Press.

YAQUI LENT AND EASTER CEREMONIES (NATIVE AMERICAN RELIGIOUS CEREMONIES)

The Yaqui are a native tribe resident in the southwest of the USA and northern Mexico. They adopted Christianity during an intense period of contact with Jesuit missionaries from the early 1600s to the mid-eighteenth century. However, they also adapted it to their own local experience (of geography, for example) as well as to their own cultural practices – their myths, social structures, architecture, pre-Christian ceremonies, and so on. Thus, they created new ways of **performing** important Christian events, the most famous of which are their Lent and Easter ceremonies. These are traditionally Christian in many ways: they portray Jesus's time in the wilderness, his betrayal by Judas, his burial and resurrection; they follow a Christian calendar; and they incorporate sermons. But they are also traditionally Yaqui: they take place within the Church but also in other significant **sites** around the community, many outdoors; they incorporate Yaqui characters (deer **dancers** and other tricksters, including the **masked** Chapayekas, who simultaneously represent Pharisees); and they are led by an orchestrating maestro rather than a cleric.

Anthropologists and performance scholars – **Richard Schechner** chief among them – have studied and employed Yaqui Lenten **rituals** to develop many arguments and analyses. For these critics, the Yaqui ceremonies demonstrate ritual's social value, here as a performance of the Passion, an **Artaudian** exploration of cruelty, and a re-enactment of the survival of the Yaqui, who have historically been attacked by the Spanish and the Mexicans and oppressed by the USA. The rituals demonstrate cross-cultural differences – for example, by being led by a maestro instead of a cleric – and similarities – the tricksters resembling the mummers common in European religious celebrations. They indicate how **intercultural** contact produces new hybrid or syncretic practices, as demonstrated also, for example, in the post-colonial playwriting of **Wole Soyinka**. The ceremonies facilitate critical exploration of the **performative** significances of site, **space**, time, performer–**audience** relationships and characterization. They also demonstrate some of the challenges of documenting performance, not only because of its **liveness**, but also because its sacredness to participating communities must be respected. In this and other ways, these rituals remind scholars to be self-reflexive about their practice. Deak argues that Euro-American scholars' interest in the Yaqui rituals is a symptom of their nostalgia for pre-secular culture. Others point out that the rituals' dynamic of Euro-American observing Native American reminds us that power is distributed unevenly in intercultural anthropological observation and must itself always be carefully scrutinized.

Bibliography

The rituals are described and analysed in detail from a performance studies perspective by Deak and Schechner, and from anthropological perspectives by Spicer and Crumrine and Spicer. Valencia *et al.* provide some Yaqui perspectives on both Yaqui religious practices and their anthropological study.

Deak, Frantisek (1989) 'Yaqui Easter: A Reflection on Cross-Cultural Experience', *Performing Arts Journal*, 'The Intercultural Issue', 11.3/12.1 (PAJ 33/34): 69–78.

Schechner, Richard (1985) *Between Theater and Anthropology*, Philadelphia: University of Pennsylvania.

—— (1993) *The Future of Ritual: Writings on Culture and Performance*, London: Routledge.

Spicer, Edward H. (1980) *The Yaquis: A Cultural History*, Tucson: University of Arizona Press.

Spicer, Rosamond B. and N. Ross Crumrine (eds) (1997) *Performing the Renewal of Community: Indigenous Easter Rituals in North Mexico and Southwest United States*, Lanham, MD: University Press of America.

Valencia, Anselmo, Heather Valencia and Rosamund B. Spicer (1990) 'A Yaqui Point of View: on Yaqui Ceremonies and Anthropologists', in *By Means of Performance: Intercultural Studies of Theatre and Ritual*, Richard Schechner and Willa Appel (eds), Cambridge: Cambridge University Press, pp.96–108.

Part III

CONCEPTS AND PRACTICES

CONCEPTS AND PRACTICES

ACTING

Acting is the art of **performing** in theatre, especially using the actor's voice and body. While this may sound obvious, it makes the point that acting is both intentional and theatrical, whereas other forms of performance, such as participating in **ritual** or **protest**, may be neither. The intentional nature of acting means the actor will be self-reflexive about his or her craft, its practice, and its aesthetic and social functions. Because it is theatrical, acting happens in a social context and can have significant social effects; further, it often aims to be mimetic – to copy a recognizable reality. These three features of acting as intentional, social and mimetic are not only descriptive. They are also at the core of arguments about whether acting is an innate and spontaneous or learned and mechanical skill, the social and ideological effects it can have, and how it **performatively** produces the world.

The first question gets to the heart of debates about what the function of acting is and how that is achieved. Actors are generally expected to convey emotion and to empathize with the characters they play, especially in **naturalism**. Thus, many analysts in the West have wanted to see the emotional link between actor and character as natural. Writing in the late eighteenth century, Denis Diderot went against this prevailing opinion to argue that it was in fact necessary for actors to maintain an objective distance in order to control their own emotions, the better properly to portray those of their characters. Diderot called this dependence of emotion on technique the 'actor's paradox'. From the late nineteenth century on, the recognition that what we perceive as good acting usually depends on intellectual and physical **training** and discipline has gained wide acceptance. This is evident in the importance commonly attributed from the mid-twentieth century on to such concepts as focus, control, research, psychophysical preparation, textual interpretation, and the identification and realization of objectives, whether the performance is **devised**, **improvised** or conventionally **rehearsed**. Nevertheless, the continuing value placed on the actor's quality of **presence** and **liveness** reveals a residual ideological investment in understanding acting as spontaneous, inspired and somehow natural.

As actor training techniques have shifted across time, so have other aspects of acting, all indicating changing social understandings, not only of acting. The Elizabethan prohibition disallowing women's appearance on stage reflected gendered ideologies of the time. Western acting has practised **intercultural** borrowing at least since the early twentieth century, when **Antonin Artaud** and **Bertold Brecht**, for example, were both influenced by **Asian performance**. This borrowing persists in Western practitioners' increasing adoption of Asian forms such as yoga, Kathakali and t'ai chi ch'uan, raising questions about balances of power in intercultural economies of exchange. From the late nineteenth century on, naturalism's emphasis on character and psychology has been continuously reinforced by training methods derived from **Konstantin Stanislavsky**'s system and has reflected understandings of identity as whole, autonomous and self-actualizing. **Postmodern** acting has interrogated this idea of a unified subject and individual agency in a variety of ways. The **Wooster Group**'s *Route 1 & 9* (1981) explicitly demonstrated the acting conventions it used to construct character and emotion. **Robert Wilson**'s **theatre of images** frequently prioritizes the actor's role as a **scenographic** element over his or her role as a whole, emotive character. Chicago's Goat Island and Sheffield's Forced Entertainment often compose performance as a set of tasks to be executed rather than an arc of emotions to be played through. Partly because it resists psychological characterization in these ways, postmodern acting is often understood more broadly as performance/performing. Further, as all of these examples indicate, from the late nineteenth century on acting has been directly developed and deployed by **directors** to realize their aims.

Acting's social status has had a chequered history. While tragic actors were highly regarded in ancient Greece, acting has often been seen as disreputable. This can partly be attributed to anti-theatrical prejudices – the actor is distrusted precisely because of his or her very skill in mimetic representation, disguise and dissembling. Throughout the twentieth century into the twenty-first, the actor's status has been variable. It has risen with the cult of the celebrity and repeatedly sunk as the actor's paradox persists in fuelling acting's associations with both artlessness and artifice, sometimes configured as self-indulgence and self-importance. What also endures, however, is a continuing fascination with acting for both performers and **audiences** alike, indicating acting's specific potential to engage intellectually and **phenomenologically** with questions of, amongst other things, subjectivity and representation.

Bibliography

Roach analyses Western theories of acting from the seventeenth century into the twentieth. Harrop provides an accessible introduction to many aspects of twentieth-century acting. Hodge collects useful introductions to the training methods of important Western director-practitioners. Zarrilli collects influential and thought-provoking essays, including Kirby's early attempt to distinguish between acting and not-acting/performing. Auslander traces some of the recent changes in acting that have transformed it into performance.

Auslander, Philip (1997) *From Acting to Performance: Essays in Modernism and Postmodernism*, London: Routledge.

Harrop, John (1992) *Acting*, London: Routledge.
Hodge, Alison (ed.) (2000) *Twentieth Century Actor Training*, London: Routledge.
Kirby, Michael (1972) 'On Acting and Not-acting', *TDR: The Drama Review* 16.1: 3–15. Reprinted in Phillip Zarrilli (ed.) (2002) *Acting (Re)Considered: A Theoretical and Practical Guide*, 2nd edition, London: Routledge, pp.40–52.
Roach, Joseph (1985) *The Player's Passion: Studies in the Science of Acting*, Newark: University of Delaware Press.
Zarrilli, Phillip B. (ed.) (2002) *Acting (Re)Considered: A Theoretical and Practical Guide*, 2nd edition, London: Routledge.

ANIMALS

Anecdotally, the presence of animals on stage, like that of children, is best avoided, because their behaviour is unpredictable and difficult to control. Yet animals have often been used in performance by many groups and artists, exploiting these very qualities of surprise and unpredictability. This ranges from England's Rose English and France's Théâtre Equestre Zingaro, who both perform regularly with horses, through Italy's Socíetas Rafaello Sanzio, who work with children and animals, to **Pina Bausch**'s **Wuppertal Dance Theatre**. Bausch has frequently used the much more predictable, though still challenging, devices of performers dressed as animals and even a stuffed deer (in *1980*), which provided an enigmatic stillness in the surrounding vortex of **movement**.

Historically, the **circus** was at the forefront of performance with live animals until increasing concerns about exploitation in the 1980s led to the development of human-only circus events, led now by the hugely successful Canadian company Cirque du Soleil. In various actions and **happenings**, **performance artists** have provoked sensitivities with their exploitation of dead and live animals. Most notorious amongst these is Hermann Nitsch, who from 1962 onwards **ritualistically** played with dead chickens and blood as visual media with which to paint the body and adorn the **space**, perhaps inevitably causing a scandal. Joseph Beuys used a dead hare and a live coyote in *Coyote: I Like America and America Likes Me* (1974) as performance partners. He deployed these animals not so much for their potential as spectacle (though this is inevitable), but more to provoke questions about our identity, about the function of art as communication (by asking how animals communicate), and about human responsibility for nature and for other beings. The juxtaposition of human performers alongside animals enables the **spectator** to scrutinize both stage **presences** closely – and comparatively – within the objectifying frame that performance provides. A performance's **liveness** is also accentuated by the risk of animals' unpredictability.

Other correspondences between humans and animals exist in concepts of actor **training** and performance, like **Tadashi Suzuki**'s idea of performers utilizing 'animal energy'. Several **directors** and teachers, like **Eugenio Barba** and **Jerzy Grotowski**, have also attempted to emphasize the 'extra-daily' or non-social aspects of performance, implicitly advocating a return to nature and ritual that goes back to the goat song (*tragos*) at the source of tragedy. These artists espouse biologically driven, impulsive, even irrational (or at least non-cognitive) behaviour, that is somehow animalistic. This is different from, though not completely unrelated to, the imitative animal exercises that have become familiar in many **acting** processes, notable in **Jacques Copeau** and **Jacques Lecoq**'s training. Such processes of transformation and imitation may have little relation to the overt display acts of '**performing**' dolphins or bears. But the presence of animals in performance, the challenges they pose theoretically, and the models of behaviour they offer, all add unusual complexity and richness to investigations of what performing might be.

Bibliography

Read collates theoretical reflections as well as more descriptive pieces by and on various practitioners who work with animals. Chaudhuri examines zoos and circuses in order to understand better the crossovers between human and animal performance, thereby building on Bouissac's early and unusual study.

Bouissac, Paul (1976) *Circus and Culture: A Semiotic Approach*, Bloomington: Indiana University Press.

Chaudhuri, Una (2003) 'Zoo Stories: "Boundary Work" in Theater History', in *Theorizing Practice: Redefining Theater History*, W. B. Worthen with Peter Holland (eds), Hampshire: Palgrave Macmillan.

Read, Alan (ed.) (2000) 'On Animals', a special issue of *Performance Research* 5.2, London: Routledge.

ASIAN PERFORMANCE

There is an overt problem in trying to write a single entry on the performance forms of a continent, for it will inevitably limit, simplify, exclude and possibly mislead. Yet, from the Western perspective this book adopts, Asian performance has long appeared as a challenging and enticing corollary to Western practices. Interest in **interculturalism** cemented this, but only at the very end of a century of fascination, misunderstanding and appropriation, to name some of the worst aspects of this cross-cultural interaction. Asian performance has also offered inspiration, education and a constant reminder of the **ritual** sources of, and possibilities for, Western theatre, **dance** and other art forms that, amongst many others, **director** Ariane Mnouchkine has explored. For these reasons it is important to attempt to summarize the complex impact traditional Asian performance (the focus here is not on contemporary practices) has had on the West, while being sensitive to ethical issues.

Much interest in Asian performance has been driven by fascination with the exotic, as articulated broadly by the late Edward Said in his influential writings on Orientalism. The codified performance forms of Kathakali and noh, for example, might distance outsiders because of their specific gestural languages or *mudras* (Kathakali's symbolic hand gestures), but they obviate this with their emphasis on physical and energetic techniques, which can be felt and seen (if not understood) cross-culturally. The skill these forms require depends on long-term **training** from an early age that has an equivalence in the West in **sports**, ballet and **music** rather than in the theatre itself, and which is markedly different from relatively short-term theatre training programmes in the West.

Equally compelling for Western theatre practitioners and historians alike are the still evident roots of these forms in ritual practices and an overt connection to spirituality, as in **Balinese dance-theatre**. Contemporary or experimental Asian forms like **butoh** have not totally cut themselves off from these traditions, even if they have called into question any dogmatism with which they might be associated or practised. This metaphysical dimension is what **Antonin Artaud** wanted to capture, just as **Peter Brook** and **Jerzy Grotowski** were also animated by the idea of a holy theatre or actor. But the very idea of performance in Asian cultures is fundamentally different from that in the West, especially in relation to its role in society. Asian forms often have a central role in their communities, which many feel is lacking in the West, even if practitioners of **popular theatre** and community arts workers have tried hard to develop this political purpose.

Asian performance forms have also helped establish the notion of the performer as someone who might sing, dance or recite text – a challenge to the Western Aristotelian model of **acting** based on mimesis. Correspondingly, performer training in Asia has other priorities from Western approaches. Achievement in later life is emphasized rather than youth and talent, just as originality is secondary to perpetuating traditions. Such notions have been picked up by many in the West including **Eugenio Barba**, Grotowski and American director Anne Bogart. The importance of mastery of techniques and rules of training, for example in **Motokiyo Zeami**'s treatises, have inspired practitioners like Phillip Zarrilli to follow and then translate methods of transmission and instruction found in Asian practices into Western contexts.

The differences between Asian and Western performance can too easily be overstated, but it is important to counterbalance these by recognizing that there are also many shared principles and practices. Barba's **theatre anthropology** is a well-documented example of an approach which looks for such common ground. Similarly, it is vital to remember that there is a two-way traffic of ideas and practices, as in Japan's *shingeki*, the term for a hybrid of Japanese theatre based on a Western, mostly **naturalist** model. Dynamic explorations of contemporary forms like **multimedia** work fused with traditional practices have been the result of recent pan-Asian projects based in Singapore (Theatre Works' 'Flying Circus' is one example), and ongoing collaborations between Singaporean artists and Australian groups like Melbourne's Playbox Theatre, who produced **Tadashi Suzuki**'s Australian version of *Macbeth* in 1992. Asian performance must not be further set in stone or falsely exoticized as locked in its past – traditions evolve and can be home to innovation, though perhaps at a rate that is slower than is usual in the West. The respect for both tradition and experimentation in much of Asia adds weight to arguments that Western theatre is too often driven by commercial rather than aesthetic or even spiritual considerations, and increasingly lacks social or political purpose.

Bibliography

The literature even on singular Asian performance forms is vast, as Brandon's important panoptical guide illustrates. These are a few examples that begin to explore the inter-relationship between Western and Asian performance practices and some of the theoretical concerns that surround them. The two edited collections cover a range of materials, forms and approaches.

Brandon, James R. (ed.) (1993) *The Cambridge Guide to Asian Theatre*, Cambridge: Cambridge University Press.

Brown, John Russell (1998) *New Sites for Shakespeare*, London: Routledge.

Fischer-Lichte, Erika, Josephine Riley and Michael Gissenwehrer (eds) (1990) *The Dramatic Touch of Difference: Theatre, Own and Foreign*, Tübingen: Gunter Narr Verlag.

Pavis, Patrice (ed.) (1996) *The Intercultural Performance Reader*, London: Routledge.

Said, Edward (1995) *Orientalism*, Harmondsworth: Penguin. Reprinted from the 1978 original with a new afterword.

AUDIENCE AND SPECTATOR

Literally speaking, an audience is a group of people who listen and a spectator is one who watches. By most definitions, the audience and/or the spectator fundamentally constitute theatre and performance by witnessing it and at least partially producing its meanings. Beyond these basic points of definition, however, the precise nature of the audience and/or spectator is troubled by questions about who the audience actually is and what it does.

As an abstract collective noun, the term 'audience' tends to homogenize the sense of who is in it, both across different times and places and within audiences at particular events. The idea of the audience as a collective is appropriate in some instances (for example, in Aristotle's understanding of the function of tragedy as an event which spiritually cleanses the community) as well as in certain models of theatre – such as black theatre or women's theatre – which aim intentionally to address and validate particular communities that may otherwise be marginalized. But often this sense of the audience's coherence and consistency is not only inaccurate but also deceptive. This is because it produces an impression of shared identity, mutual ideologies and community – or **Victor Turner**'s communitas – that might not actually exist. Historically, for example, the class, gender and ethnic constituency of theatre audiences has varied according to shifting ideas about who is permitted to attend and whether or not theatre-going is proper or fashionable. That said, while an audience may appear to be mixed, the performance's address to the audience can constitute it as homogeneous. Many **feminists**, for example, have pointed out that much Western theatre often assumes an 'ideal' spectator who is white, middle class and male. They argue that to maintain another perspective in the face of this assumption is to sustain one's exclusion from the show's projected meaning and from the dominant class.

This homogenization of the audience also problematically presumes that audiences consistently do the same thing. But there clearly exist many different understandings about what audiences do, and especially about whether audience participation is fundamentally active or passive. In some models, often associated with commercial forms such as Broadway and West End theatre, audiences bank-roll the show, look and hear, sit back and expect to be entertained. In other models, they become voyeurs, or are spiritually uplifted, or emotionally moved. Sometimes they watch and listen, applaud or jeer, witness and take responsibility, or are compelled to act. In different configurations of theatre and performance **space**, audience involvement can range from the passivity encouraged by the darkened, segregated auditoria of traditional proscenium-arch theatres, to the mobility necessitated by **environmental and site-specific performance** and **installation art**.

For Aristotle, the audience identified with the tragic hero and experienced catharsis, or the purgation of difficult feelings. This analysis of the audience's experience persisted for a long time – and still persists. But it drew criticism for modelling a fundamentally passive spectator: the spectator might recognize hardship in a play's narrative but would not act on it in real life because the will to act had been quelled by the experience of catharsis in the theatre. Arguing against what he saw as **naturalism**'s inherently passive spectator, **Bertold Brecht** advocated an active spectator who would be compelled by epic theatre to go out after the show and take direct political action. **Augusto Boal** has proposed a 'spectactor', who literally participates in both forum theatre – by deliberately entering the performance as a vocal, thinking participant – and invisible theatre, which surreptitiously draws 'innocent' bystanders into public altercations. Many playwrights, movements and practitioners, including Samuel Beckett, Peter Handke, **Dada**, **futurism** and the **Wooster Group**, have tried to challenge the inherent passivity of assumed rules about being an audience by deliberately provoking and even offending their audiences. **Jerzy Grotowski** moved from a strong belief in the importance of the audience in constituting the show's meaning to favour instead a **paratheatre**, where the powers of catharsis were fundamentally designed to transform the performers rather than the audience. While an audience is nearly always an essential part of theatre and performance, therefore, what an audience is understood to mean and do shifts according to changing ideas, not only of what theatre and performance are and how they make meaning, but also of what community and identity are.

Bibliography

Bennett offers a detailed survey of theoretical understandings of the audience, concentrating on twentieth-century theatre practice and active audiences. Blau's book is a well-informed rumination on the audience, grounded in **psychoanalytic** theory and asking important questions about what the social and political function of a community or public is, and whether one is possible. Dolan's book is a foundational feminist critique.

Bennett, Susan (1997) *Theatre Audiences: A Theory of Production and Reception*, 2nd edition, London: Routledge.

Blau, Herbert (1990) *The Audience*, Baltimore: Johns Hopkins University Press.

Dolan, Jill (1988) *The Feminist Spectator as Critic*, Ann Arbor: University of Michigan Press.

BODY ART

Body art is radical **performance art** that explicitly uses the artist's own body, to comment visually, sensually and often viscerally on identity and to enact the body's social meanings and expressive possibilities. It began after the Second World War with artists actually using their own and others' bodies in their art; in the 1950s, a fully dressed Yves Klein infamously deployed naked women's painted bodies as 'paintbrushes', **directing** their **movement** on canvases to leave paint marks. Body art came to prominence in the 1970s as part of a growing recognition that the body's specificity and social significations mean it can never be neutral, either as an artistic medium – the actor's body – or as the author of meaning – the artist's body.

Body art was led by **feminist** artists who put themselves in their work, collapsing the distance between artist and artwork, subject and object, and process and product, and insisting that their embodied gendered experiences affected their work, its reception and its meanings. Body art has consistently challenged the ways that bodies signify – or are made to signify – within dominant cultures. Feminist body art has explored how the female body is controlled by, for example, dominant conceptions of beauty and sexuality, such as the kind of sexual objectification of women demonstrated by Klein. **Orlan**'s series of plastic surgery operations, *The Reincarnation of Saint Orlan* (1990–93), simultaneously acknowledges icons of beauty in Western art history by adopting elements from famous portraits, and undermines them by combining them in hybrid new configurations. Carolee Schneemann, Yayoi Kusama, Karen Finley, **Annie Sprinkle** and numerous other artists have performed naked or semi-naked to challenge **audiences** to confront the ways pornography, fine art and other forms of representation persistently portray women as commodified sexual objects, rather than as active subjects.

As well as exploring the social significations of bodies differentiated by gender, sexuality, 'race', ethnicity, illness and so on, body art has explored the body's material capabilities and limits. This work has focused on and tested the body's material borders – such as its skin – as well as the limits of mental endurance. Numerous artists, including Chris Burden, **Marina Abramović**, Ulay, Ron Athey, Fakir Musafar and Franko B, have shot, cut and/or pierced their bodies in performance, with a variety of effects – provoking audiences to consider the ethics of their passive **spectatorship**, and exploring responses to pain, transgressed taboos, the putatively 'obscene', masochism, the **presence** of the performer and the mortality of the body. **Stelarc**'s early 'body suspensions' with meat hooks viscerally illustrated the material body's vulnerability, leading to his subsequent work exploring the relationship of the body to its technological environment in body work incorporating **multimedia**, robotic machines and the **internet**.

Much body art has explored the complexities of subjectivity as conceived within **postmodern** theory, recognizing it as fragmented – partially constituted by culture and partly by the body's given material conditions. It has interrogated the limits of personal volition as well as conceptions of identity as coterminous with the body. Work by artists including Abramović, Cindy Sherman, Hannah Wilke and Gilbert and George self-consciously enacts the repetitions through which identity is produced and changed, demonstrating identity's **performativity** – a critical concept developed by **Judith Butler**.

Body art is practised in artistic contexts such as theatres and galleries, but it also occurs much more widely – and with many of the same meanings – through **everyday-life** activities of costuming/**body adornment** such as tattooing, piercing and scarring. Other forms of body modification might be seen to include eating disorders such as anorexia and bulimia. Like the gallery's body art, these everyday forms articulate bodies' social relationships of oppression and resistance. They also engage with **ritual** practices and rites of passage, mark the body in time, explore **psychoanalytic** understandings of pain and pleasure, and provoke varied interpretations as celebratory, exhibitionist, self-abusive or liberating.

Bibliography

All three books provide strong critical overviews. Warr also provides extensive illustration and supporting critical reading.

Jones, Amelia (1998) *Body Art: Performing the Subject*, Minneapolis: University of Minnesota Press.
O'Dell, Kathy (1998) *Contract with the Skin: Masochism, Performance Art and the 1970s*, Minneapolis: University of Minnesota Press.
Warr, Tracey (ed.), survey by Amelia Jones (2000) *The Artist's Body*, London: Phaidon.

BUTOH

Butoh was part of a powerful new movement of underground or alternative performance forms in Japan that emerged in the late 1950s and (more forcefully) the 1960s, a decade of radical **protest** amongst students in Japan, as elsewhere in the world. Butoh performers were highly critical of 1950s Japanese culture and politics. Against the troubled background of the economic and material destruction of Japan during the Second World War – exemplified by the atom bombings of Hiroshima and Nagasaki – and the subsequent American Occupation, debates shifted between the conservative right-wing forces espousing the preservation of traditions and cultural autonomy, and the reformists championing Western influences and change, with which butoh aligned itself. **Expressionism**, for example, was a significant influence on butoh. Initially, butoh was led by individual artists such as dancer/choreographers **Tatsumi Hijikata** and Kazuo Ohno. Ohno was Hijikata's collaborator, then pupil. His **dance** style emphasized personal expressivity, in part derived from his work with a student of German expressionist dancer Mary Wigman. Only in 1972 was the standing of butoh in Japan reinforced by the founding of the first butoh group, Dairakudakan (which translates as 'Dance Apricot Machine'), led by Maro Akaji. And it was only in the 1980s that butoh achieved widespread popularity in Europe and the rest of the world through touring groups like Paris-based Sankai Juku (founded in 1975).

Butoh – or 'the dance of darkness' as it is known – turns the **spectator**'s attention to the simplicity of the stripped-bare, almost **animal** body and the innermost recesses of the Japanese psyche. To the West it reiterated the image of Japan as a suffering nation after the Second World War. Its painted white figures with shaved heads, moving in painfully slow, acutely controlled and contorted sequences on bleak sets, recall the ghosts of the traditional noh theatre as well as the victims of radiation. Even if it still demanded strict allegiance in terms of company dynamics and a certain uniformity of expression, butoh demonstrated an innovative progression from strict **Asian performance** forms like Japanese noh and kabuki. Whereas these had set patterns or *kata*, many of which are centuries-old, **movement** in butoh is **devised** largely though **improvisation**, even if the performance ultimately appears as precise, detailed choreography. Its intense physicality is meant to derive from the flow of deep atavistic inner impulses of an animal nature that reveal the performer's very soul. The 'dance of death', which butoh is also called, should somehow transcend the body's material **presence**. **Training** for, and practising, this form is frequently rigorous and intensely demanding of personal sacrifice, crossing over into **everyday life**. This principle was taken to its extreme in 1985, when one member of Sankai Juku fell to his death during a performance in Seattle, when the rope he was suspended from, high above the streets, snapped. Butoh continues to challenge orthodoxies on an artistic, personal as well as political level, in its questioning of conformity and its emphasis on individual instinctive creativity. It is also, in many ways, still largely an enigma. Butoh sits awkwardly, though challengingly, in a liminal space between dance, therapy, protest and **acting**.

Bibliography

There is very little written in English on butoh, other than these three core texts. The commercially available Blackwood video therefore offers an indispensable companion to these, especially since the form is so difficult to describe verbally.

Blackwood, Michael (1990) *Butoh: Body on the Edge of Crisis*, New York: Michael Blackwood Productions. Film.

Fraleigh, Sondra (1999) *Dancing into Darkness: Butoh, Zen and Japan*, Pittsburgh: University of Pittsburgh Press.

Klein, Susan Blakeley (1988) *Ankoku Butō: The Premodern and Postmodern Influences on the Dance of Utter Darkness*, Ithaca, NY: Cornell University.

Viala, Jean and Nourit Masson-Sekine (eds) (1988) *Butoh: Shades of Darkness*, Tokyo: Shufunotomo Co. Ltd.

CAMP

Camp exemplifies **Judith Butler**'s conception of identity as **performative** – constructed through repetition, therefore provisional, and indicative of the potential of cultural identities not to be predetermined by biology but to be articulated and changed through cultural practice. However, the precise meanings of the term 'camp' and the practices it represents have been strongly disputed in cultural criticism – especially queer criticism. In her famous 1964 essay, 'Notes on "Camp"', cultural critic and theatre **director** Susan Sontag defined camp as a sensibility and a style characterized by artificiality, excess and a lack of political commitment. By suggesting that camp values the apparently vulgar and the popular over fine art, high culture and received notions of beauty, she usefully indicated the ways camp implicitly promotes cultural democratization by playfully challenging dominant cultural hierarchies. By identifying it as simultaneously attractive and repulsive, she acknowledged this anti-hegemonic cultural value, but also camp's potential problems. While she did not specify what these were, other critics have, suggesting that camp is potentially misogynist, sometimes celebrating restrictive clichés of femininity; not egalitarian but elitist, as a sensibility shared only by those with the requisite 'queer eye'; seduced by consumer culture; and desexualizing – engaged with eroticism and desire, but not linking them to any particular sexual practices. Some of these problems with camp are epitomized in the television programme *Queer Eye for the Straight Guy* (2003), which plays on ideas of gay men as stylish but somewhat superficial elitist consumers.

Sontag's analysis has been criticized on a number of counts, especially for downplaying the link between camp and homosexual and/or queer sexual identities, and for identifying camp as apolitical. For many queer theorists, camp is queer activism: parodying dominant heteronormative culture in both **everyday life** contexts and at such events as **parades** and **carnivals**; challenging binary understandings of male and female genders, especially through cross-dressed or drag performance like that of **Split Britches**; and consuming excessively, not in a capitulation to capitalist culture, but to claim queer purchase within a dominant culture that otherwise marginalizes the queer.

Bibliography

All three collections contain numerous good articles. Cleto's is most substantial and includes Sontag's essay, as well as a full bibliography dating back to the nineteenth century.

Bergman, David (ed.) (1993) *Camp Grounds: Style and Homosexuality*, Amherst: University of Massachusetts Press.

Cleto, Fabio (ed.) (1999) *Camp: Queer Aesthetics and the Performing Subject: A Reader*, Edinburgh: Edinburgh University Press.

Meyer, Moe (ed.) (1994) *The Politics and Poetics of Camp*, London: Routledge.

Sontag, Susan ([1964] 1987) 'Notes on "Camp"', in *Against Interpretation*, London: André Deutsch, pp.275–92. Reprinted in Fabio Cleto (ed.) (1999) *Camp: Queer Aesthetics and the Performing Subject: A Reader*, Edinburgh: Edinburgh University Press, pp.53–65.

CARNIVAL

Carnival is popular street **festival** that usually combines **music**, **masking** or costume, **dance**, food, eroticism, and performances such as **parades**, street theatre and **puppetry**. Its practices raise key debates about cultural power and cultural identities. Theorist **Mikhail Bakhtin** influentially argued that carnival is socially liberating because it licenses the crossing of boundaries, especially between classes. As others have noted, carnival's transgressive potential can also challenge the conventional separation of **audiences** and performers, as well as boundaries of gender, race, ethnicity and sexuality in events such as Gay Pride festivals. It can also challenge dominant social rules regarding time and **space** – as in women's 'Take Back the Night' marches, which advocate women's right to walk safely in the city at night, or in events where anti-globalization campaigners occupy the streets and prevent the usual flow of traffic and commerce. And it can challenge hegemonic assumptions of value, most importantly by celebrating marginalized communities, as in the community plays and events of Welfare State International (UK) and the **Bread and Puppet Theatre** (USA). However, in a debate subsequently extended by Stallybrass and White, Bakhtin acknowledged that carnival also has socially *repressive* potential because its licence to exist is granted only temporarily, in a circumscribed space and by the State. Thus, carnival produces an illusion of democratically dispersed cultural power while actually reinforcing hegemony: by allowing the oppressed classes to 'let off steam' temporarily, carnival evacuates their oppositional energies.

These debates about carnival's inherently ambivalent political potential can be demonstrated through the form that is now most pervasive in the West: carnival that originated in the Caribbean and has spread throughout the black diaspora to Europe, North America and beyond. Historically, this form combined imported European carnival practices that originated in Christian pre-Lent festivities with black and indigenous Caribbean forms of music and dance. The resulting hybrid combination can be considered both liberating for, and oppressive of, black communities. It is oppressive if the new hybrid form of carnival is seen as predominantly imposing European cultural practices on black cultures, and liberating if the carnival seems more significantly to challenge imposed culture through the black communities' claiming of space, **presence**, music, dance, food, and so on.

In contemporary contexts as far dispersed as Rio de Janeiro, London's Notting Hill and Toronto, carnivals often function to articulate minority communities' national, ethnic and/or 'racial' cultural identities, temporarily but powerfully contesting racism and oppression. Carnival nevertheless remains vulnerable to appropriation. While hegemonic governments may promote themselves as benignly multicultural by supporting carnival, they may simultaneously exploit it by presenting it as **intercultural** exotica and using it to attract tourists and to stimulate regional regeneration. Carnival is also vulnerable to capitalist exploitation. In the 1990s, the Notting Hill Carnival's sponsorship by a soft-drink company meant it temporarily changed its name to the Lilt Notting Hill Carnival. This association of product and event was obviously meant to attach street credibility to the soft drink, but it is possible instead to see its actual effect as detracting from the Carnival's oppositional status, linking the event with commercial rather than cultural priorities.

Bibliography

Bakhtin's book lays down ideas subsequently developed by Bristol, Schechner and Stallybrass and White. Carver discusses issues raised by Lilt's sponsorship of the Notting Hill Carnival. Riggio's book indicates the growing interest in this topic.

Bakhtin, Mikhail (1984) *Rabelais and His World*, trans. Hélène Iswolsky, Bloomington: Indiana University Press.
Bristol, Michael D. (1985) *Carnival and Theatre: Plebeian Culture and the Structure of Authority in Renaissance England*, London: Methuen.
Carver, Gavin (2000) 'The Effervescent Carnival: Performance, Context and Mediation at Notting Hill', *NTQ: New Theatre Quarterly* 16.1 (NTQ 61): 34–49.
Riggio, Milla Cozart (2004) *Carnival*, London: Routledge.
Schechner, Richard (1993) *The Future of Ritual: Writings on Culture and Performance*, London: Routledge.
Stallybrass, Peter and Allon White (1986) *The Politics and Poetics of Transgression*, London: Methuen.

CIRCUS

An emphasis on large-scale spectacle and virtuosic achievement has always been integral to circus, an influential and continually evolving **popular theatre** form. Although demonstrations of skill and exotica may have much older roots, the idea of mass public circuses stems concretely from early Roman times. The term then denoted both the open-air stadia built for entertainment – like chariot racing at the Circus Maximus, for example – as well as the name of such events themselves. The circular shape of circus tents echoes these ancient counterparts and presents a non-hierarchical auditorium for the **spectators**, encouraging a participatory inclusivity, where vocal responses, eating and drinking are encouraged, and the audience see each other across the dirt stage. Tents are portable and easy to tour and are thus germane to its popularity. The collective nature of circus spectatorship was alluded to by Karl Marx in his phrase 'bread and circuses' (from the Latin *panem et circenses*), though he was suggesting that the masses could be fobbed off with such spectacles. Following Marx's statement, debates focus (as with **carnival**) on whether circus is socially liberating or oppressive for performers and spectators alike.

Circus went through extensive transformation following the public rejection of **animal** participation in the 1980s. Now the popular Moscow and Chinese State Circuses, for example, with their multiple franchises operating simultaneously in different countries, rely instead on human skill and invention. Such companies draw their personnel worldwide from national circus schools with their intensive **training** programmes. The specialist skills that circuses depend on take years to acquire, and performers need constant practice. Canadian group Cirque du Soleil (founded in 1984) have taken virtuosity to an unprecedented level and an astonishing scale, and now runs a multi-million-dollar international business. As well as touring, the company is based at major leisure destinations like Orlando, Florida and Las Vegas, and merchandises its work extensively. In the face of such competition and promotion, small travelling troupes – of the kind immortalized in Federico Fellini's films like *The Clowns* (1970) – are having to adapt quickly.

The commodification of circus has removed it from its former marginal and excluded position into mainstream consciousness. The broad appeal touring allows is at odds **spatially** with the liminal places at the edges of towns and cities that circuses have historically inhabited. This marginal position is a reminder that circus has the potential to provoke and challenge public perceptions of norms as well as just entertain. There have been exciting innovations in what has been termed 'new vaudeville' (in the United States) or 'new circus', following the lead of experimental groups like Australia's Circus Oz, France's now-disbanded Archaos and American clown Bill Irwin. Archaos were renowned for working on the edge of safety, juggling with chainsaws in performances based on a heavy metal aesthetic. As well as taking circus skills into schools and communities, new circus practitioners in the United Kingdom have investigated how their form can create hybrids with other media, opening up what was once centred on relatively closed, transient troupes. Even the traditional role of the clown has disappeared from some circus performances. Notions drawn from **performance art**, **dance** and the theatre are energizing circus, which (relieved from its heritage of animal exploitation) is undergoing a renaissance.

Bibliography

Few academics or critics, with the notable exception of Bouissac, have engaged with theoretical issues about circus, and there is little other than scattered articles, five of which are collated in Schechter's edition. Bolton gives a lively report on the changing face of circus in a range of countries and Jenkins looks at American performance that has been inspired by circus practices and other popular forms. One way to appreciate developments in circus is to compare videos like that from 1988 with more recent ones. Sixteen videos are available through Cirque du Soleil's website, including *Quidam* (1999), *Saltimbanco* (2001) and *Alegria* (2003).

Birch, Miriam (1988) *Inside the Soviet Circus*, National Geographic Society. Film.

Bolton, Reg (1987) *New Circus*, London: Calouste Gulbenkian Foundation.

Bouissac, Paul (1976) *Circus and Culture: A Semiotic Approach*, Bloomington: Indiana University Press.

Cirque du Soleil. Online. Available <http://www.cirquedusoleil.com> (accessed 25 February 2005).

Jenkins, Ron (1988) *Acrobats of the Soul: Comedy and Virtuosity in Contemporary American Theatre*, New York: Theatre Communications Group.

Schechter, Joel (2003) *Popular Theatre: A Sourcebook*, London and New York: Routledge.

DADA AND SURREALISM

Dada is an 'anti-art' form that came into being in 1916, partly as a deliberately illogical response to the perceived irrationality of the First World War. It was pioneered by a trans-European group of artists who fled their war-ravaged countries to gather – partially by chance – in the neutral domain of Switzerland. Here, in a Zurich nightclub in February 1916, the German poet and theatre-maker Hugo Ball opened the infamous **Cabaret Voltaire**. The Cabaret exhibited paintings and other graphic artworks, but its main function was to present performance. Initially, the performances resembled conventional cabaret, staging poetry readings alongside musical turns. However, they quickly became much more experimental, combining **dances** and skits that were often performed in **masks** to avoid **naturalistic** characterization; cubist costumes; recitations of manifestos; **music** exploring silence, rhythm, noise and sounds produced by the body; and, most famously, unconventional poetry readings. These emphasized sound rather than literal meaning by simultaneously combining drumming and bell-ringing with multiple voices speaking different languages, singing, whistling and simply making noises. In contrast to the dominant performance of their time, the Dadaists' performances rejected rationality and its oppressive hierarchies in favour of apparent nonsense and freedom, fantasy, the abstract, process, chance and spontaneity.

Like **futurism**, Dada aimed deliberately to challenge its **audience**, even to scandalize them, provoking them to respond actively. It also shared futurism's forms of cabaret, phonic poetry and manifestos. However, where futurism celebrated war, Dada's artists were fleeing war; where futurism extolled the machine, Dada was interested in the primitive and the infantile, including the nonsense of pre-linguistic speech; and where futurism had a sense of mission, Dada was characterized by anarchic **play**. The name 'dada' itself ambiguously invokes a horse in French, 'yes, yes' in Russian, and in many languages a sense of childish precocity and deliberate obstruction. Dada, of course, cultivated this ambiguity.

The Cabaret Voltaire shut after only five months, but Dada's practice spread to Paris, Berlin and elsewhere in Germany, Holland, New York and Barcelona. The publication of Dada magazines, books and posters, and the foundation of dedicated gallery spaces, led to a split among its primary exponents, who argued for and against Dada's institutionalization. However, despite Dada's relative brevity as a movement, its influence has been enormous. Its deliberate irrationality was taken up in the surrealism which flourished in the graphic art of, for example, Salvador Dalí, and in films such as Dalí and Luis Buñuel's *Un Chien Andalou* (1928). Surrealism was less developed in theatre but its absurdity is visible in the earlier plays of Alfred Jarry, like *Ubu Roi* (1896), and later writers of the theatre of the absurd. Like **expressionism**, surrealist work featured illogical, often dreamlike and sometimes menacing narratives and images, it externalized otherwise repressed feelings, and it experimented with dreams, as both form and content. Dada's expressive principles also worked their way into the **dance** of choreographers **Rudolf von Laban** and Mary Wigman, who attended the Cabaret Voltaire. Its collage composition extended later into the epic style developed by Erwin Piscator and **Bertold Brecht**, and its exploration of theatre's many arts led to **Antonin Artaud**'s advocacy of a total theatre. Its anti-naturalistic avant-gardism worked its way into a range of **performance and body art** practices as well as **happenings**. And its experiments with chance were later extended in music by composers including **John Cage** in *4' 33"* and in dance by choreographers including **Pina Bausch**. While it resisted being a coherent movement, Dada nevertheless articulated a clear sense of social resistance, demonstrating some of the ways art could operate as anti-art, challenging contemporary artistic and social conventions.

Bibliography

Through extensive, accessible documentation and narrative, Goldberg locates Dada within a series of avant-garde movements that led to the development of performance art. Matthews' and Melzer's histories focus on, respectively, playwriting (by authors including Tristan Tzara, Louis Aragon and Artaud) and performance (including theatre and dance). Richter was one of the original Dadaists.

Goldberg, RoseLee (2001) *Performance Art: From Futurism to the Present*, revised and expanded edition, London: Thames and Hudson.
Matthews, John Herbert (1974) *Theatre in Dada and Surrealism*, Syracuse: Syracuse University Press.
Melzer, Annabelle Henkin ([1976] 1994) *Dada and Surrealist Performance*, Baltimore: Johns Hopkins University Press.
Richter, Hans ([1965] 1997) *Dada: Art and Anti-Art*, London: Thames and Hudson.

DANCE

Dance is central to any study of performance and needs to be considered even in this *Companion*, which focuses mostly on theatre practice, a form with which it shares many elements. Indeed, in non-Western cultures, dance's many manifestations are often inseparable from the theatre. **Asian performance** forms often integrate text, character and stylized **movement**, their performers operating as dancer/actors with little distinction discernible between the two. Dance in the West, however, is primarily concerned with movement in **space** rather than with text or **acting**. Western dance is usually choreographed, or at least follows a structure based on rhythmic patterns, sounds or **music**. As a phenomenon, dance

– like **play** or **ritual** – is vast in its potential frameworks and in encompassing a ubiquitous part of human and even **animal** behaviour, with multiple motivations and functions. But, whereas play can often be solitary, dance mostly has a social dimension. As such it bonds, celebrates, integrates and identifies people through a particular affiliation (as in Mods' or Rockers' styles of dancing). This social role recalls dance's origins in ritual practices, where communal dance accompanied by music would be a primary component of rites that brought a community together for calendrical or celebratory purposes. From such public participation evolved the individualized dances of shamans, for example, the beginnings of dance as performance presented for the aesthetic admiration and appreciation of **spectators**.

While still predominantly using choreographed human movement, many Western dance experimenters have also explored text, character and **site-specificity**, concepts more familiar to the theatre. Anna Teresa de Keersmaeker's *Rosas Danst Rosas* (1983) was performed and later filmed (1997) in a disused factory. Many practitioners have consciously explored the boundaries between genres, like German choreographer **Pina Bausch** with her decades of dance theatre. British group DV8 describe themselves as a physical theatre company, yet they build on the 1980s Eurocrash dance movement, which pushed the body to its limits. They have challenged narrow-minded views of the ideal dance performer by employing older dancers, questioning the fact that performers are assumed to be finished after their early thirties. The success of British dance company CanDoCo, who consciously integrate disabled with able-bodied dancers, has also nudged this important issue forward. Such groups have succeeded in making dance and movement explicitly political, in content as much as in its processes and context. DV8 have consistently explored gay issues, for example, most notably in *Dead Dreams of Monochrome Men* (1988). This was partly an exploration of the body-conscious competitiveness of gay club culture and a response to Denis Nielsen's murder of several homosexual men, but also an outcry against the British Conservative government's homophobic Clause 28, which restricted teaching about homosexuality in British schools.

Dance has frequently contended with the question of how to speak with the body or present concrete concepts or themes through abstract movement. Like DV8, **postmodern** dancers such as New York's Judson Group tried to combine formal experimentation with politics. A piece like *Trio A* (1966) purposefully devalued virtuosity and technique and replaced it with **everyday** movement, rejecting the politics of body use and the aesthetics inherent in classical forms. The fact that dance scholar Sally Banes has subsumed such work under the title *Democracy's Body* reveals how wider social agendas can be implicit in an aesthetic approach. Indeed, it can be argued that all movement, however abstract, contains, reflects or endorses an ideology. Battle lines have frequently been drawn against traditional forms like ballet, which is based on fantastical narratives, is removed from any political implications and in which movement is aestheticized and remote from the spectator, using an archaic codified language. The dominance of classical dance has also led many contemporary or modern dancers like Martha Graham and

Merce Cunningham to create their own techniques, focusing their experimentations on form. For Cunningham, for example, movement is about position and space rather than the development of narratives through danced action.

For the scholar, dance shares the difficulty of all live performance forms in that it is inherently transitory. Dance studies range widely: from **phenomenological** approaches, which emphasize the experience of movement; through the techniques and precise vocabulary of physical processes such as those articulated by **Rudolf von Laban**; through questions of interpretation; to the placing of works in a historical, political and social context. Problems inherent in dance analysis are partly remedied by the fact that there have been some very good attempts to document dance on film from avant-garde filmmaker Maya Deren's 1940s and 1950s works onwards. The visual nature of dance and the ability of cameras to zoom in on details have led to many rich and informative film documents. Filmed dance has also fed back into performance in the works of companies like British group VTol Dance and Belgium's Charleroi Danses/Plan K, who have experimented extensively with new technologies. Live performers have danced with virtual partners streamed through the **internet** or on film, and there has been much exploitation of motion capture technology, which, amongst other properties, allows dancers themselves to trigger **lighting and sound** cues. As is evident, the possibilities for dance analysis are as many as the forms and processes dance inhabits, the theories pushed to their limits by the moving body.

Bibliography

The range of styles and modes of dance is reflected in a huge dance bibliography, of which this is a very small selection. Some works on specific dancers can be found in entries on choreographers in Part I ('People'). Thomas, a sociologist, gives a cross-disciplinary view. Foster's various writings on dance have been eagerly picked up by theatre and performance scholars, and Carter offers a comprehensive reader on the study of dance. The DVD accompanying the Mitoma book is an excellent resource that includes almost two hours of dance footage. The *Rosas* website contains information on buying the films *Rosas Danst Rosas* (1997), directed by Thierry de Mey; *Rosa* (1992), directed by Peter Greenaway; and *Achterland* (1994), directed by De Keersmaeker.

Banes, Sally (1981) *Democracy's Body: Judson Dance Theatre 1962–1964*, Ann Arbor: University of Michigan Press.
Carter, Alexandra (ed.) (1998) *The Routledge Dance Studies Reader*, London: Routledge.
DV8 (1990) *Dead Dreams of Monochrome Men*, Millennium Productions/DV8 Physical Theatre. Film.
Foster, Susan Leigh (1996) *Corporealities*, London: Routledge.
Maya Deren (1945–55) London: Dance Films, Collected films.
Mitoma, Judy (ed.) (2002) *Envisioning Dance on Film and Video*, London: Routledge.
Rosas. Online. Available HTTP: <http://www.rosas.be/Rosas/center_films.html> (accessed 30 April 2004).
Thomas, Helen (1995) *Dance – Modernity and Culture: Explorations in the Sociology of Dance*, London: Routledge.

DEVISING

Devising is a method of making performance that is often non-text-based and includes the collaborative participation of the whole creative company in all stages and aspects of performance-making, from **scenographic** design, to textual development, **lighting and sound** design, and actual performance. Companies that devise begin with one or more stimulus, such as an idea, question, theme, story, object, image, light, smell, **movement**, place or a piece of text or **music**. They then use a variety of methods first to develop performance material and then to **rehearse** and edit it into a performance event. Methods of generating material vary but may include **improvisation** exercises, writing, drawing, filming, **play** and games, research and discussion. Having developed material, the company selects, structures and edits it, practises it – sometimes seeking **training** to develop necessary skills – and often shows work in progress to solicit **audience** feedback.

Devising methods can be seen in many earlier forms of performance such as commedia dell'arte, which directly influenced teacher **Jacques Lecoq**. However, these methods achieved newfound currency (if not yet the name 'devising'), from the 1960s on, in the work of avant-garde companies that aimed explicitly to challenge conventional theatre-making methods. Such companies included the Living Theatre, **Richard Schechner**'s Performance Group and the **Wooster Group** in the USA; Theatre Passe Muraille in Canada; **Pina Bausch**'s **Wuppertal Dance Theatre** in Germany; and, in Britain, the People Show, Joint Stock, Monstrous Regiment, Complicité and, later, Forced Entertainment and DV8 Physical Theatre. They challenged conventional theatre's usual prioritization of text, **director** and performance product by using collaborative and/or collective methods to explore the possibilities and challenges of a less hierarchical theatre practice and an emphasis on all participants' artistic processes. Thus, before the term 'devising' gained currency in the UK in the 1990s, the work of such companies was often known as 'collaborative' in the UK and as 'collective creation' in Canada. These makers frequently rejected dominant generic patterns and formal categories, often producing non-linear **postmodern** performance and cross-disciplinary performance as epitomized in the **theatre of images**. Because devised theatre is often temporally and **site-specific**, these companies also provoked audiences' ethical engagement with controversial current social issues. For example, Caryl Churchill's collaboratively developed *Cloud Nine* (1979) explored gender and colonial relations, the Wooster Group's *Route 1 & 9 (The Last Act)* (1981) addressed 'race' relations, the work of playwright Howard Brenton interrogated the ethics of witnessing violence, and director Mike Leigh explored class aspirations and animosities.

Devised theatre frequently addresses a particular audience, such as children or people from a specific region. Because it requires enormous personal commitment from its makers, it often works to enhance the risk taken and investment made in the performance, by both performers and audiences, and it is often auto-biographical, as in the work of **Robert Lepage** and Bausch. However, because it sometimes lacks big-'name' directors or playwrights and does not have the draw of a familiar (let alone classic) title, it can also be financially risky, sometimes having difficulty securing both development funding and box office sales. Its anti-hierarchical origins have perhaps been developed most extensively in the invisible and forum theatre work of **Augusto Boal**, for whom it is a universal method of rehearsal for revolution. It is worth noting, though, that as well as suggesting models of anti-hierarchical, more democratic theatre practice, devised theatre sometimes points up – whether inadvertently or knowingly – the challenges of a truly democratic theatre, questioning the necessity of a director or another figure who takes final decisions. While many companies worldwide still use devising practices, some of the utopian collectivism characteristic of devising from the 1960s to the 1980s has now dissipated.

Bibliography

Etchells' inspirational book is a creative memoir and history of his company, Forced Entertainment. Oddey provides an overview of devising practices, with many specific examples from British companies' work. All the recommended texts suggest practices for devising theatre.

Bicât, Tina and Chris Baldwin (2002) *Devised and Collaborative Theatre: A Practical Guide*, Ramsbury, England: Crowood Press.
Boal, Augusto (2002) *Games for Actors and Non-Actors*, trans. Adrian Jackson, 2nd edition, London: Routledge.
Etchells, Tim (1999) *Certain Fragments: Contemporary Performance and Forced Entertainment*, London: Routledge.
Oddey, Alison (1994) *Devising Theatre: A Practical and Theoretical Handbook*, London: Routledge.

DIRECTING

Today it seems surprising that Western theatre existed for so long without a director – or at least a director in the form with which we are now familiar. It was as late as the second half of the nineteenth century when Duke Georg II of Saxe-Meiningen (in what is Germany today) took responsibility in the Meiningen company for both coordinating a **mise en scène** and interpreting the text. This concept of a director was quickly picked up by artists linked to **naturalist** theatre, especially André Antoine and **Konstantin Stanislavsky**, with whom the title became firmly established. Their primary concern was to create the coherent aesthetic central to naturalist theatre, focusing, for example, on psychologically believable characters and group cohesion, rather than creating vehicles for the star actors who had previously dominated the theatre. Before naturalism, the director's role had often been taken on by an **acting** company member, an actor-manager or producer figure, or the playwright. However similar their work might have been in practice to that of the director we know today, the role was not recognized as a discrete one with its own expertise or responsibilities, and did not share the dominant position in theatre hierarchy that directing has today. Directors like **Vsevolod Meyerhold** and **Bertold Brecht** then emerged. They wanted control of a production in order to embody their own vision and style, which then led to the creation of a range of approaches to acting.

What, though, are the director's responsibilities as we now understand them, and what does directing actually involve? The answer of course depends on the work being directed, but the broad responsibilities do not vary extensively between different materials. Whether the director's task is the interpretation of playtexts, the construction of a performance through a **devising** process or the creation of a **visual theatre** environment according to the model of director-auteurs **Robert Wilson**, **Robert Lepage** and **Tadeusz Kantor**, directing usually evolves from extensive planning into a **rehearsal** process. This may or may not involve **training** *per se* but will inevitably focus on acting techniques. Rehearsals culminate with the addition of costumes, **lighting and sound** in the eventual construction of a mise en scène or **scenography**. This grows from collaboration with the technical team before and throughout the rehearsals, following on into runs or touring.

Some directors work repeatedly with particular individuals in a collaboration that is central to their vision. Declan Donnellan and Nick Ormerod, who established the British company Cheek by Jowl, are a notable director–designer team. But at the heart of all directing processes is the director–performer relationship. This may vary from ensembles where a director works with a group over many years, as **Eugenio Barba** has done with Odin Teatret, to a situation where casting managed by an agent brings in people new to the director but appropriate to the material or methodology of his or her chosen production. The director's main task is to make these performers comfortable with their characters, roles or tasks so they can perform them to the best of their abilities, whatever the stylistic conventions. In rehearsal, the director works almost as a proxy **audience**, reflecting the actor's work back to him or her and providing what is often described as an 'outside eye'. Work that is made without such an outside eye, in theatre collectives for example, has often been criticized for being indulgent or shapeless, perhaps indicating through this absence crucial aspects of the director's job. Directors need to find a dramaturgical or structural shape to their work, a well-formulated and articulated rhythmical pattern, cultivate focused performers and a sense of shared purpose among the company, and build a staging or **spatial** environment that is consistent with their material and the acting style. A further vital part of the director's work is to instil confidence in, and integrate, the entire cast and production team, to manage the inevitable nervousness that is generated by the expectations and actuality of public performance. These feelings of trust, balanced against carefully selected challenges and risks, are enabled by the constant evaluation and feedback that a director gives. The role is organizational as much as it is artistic, but too much organization of the performances can stifle the performers' creativity. Subsequently, most directors do not have a strict methodology which they apply to all texts or concepts. The nature of the job is rather more pragmatic and serendipitous, the primary virtue of a good director perhaps being his or her ability to adapt to the particular conditions and given resources of each production.

There is no denying the central place that directors have held, shaping (through their theories as well as their practices) the innovations that have revolutionized twentieth-century theatre and performance, as a glance at our list of 'People' in Part I confirms. But the public perception of theatre directors' work is that it is often invisible. It might be sidelined by star actors or celebrated writers, but also most of their work is over by the time a production reaches the public. If directors have done their job well, the **spectator** will perhaps focus more on the content or the performers than on the staging, though directing cannot of course be extricated from these. Some directors cross over between the stage and television and film, building a reputation through the wider reception that these formats bring. Sam Mendes, formerly of the Donmar Warehouse, London, did just this with his first film *American Beauty* (1999). But for many directors public or critical acceptance can be a double-edged sword, especially if they want to challenge established orthodoxies or be 'cultural critics', with radical interpretations of classics or new works, as the **Wooster Group** have done. Whether freelance or company-based, directing requires resourcefulness, imagination and perseverance.

Bibliography

There are numerous books on directing, many by directors articulating their own theories or approach. Several of these can be found in the individual bibliographies in the 'People' section. Below is a sample of books about directing that covers a range of approaches: from Delgado and Heritage's interviews; Mitter and Shevtsova's collection; to Schneider and Cody's collection of materials previously published in *The Drama Review*; and Braun's thoughtful historical survey.

Braun, Edward (1982) *The Director and the Stage: From Naturalism to Grotowski*, London: Methuen.

Delgado, Maria M. and Paul Heritage (eds) (1996) *In Contact with the Gods? Directors Talk Theatre*, Manchester: Manchester University Press.

Mitter, Shomit and Maria Shevtsova (eds) (2005) *Fifty Key Theatre Directors*, London: Routledge.

Schneider, Rebecca and Gabrielle Cody (eds) (2002) *Re:Direction: A Theoretical and Practical Guide*, London: Routledge.

ENVIRONMENTAL THEATRE AND SITE-SPECIFIC PERFORMANCE

These two forms aim explicitly to alter the conventional spatial practices of performance to enhance both the relationship between performers and **audience** and the performance's engagement with its **space** and site of production. The term 'environmental theatre' was popularized in the early 1970s through the writings of **Richard Schechner**, works made by his company The Performance Group, and the practices of other innovative makers such as **Jerzy Grotowski**. Schechner intended to include a broad range of theatre practices in this term, including theatre made in found spaces. In practice, however, The Performance Group concentrated on making work in their studio, which they altered radically for each performance. These physical alterations focused on producing for each show a specially constructed **scenography** that would provoke performers and audiences to interact, through both looking and contact. Productions such as *Dionysus in 69* (1968–69) avoided end-on perspectives, put audiences closer to and often in the action, encouraged them to move around, and sometimes provided multiple, simultaneous focal points.

Site-specific performance shares many of these features. However, it achieved currency as a name in the 1980s and 1990s to identify performance that was produced in non-theatre sites, aimed to engage directly with the meaning and history of those sites, and went out to audiences who might not normally come to the theatre. This shift in production practices reflected an increasing imperative felt by many makers to address local audiences in the face of advancing globalization. Coincidentally, the shift in name also responded to the increasing association of 'environmental' with ecological issues. The Welsh company Brith Gof produced **devised** shows in rural outdoor sites (*Tri Bywyd*, 'Three Lives', 1995) and a disused urban factory (*Gododdin*, 1988–90), provoking audiences to think about the significance of these sites in Wales's recent post-industrial economy and culture. **Orlan**'s choice of an operating theatre as her site for *The Reincarnation of Saint Orlan* (1990–93) invited audiences to reflect on various aspects of such a site's usual use, including its gender divisions. Tinderbox Theatre Company's *convictions* (2000) staged seven short plays in Belfast's disused Crumlin Road Courthouse, site of many 'Troubles' trials, to reflect on issues of justice and Northern Irish identity in the context of a faltering peace process.

Although the terms 'environmental theatre' and 'site-specific performance' only came into common use in the twentieth century, the spatial practices they name have a much longer Western history, from Greek amphitheatres set in spectacular natural environments, to medieval religious processions through towns, to **Dada** performance like the **Cabaret Voltaire** in cafés, to **festivals**, **carnivals** and **protests** – in all of which people occupy familiar **everyday** sites in unfamiliar ways. These practices also share similarities with **performance art**, **installation art**, **happenings** and **Augusto Boal**'s invisible theatre, which put creative and often critical work in unusual sites in order to ask questions about those sites and the ways people behave in them (compare with **Erving Goffman**).

Environmental theatre and site-specific performance almost always aim to make political interventions in relation to their audiences and sites, but the effectiveness of these aims is sometimes questionable. Some performances exploit the novelty of site-specific performance to attract large audiences without necessarily developing a critique of the site – an example might be the Cirque du Soleil, which commonly exploits rather than interrogates the cultural cachet of the urban sites in which it pitches its tent (such as lower Manhattan's Battery Park). Physical proximity between performers and audience does not necessarily produce critical or democratic interaction. What such work does consistently do is raise questions about the effectiveness of different performance sites, asking whether performance is more effective in a 'neutral' space that can be adapted or in a specifically selected space to which it explicitly refers.

Bibliography

Aronson and Schechner write on environmental theatre; Kaye, Pearson (former co-director of Brith Gof) and Shanks discuss site-specific performance.

Aronson, Arnold (1981) *The History and Theory of Environmental Scenography*, Ann Arbor: UMI Research Press.
Kaye, Nick (2000) *Site-Specific Art: Performance, Place, and Documentation*, London: Routledge.
Pearson, Mike, and Michael Shanks (2001) *Theatre/Archaeology*, London: Routledge.
Schechner, Richard ([1973] 1994) *Environmental Theatre*, New York: Applause Books.

EVERYDAY LIFE

'Everyday life' is both a descriptive and a theoretical term. It describes what people do every day, especially such repetitive activities as working, consuming food, and interacting. From that basic description, at least three related critical applications of the term arose in the twentieth century. Cultural theorists and historians used it to emphasize how all culture is grounded in everyday activity, to argue for the importance of popular culture (as distinguished from elite culture) and to refocus critical study on what had previously been considered unworthy of analysis, such as the lives of workers, women and immigrants. This shift in thought influenced theatre studies by propelling the development of performance studies through the analysis of such popular forms as **ritual** and **festivals**. Activists known as the Situationist International and French sociologists Henri Lefebvre and Michel de Certeau developed this first understanding of everyday life by identifying it as the medium both of people's oppression but also of their emancipation. Everyday life was oppressive because it was organized by state and capitalist control. It consigned people to the alienating drudgery of repetitive work and, even in the apparent safety of their own homes, it 'terrorized' them through such means as advertising into the equally alienating drudgery of unthinking consumption. It was nevertheless emancipating because it was through activities such as **carnivals**, face-to-face communication and other small acts of resistance that individuals could tactically challenge the alienations of capitalist life and claim subjectivity and agency. Lefebvre wrote, 'Everyday life should be a work of art', indicating that **performative** interventions could change and enhance people's lives.

A related performative analysis of everyday life had already been developed by the Canadian sociologist **Erving Goffman**, who focused on how people's daily behaviour could be understood through dramaturgical analysis. Goffman observed that in regular social interactions such as communicating with colleagues people are not simply being, they are **performing**, both consciously and unconsciously. Identity is not what we are (a given), it is something we make and do through the deployment of dress (costume), objects (props) and behaviour (**acting**). Where many critics had previously distinguished rigidly between 'real' life and theatre, Goffman argued that real life *was* theatre. He did not denigrate real life as false but simply recognized that real life shares features with theatre, and that performance analysis can therefore be used to help understand human behaviour. Goffman's argument has certainly been corroborated in performance studies. Michael Kirby's influential analysis of acting put all behaviour from acting to 'being' on a continuum, and claimed that certain activities were seen as acting, not because of what they were but because of how they were framed for an **audience**.

The twentieth-century critical preoccupation with everyday life has other important links to theatre and performance. It inspired many **performance artists**, especially those who did durational work that explicitly challenged the separation of life and performance. In *Coyote: I Like America and America Likes Me* (1974), Joseph Beuys lived with a coyote in a New York gallery for a week, literally staging his lived daily experience as a European in the constant **presence** of American culture, embodied by the coyote. Analyses of everyday life similarly influenced much **environmental theatre and site-specific performance**. Frequently set in everyday contexts such as people's homes, factories and familiar landscapes, this work emphasizes performance's ethical responsibility to function directly in people's everyday lives, rather than removed from that context in theatres. The rise of reality television at the turn of the millennium, where people's daily lives are explicitly presented as entertainment, once again tests distinctions between real life and performance and presents new challenges for critical understandings of everyday life.

Bibliography

Goffman's book is foundational to analyses of life as performative. Lefebvre and de Certeau argue for the revolutionary potential of everyday life. Read proposes that the imbrication of theatre and everyday life gives theatre the responsibility – and opportunity – to be an influentially ethical practice. Highmore collects an excellent range of critical and creative texts.

de Certeau, Michel (1984) *The Practice of Everyday Life*, trans. Steven Rendall, Berkeley: University of California Press.
Goffman, Erving (1959) *The Presentation of Self in Everyday Life*, New York: Doubleday.
Highmore, Ben (ed.) (2002) *The Everyday Life Reader*, London: Routledge.
Kirby, Michael (2002) 'On Acting and Non-Acting', in *Acting (Re)Considered: A Theoretical and Practical Guide*, Phillip B. Zarrilli (ed.), London: Routledge, pp.40–52.
Lefebvre, Henri ([1968] 1984) *Everyday Life in the Modern World*, trans. Sacha Rabinovitch, New Brunswick, NJ: Transactions Publishers.
Read, Alan (1993) *Performance and Everyday Life: An Ethics of Performance*, London: Routledge.

EXPRESSIONISM

The term 'expressionism' was first used most widely near the turn of the twentieth century to describe a radical style of visual art that aimed to express emotion non-naturalistically, in violent protest against the perceived bourgeois repression of **naturalism**. It is exemplified in Edvard Munch's well-known lithograph *The Scream* (1893), where the central figure's scream sends powerful shockwaves through the entire surrounding environment. Practised across a range of art forms, expressionism's roots stretch back to the nineteenth century and the advent of **psychoanalysis**, with its interests in people's emotional life and in dreams. Theatrical expressionism begins with the work of playwrights such as Frank Wedekind and August Strindberg, but it was especially prevalent in Germany from about 1907 to the early 1920s, largely in response to the First World War and its aftermath. Expressionist plays by such writers as Oscar Kokoschka, Ernst Toller and Georg Kaiser are polemical but highly poetic. They often focus on a single male protagonist who declaims long self-exploratory monologues interspersed with brief dialogue with often nameless supporting characters acting as representative social beings. Often, the plays are violent, are concerned with human conflict (especially generational and class conflict), challenge taboos (particularly sexual taboos), and adopt the associative and highly visual qualities of dreams. Expressionist **acting** developed a complementary declamatory, intensely physically committed style featuring actors with haunted, emaciated physiognomies; action that was spare and often allegorical; and the intention to move its **audience** to ecstasy through empathy with the protagonist. Other aspects of expressionist theatre, most notably its **scenography** and **lighting**, were also revolutionary, eschewing naturalism in favour of strong lighting and colours, stark contrast and asymmetry, and the kind of emotionally suggestive abstraction familiar from *The Scream*. A good extant visual example of expressionism's early performance and scenographic styles is Robert Wiene's 1919 film *The Cabinet of Dr Caligari*, with its intensely energized performances and sinister angular, disproportionate sets (compare with **Vsevolod Meyerhold**'s constructivist sets).

The impetus behind expressionism – as with its near-contemporaries **Dada** and **futurism** – was to effect revolutionary change. David F. Kuhns argues, for example, that expressionist performance could **performatively** regenerate German society by fostering the audience's ecstatic engagement with alternative social possibilities and visions. Expressionism was distinctive from those other movements, however, in its initial emphasis on stimulating empathy for human suffering. Even as expressionist artists gradually grew disaffected with the lack of social change occurring, they maintained their focus on human emotion and developed a cynicism quite different from the nihilism of Dada's absurdity. Despite the relatively brief life of a wholly expressionist theatre, many aspects of theatrical expressionism have persisted. Beyond Germany, expressionist playwrights include the American Eugene O'Neill and the Irish Sean O'Casey. **Bertold Brecht** adopted and developed expressionism's iconic imagery and declamatory speech as well as its social impetus. Adolphe Appia, **Edward Gordon Craig** and **Robert Wilson** developed its revolutionary scenography. Choreographers Mary Wigman and, later, **Pina Bausch** and **butoh** practitioners have all explored emotional material through performance in ways that expressionism pioneered and legitimated. Theatrical expressionism's wordiness and abstraction have made its production somewhat uncommon, but it is still produced by **directors** such as Katie Mitchell and Wilson, who want to test theatre's expressive possibilities as well as their own craft.

Bibliography

Styan analyses the broad historical and geographical range of expressionist drama. Richard and (especially) Kuhns provide more sustained analysis of expressionist theatre and performance.

Kuhns, David F. (1968) *Seven Expressionist Plays: Kokoschka to Barlach*, London: Calder and Boyars.
—— (1997) *German Expressionist Theatre: The Actor and the Stage*, Cambridge: Cambridge University Press.
Richard, Lionel (1978) *Phaidon Encyclopedia of Expressionism*, Oxford: Phaidon.
Styan, J. L. (1981) *Modern Drama in Theory and Practice*, vol. 3, *Expressionism and Epic Theatre*, Cambridge: Cambridge University Press.

FEMINISM

Feminism is a political practice which addresses gender identities, relationships and representations in order particularly to redress inequalities which disadvantage women. 'First wave' feminism spanned the late nineteenth and early twentieth centuries in the West and focused on improving women's rights, especially their access to education and suffrage (the right to vote). 'Second wave' feminism burgeoned in the 1960s and 1970s as part of a broader escalation in civil rights **protest** and identity politics. This included protests against the Vietnam War and for black and gay rights in the USA especially, and French student demonstrations against institutional and state oppression, notably in 1968. Among other things, second wave feminism advocated greater equality in conditions of labour and pay, better childcare provision, and women's right to control their reproduction, for example through access to contraception and abortion. But it was also increasingly concerned not only with the explicit legislation that controlled women, but moreover with how women were controlled in more implicit, **everyday** material and social practices, such as through daily language, the personal politics of family relations, and representation, for example in advertising, film and theatre.

Feminist precepts have been articulated through theatre, **dance** and performance throughout the twentieth century and into the twenty-first. Several first wave feminists wrote and performed plays advocating female suffrage and decrying double standards in the social behaviour expected of women and men (for example, Elizabeth Robins's *Votes for Women* [1907]). Christabel Pankhurst and others might be seen as early makers of **performance art** and **body art**, staging public protests and hunger strikes in pursuit of suffrage. Throughout the twentieth century, feminist theatre and dance have interrogated the ways women's conventional representation is often derogatory, exploitative or at least patronizing, reproducing relationships of representation and **audience** spectatorship that disempower women. They have indicated how women's representation is often founded on clichés and stereotypes that invite voyeuristic consumption; how female characters serve as foils in plots centred around male characters; and how the dominant theatre simply offers fewer roles for women. Many theatre- and dance-makers have drawn attention to these inequalities. **Pina Bausch**'s dance theatre, for example, intentionally stages clichés of femininity and masculinity in order to explore how they are socially constructed or **performatively** produced. Other makers overturn these inequalities by producing theatre run by women (**Sistren**), and sometimes for women-only audiences (**Split Britches**). Some feminist theatre-makers deploy **postmodern** strategies of deconstruction to interrogate conventional practices of representing women, for example by engaging with both pornography and the conventional family structures of classic American drama, as in the **Wooster Group**'s *Route 1 & 9 (The Last Act)* (1981). Feminists including **Hélène Cixous** have challenged what they perceive as male-dominated languages and structures of representation, using *écriture féminine* and non-linear structures to explore non-patriarchal strategies of representation. Feminist theatre-makers have also adopted **devising** and **improvisation** techniques to evade theatre's conventionally hierarchical structuring. And feminist **historiographers** have retrieved women's 'lost' theatre histories. Across these critical and creative practices, feminist theatre-makers and analysts have worked to strengthen women's communities and to change gender inequalities.

Feminist performance has pursued many of the same objectives through parallel strategies. Protesters such as **las Madres de la Plaza de Mayo** have congregated to strengthen female communities and to display their gender (and age) to advocate social change. Numerous performance and body artists – including **Marina Abramović**, **Laurie Anderson**, Bobby Baker, **Orlan** and **Annie Sprinkle** – have redressed conditions of women's oppression through the use of direct address and autobiography.

Feminist critics have explored not only how feminism can inform theatre and performance, but also how ideas developed through theatre and performance can inform and progress feminism. **Judith Butler** and others have pioneered understandings of how sexist identities are performatively produced through naturalized, repeated behaviours. They have suggested, further, that these identities might therefore be transformed by interrupting that repetition. **Peggy Phelan** has advocated a feminist political practice which unusually does not advocate visibility and rights. Instead, she embraces women's status as 'unmarked' or less visible culturally, proposing that this marginalized position is actually enabling because it allows women to evade voyeurism and surveillance.

Theatre, dance and performance have been crucial media for enacting feminist concerns because they facilitate detailed interrogation of the ways gender inequalities are produced, most importantly through acts of representation and through embodied behaviours. In the context of theatre, performance and feminist theory, some critics' heralding of post-feminism in the early 1990s seems to have been premature, as all three continue to challenge and work to change gendered representations and behaviours.

Bibliography

Publishing on feminism and theatre exploded in the late 1980s, and continues. Early influential texts are the journal *Women & Performance* (founded in 1983, and published twice annually by New York University's Department of Performance Studies), Case's 1988 book, and books by Dolan, Aston, and Chinoy and Jenkins. Strong collections of articles include those edited by Case, Goodman and du Gay, Hart and Phelan, and Martin. Chothia's edited collection of suffrage plays contains Robins's *Votes for Women*. Baker is an influential performance artist in the UK.

Aston, Elaine (1995) *An Introduction to Feminism and Theatre*, London: Routledge.

Baker, Bobby (1991) *Kitchen Show: One Dozen Kitchen Actions Made Public*, programme with performance text, London: Arts Admin.

Case, Sue-Ellen (1988) *Feminism and Theatre*, New York: Methuen.

—— (ed.) (1990) *Performing Feminisms: Feminist Critical Theory and Theatre*, Baltimore: Johns Hopkins University Press.

Chinoy, Helen Krich and Linda Walsh Jenkins (1987) *Women in American Theatre*, revised and expanded edition, New York: Theatre Communications Group.

Chothia, Jean (ed.) (1998) *The New Woman and Other Emancipated Woman Plays*, Oxford: Oxford University Press.

Dolan, Jill (1988) *The Feminist Spectator as Critic*, Ann Arbor: University of Michigan Press.

Goodman, Lizbeth with Jane du Gay (eds) (1998) *The Routledge Reader in Gender and Performance*, London: Routledge.

Hart, Lynda and Peggy Phelan (eds) (1993) *Acting Out: Feminist Performances*, Ann Arbor: University of Michigan Press.

Martin, Carol (ed.) (1996) *A Sourcebook of Feminist Theatre: On and Beyond the Stage*, London: Routledge.

Women & Performance: A Journal of Feminist Theory. Online. Available <http://www.womenandperformance.org/> (accessed 22 November 2004).

FESTIVALS

Festivals are spatially and temporally limited events, usually held annually, where theatre and/or performance is staged and celebrated. Like **carnival**, they often serve significant social functions, such as honouring the host community or encouraging artistic innovation. However, they also pose certain risks, for example, the possibility that a select few may exploit a festival to serve their own interests rather than those of the broader community. These ambivalent potentials are demonstrated in the West as far back as the fifth century BC in Athens's Festival Dionysia, a major civic competition that presented both comedy and tragedy. The Festival Dionysia aimed to serve a **ritual** function for all of Athens' citizens through the mimetic enactment of symbolic sacrifice. Because it was grounded in a system of patronage, however, the Festival Dionysia nevertheless privileged the city's leaders.

Festivals take many forms in the twentieth and twenty-first centuries: presenting international, national, local, amateur or professional work; combining **dance**, theatre, **music**, opera, **sports**, workshops and/or debates; or exploring in detail a particular form, as at the London International Mime Festival (founded in 1977). Many theatre festivals are dedicated to the work of a single playwright, most frequently Shakespeare. Such festivals are partly designed to celebrate the genius of an individual, but these and other festivals also function to acclaim the 'genius' and achievement of their host city, nation or region – as the **Olympics** do. Many European international theatre festivals founded after the destruction and alienation of the Second World War – including Edinburgh, Avignon and Holland (all 1947), the Berliner Festwochen (1951) and the Théâtre des Nations (Paris, 1954) – were created to demonstrate Europe's cultural accomplishments as well as to facilitate European regeneration and international communication. Festivals continue to foster diverse community identities through the proliferation of black, women's, children's and queer theatre festivals.

Festivals have many potential benefits for their sites, art forms and participants. They can benefit their sites by fostering economic development and urban regeneration. They can foster artistic appreciation and development, providing opportunities for artistic experimentation and introducing **audiences** to new work through innovative programming and producing. Given their frequently amenable conditions of big budgets and well-equipped theatre **spaces**, major international festivals significantly support the work of such eminent **directors** as, for example, **Peter Brook**, **Robert Wilson**, **Robert Lepage** and **Tadashi Suzuki**. Through such activities as the 'Enquiries' of the London International Festival of Theatre (founded 1981), festivals can also provoke reflection on the (potential) purposes of theatre, as well as the nature of community. Both the Edinburgh Festival Fringe (founded 1947) and the Edinburgh People's Festival (founded 1951) challenged the perceived elitism and exclusivity of the Edinburgh International Festival. The 1990 Los Angeles Festival curated by director Peter Sellars excluded much work from the Euro-American pool that international festivals usually draw on, and included Asian and Mexican practices and groups that represented the backgrounds of many of LA's marginalized immigrant communities. It thus asked who and what LA was and what communities the festival should both represent and serve.

Despite all these positive potentials, there are a number of festival characteristics that bear critical scrutiny, especially as festivals continue to proliferate alongside growing international trade and tourism. First, as in any context of **intercultural** exchange, festivals risk trivializing and commodifying the cultures they represent. Second, given the standardization of international theatre festivals' conditions of production, they risk internationalizing aesthetic trends, producing homogenized festival fare (which is recognizably large-scale, auteur-directed/branded so it will sell), and often **visual theatre**, so it can trade across linguistic barriers. Finally, they risk producing an acute elitism, certainly because they are often financially expensive, but also because they frequently deploy rarefied theatre vocabularies that address specialist (international) audiences but may be less accessible to local audiences.

Bibliography

Contemporary Theatre Review's special issue includes useful articles on festivals in Avignon, Edinburgh, Africa and the Arab world, and on how festival conditions affect the work of Robert Lepage. Knowles details how international festival conditions affect theatre's meanings.
Contemporary Theatre Review (2003) special issue on festivals, 13.4, London: Routledge.
Knowles, Ric (2004) *Reading the Material Theatre*, Cambridge: Cambridge University Press.

FUTURISM

Futurism is an avant-garde artistic movement and ideology that originated in Italy before the First World War. Its founding manifesto by poet and playwright F. T. Marinetti published in 1909 in Paris's *Le Figaro* newspaper espoused the destruction of museums and libraries – as enervating sites of reflection on the past – and celebrated machines, speed, youth, masculinity and war. Automobiles, aeroplanes and other machines and technology provided models for a new era driven by an aggressive masculine energy focusing on the future. Futurist art often took literary and graphic form, but it keenly adopted and developed many performance techniques in order directly to shock **audiences** out of lazy conformity by actively provoking debate, **protest** and – ideally, for many of its proponents – riots. Its numerous manifestos were rhetorically conceived less to be privately read than to be publicly declaimed. Futurist cabaret-style performance evenings were inspired by traditions of **popular performance** and variety theatre, encouraged **improvisation** to be as provocative as possible, and combined several unrelated acts such as sequences of noise **music**, poetry readings and brief plays designed to produce a sense of acceleration in their stripped-down compression. Eventually earning the name 'synthetics' for their dynamic synthesis of numerous disparate elements, these events embraced abstraction and rejected the dominant theatre's focus on artifice, linear narrative, psychology and **naturalism**. They were similar to **Dada**'s cabarets, such as the **Cabaret Voltaire**, but more destructive and assertive of a world view than was Dada's absurd questioning. **Scenographically**, futurist theatre often emphasized the mechanical by using machine-like costumes, automatons and marionettes, realizing the performance of *Übermarionetten* that **Edward Gordon Craig** had advocated but not fully achieved. Because it glorified war and was linked to Fascism, futurism was somewhat discredited with the coming of the First World War, although its experiments continued in theatre, **dance**, film and radio through the 1920s until the early 1930s, primarily in Italy but also, for example, in Russia. From the 1970s on, theatre historians have recuperated futurism as an important progenitor of numerous twentieth-century avant-garde and political performance practices, from Dada, to the theatre of the absurd that developed in Italy (for example, in the plays of Luigi Pirandello) and elsewhere in Europe (in the work of Samuel Beckett, for instance), to the interventionist practices of **happenings**, to **multimedia performance**. Elements of futurism's aggressive experimentation have certainly been influential, but its advocacy of violence and war has resulted in the critical, highly selective adoption of its practices.

Bibliography

The Kirbys collect archival material and develop a detailed analysis in order to recuperate futurist theatre from critical neglect and demonstrate its contribution to other non-naturalistic twentieth-century theatre practices. Goldberg draws out this link to other avant-garde practices.

Goldberg, RoseLee (2001) *Performance Art: From Futurism to the Present*, revised and expanded edition, London: Thames and Hudson.

Kirby, Michael and Victoria Nes Kirby ([1971] 1986) *Futurist Performance*, New York: Performing Arts Journal Publications.

Marinetti, F. T. ([1909] 2002) 'The Founding and Manifesto of Futurism', reprinted in Michael Huxley and Noel Witts (eds) *The Twentieth-Century Performance Reader*, 2nd edition, London: Routledge.

HAPPENINGS

Happenings are cross-disciplinary non-text-based events that utilize all media and means at the artists' disposal, and especially those from outside the maker's own field. A central part of **artistic** experimentation of the 1960s, happenings evolved from various disciplines. They were inspired by challenges in **dance** led by the Judson Church and pieces like *Trio A* (1966), as well as the earlier pioneering explorations of **John Cage** and **Merce Cunningham** at Black Mountain College during the 1950s. Many consider Cage's work the main inspiration for happenings. But as in **Dadaist** events like the **Cabaret Voltaire**, visual and plastic artists (connected to the pop art movement) were particularly dominant. The actual term was coined by American artist Allan Kaprow and came to prominence in the 1960s, even though the notion had been in circulation in the 1950s, as Kaprow's own event *18 Happenings in 6 Parts* (1959) demonstrates. But it was only with the plethora of live and **installation** works by Jim Dine, Kaprow, George Brecht and Robert Whitman, for example, as well as later publications by Kaprow and Michael Kirby in response to these, that this distinctive genus of performance clearly emerged.

Although happenings took place mainly in America, they also had their proponents in Europe and Japan. Jean-Jacques Lebel produced and wrote about his fiercely political happenings in France, **Tadeusz Kantor** conducted events in

Poland with mannequins, found objects and eccentric home-made contraptions, and Japan's Gutai Theatre's performances led to international renown. After the 1970s, happenings, 'assemblages' and events were subsumed under the range of work labelled **performance art**.

Happenings relied predominantly on visual or material elements, many of which were deliberately impermanent or destroyed during the act of performance. Practitioners consciously avoided using artists' materials or theatre techniques, working outside their disciplines and beyond familiar gallery **spaces**. In Kaprow's *Notes to Soap* (1965), participants were smeared with jam and buried on a beach. Joseph Beuys, in what he termed 'Actions' rather than happenings, lived with a coyote in *Coyote: I Like America and America Likes Me* (1974). Such events shared much with **environmental theatre**, often taking place in outdoor or non-performance spaces like streets, shops or in the countryside. They were frequently participatory, deliberately immersed in, or intervening in, **everyday life** rather than in spaces created for the showing of art. Although these one-off unrepeatable events were loosely scored or structured rather than **improvised**, they depended on planning rather than on **rehearsal** or **training**. They were what Michael Kirby has referred to as 'non-matrixed' performance, where performers do activities, tasks or actions in the present time and in an actual place, rather than **acting** in illusionist or mimetic terms, where they are expected to fabricate an alternative here and now. Happenings demanded aesthetic re-evaluation of all processes that they utilized, deliberately blurring the boundaries between art and life.

As the name suggests, happenings were intended to make the audience aware of the **liveness** of the event, to encourage them to engage in the moment and experience what was happening. As such, they contested **realist** art forms that depend on artifice and reproduction, and what might be considered the privileged position of funded work presented with sophisticated technologies and techniques in dedicated spaces for paying audiences. In sympathy with, and emerging from, the political idealism of 1960s America, Europe and Japan, happenings shared features with (and were sometimes inseparable from) **protests and demonstrations**, particularly in their European manifestations. The 1968 demonstrations in Paris and around the world took inspiration from happenings' challenges and transgressions. Happenings were rough-and-ready events that were free and accessible and thus operated in a different economy from commercial art. With their seemingly random association of actions (which were in fact usually carefully planned), happenings posed provocative political, aesthetic and personal challenges throughout the 1960s and 1970s.

Bibliography

There are several books that focus on the evolution of postmodern performance and performance art generally, but these texts focus on the specific nature of happenings. Kaprow's has many useful black-and-white illustrations of his and others' events and a short explanatory text.

Kaprow, Allan (1966) *Assemblage, Environments and Happenings*, New York: Harry N. Abrams.

Kirby, Michael (1965) *Happenings: An Illustrated Anthology*, New York: Dutton.

Sandford, Mariellen (ed.) (1995) *Happenings and Other Acts*, London and New York: Routledge.

HISTORIOGRAPHY

Historiography is the study of the writing of history. It recognizes that because history is past and in some senses unrecoverable, recollecting and writing it will never be an objective practice, but rather one that is subjective, interpretive and fundamentally creative. Different writings of the 'same' history thus implicitly reveal the cultural conditions and ideologies of their time. The subjectivity of history writing becomes evident when we compare histories of the same topic written at different times. Variations in theatre history writing, for example, show how attitudes towards theatre – as differentiated from drama – have shifted. While early theatre histories concentrated on the playtext as the primary source of the theatre's meaning, more recent theatre histories focus overwhelmingly on the material conditions of production – or **mise en scène** – as crucial determinants of meaning. Much theatre history writing has also identified, and so produced, theatre as high cultural practice, excluding such **popular theatre** activities as offstage cross-dressing in the Renaissance, melodrama in the nineteenth century and contemporary **musical theatre**.

As these examples indicate, the fact that history writing is subjective affects not only what information it explicitly conveys, but also the ideologies or beliefs it may implicitly carry. It matters not only what history is told, but also how it is told. So, a Renaissance theatre history that concentrates on the stage and not on other theatrical cultural practices will necessarily produce a gender focus on men because women were not permitted to perform on public stages. Similarly, a history of nineteenth-century theatre that omits melodrama will simultaneously omit an enormous working-class **audience**. In the 1970s and 1980s, as part of a **postmodern** movement that rejected what critic Jean-François Lyotard called 'grand narratives' and their apparent certainties, it was increasingly recognized that 'received' histories were often the history of the dominant. It was also recognized, however, that absence from the histories did not mean absence from history, and efforts were made to redress the prevailing bias by retrieving lost histories. In the 1980s and 1990s, this led to the rise of historiographies with explicit subjective focus on, for example, **feminist**, lesbian, gay and black theatre. In the 1990s and on, it has also led to the rise of **performative** theatre histories. Drawing on the particular challenges and possibilities presented to the historian by theatre and performance's **liveness** and inevitable immediate loss or absence, these writings are explicitly self-reflexive about their own subjective formation of history and meaning.

Bibliography

Bratton provides an excellent introduction to key issues in historiography and grounds them in English theatre history. Reinelt and Roach and Postlewait and McConachie collect articles which usefully indicate historiography's practice and potential. Roach and Shepherd and Womack both demonstrate performative, self-reflexive historiography.

Bratton, Jacky (2003) *New Readings in Theatre History*, Cambridge: Cambridge University Press.

Postlewait, Thomas and Bruce A. McConachie (eds) (1989) *Interpreting the Theatrical Past: Essays in the Historiography of Performance*, Iowa City: University of Iowa Press.

Reinelt, Janelle G. and Joseph R. Roach (eds) (1992) *Critical Theory and Performance*, Ann Arbor: University of Michigan Press.

Roach, Joseph (1996) *Cities of the Dead: Circum-Atlantic Performance*, New York: Columbia University Press.

Shepherd, Simon and Peter Womack (1996) *English Drama: A Cultural History*, Oxford: Blackwell.

IMPROVISATION

Improvisation is the spontaneous invention of performance. It has a long theatre history, for example in commedia dell' arte, which has been practised in Italy from about the mid-sixteenth century. In commedia, performers improvise unique performances within set rules regarding stock characters, plots and jokes. Commedia demonstrates improvisation's particular ability to produce 'new' shows quickly and with few resources and, by responding to local contexts and current issues, to produce topical satire. Improvisation achieved popularity elsewhere in the West in the 1960s and 1970s, when its defining principles of spontaneity, creative **play**, openness to chance and group participation captured the imagination of artists and teachers. For these practitioners, improvisation seemed to hold out the possibility of escaping learned taboos, achieving freedom of expression, producing unexpected outcomes and developing more democratic group practices. These practitioners included composer **John Cage**, **dance**-makers whose contact improvisation produced choreography out of performers' unplanned **movements**, and theatre-makers and **performance artists** including **Richard Schechner**, **Laurie Anderson** and creators of **happenings**. Such practitioners were inspired partly by theatre's own history of improvisation, but also by such things as improvisational jazz and contemporary educational theories about stimulating children's learning through play. Improvisation in this context and beyond is a tool of creative stimulation both for its own sake and for **devising** performances. It is a method of facilitating better collaboration by requiring practitioners not to block a partner's proposition, but to go with it and build on it. And it is a vital **training** and **rehearsal** tool, encouraging the breaking of habit, building of character, and generation of devised performance material. It also has links with stand-up comedy – which has to respond spontaneously to heckling and other **audience** interjections – as with a lot of political comedy, such as the long-running American television programme *Saturday Night Live*.

Improvisation's capacity to be topical, to evade censorship and to facilitate democratic participation gives it enormous political potential that has been harnessed by performance artists like **Guillermo Gómez-Peña**, **body artists** such as **Orlan** and theatre artists including **Augusto Boal**, with his Forum Theatre. Improvisation's capacity to challenge the received wisdom of 'grand narratives' has also made it a favoured tool of many **postmodern** performance-makers, including the **Wooster Group**. Despite its emphasis on freedom, improvisation relies on the observation of certain rules – for example, of genre and characterization. And, while it specifies a particular form of performance, elements of improvisation are intrinsic to all performance and the quality of **liveness** it produces, as performance must constantly be prepared to adapt to its live, unpredictable conditions.

Bibliography

Spolin and Johnstone's books are early testimonies to the value of improvisation as a creative and self-actualizing practice. Frost and Yarrow provide historical and theoretical context as well as more practical exercises.

Frost, Anthony and Ralph Yarrow (1990) *Improvisation in Drama*, London: Macmillan.
Johnstone, Keith (1981) *Impro: Improvisation and the Theatre*, London: Eyre Methuen.
Spolin, Viola (1973) *Improvisation for the Theatre: A Handbook of Teaching and Directing Techniques*, London: Pitman Publishing.

INSTALLATION ART

This term has been used since the 1960s to designate art practice which is not simply displayed in a supposedly neutral site, like most paintings hung in galleries, but which explicitly aims to include and refer to its site and context as a crucial constituent of its meanings. As in the installations of **Guillermo Gómez-Peña** and **Abramović**, installation art sometimes involves the artists as performers. Usually, it is three-dimensional, temporary, and can be entered and possibly interacted with by its **audience/spectators**. Almost always both the site and the spectator are regarded as necessary to the completion of the piece and its constitution as meaningful. Sometimes installation art occupies an art gallery unconventionally, as in such pieces as **Abramović**'s *Balkan Baroque* (1997), in which she scrubbed beef bones in a gallery for hours at a time, or Tracey Emin's *My Bed* (1998), in which she challenged the putative austerity and objectivity of the public gallery by putting the intimate **space** of her dishevelled bedroom within it. Sometimes it occupies a space not normally dedicated to art, as in the 'wrappings' of **Christo and Jeanne-Claude**, where they temporarily engulf in fabric natural sites or famous buildings such as Berlin's Reichstag. Like **performance art**, installation art arose at a point in art history when, in a political assault on the status quo, boundaries between art disciplines and media were breaking down to develop hybrid new forms.

Like **environmental theatre and site-specific performance**, installation art compels its audiences to reflect on the meanings and histories of its site. Like performance art, it challenges the institutionalism of much fine art, interrogating the ways galleries feign neutrality and contain, delimit and commodify art practices. Because it is almost always temporary, it argues against universalism and for the value of seeing art's meaning as not only site-specific but also time-specific. It is directly relevant to theatre and performance for a number of reasons. For example, it often indisputably is performance, as in Gómez-Peña's work, and its interactive models of the event–audience relationship bear useful comparison to more conventional theatrical models, as well as to such ideas as **Augusto Boal**'s 'spectactor'. Perhaps most influential, however, is the way art scholar Michael Fried's 1967 condemnation of installation art explicitly blamed what he saw as its moral failure on its inherent theatricality. For Fried, installation art was morally bereft because it relied on the theatrical features of duration and audience in order to produce its meaning. Unlike such modernist forms as painting and sculpture, which he saw as inherently complete and therefore achieving subjecthood, it needed contextualization to be complete and was therefore consigned to 'objecthood'. Fried's provocative argument not only denounced installation art, it also denounced theatre and such inherent features of theatre and performance as duration and audience. It thus compelled reflection on these crucial aspects of theatre and demanded defence of what for many are precisely what makes theatre an ethical practice – its audience's responsibility to it, and its responsibility to its social, temporal and spatial contexts of production. Despite Fried's attack, the explicit relation of installation art to its audience and context actually secured its widespread acceptance and even mainstream popularity in the 1990s, as indicated by the title of Reiss's book and the fame of such British artists as Emin, Sarah Lucas and Damien Hirst.

Bibliography

Reiss provides an informative history. Both of Oliveira *et al.*'s books offer excellent illustrations.

Fried, Michael (1967) 'Art and Objecthood', *Artforum* 5.10: 12–23. Reprinted in Philip Auslander (ed.) (2003) *Performance: Critical Concepts in Literary and Cultural Studies*, vol. 4, London: Routledge, pp.165–87.
Oliveira, Nicolas de, Nicola Oxley and Michael Petry (1994) *Installation Art*, London: Thames and Hudson.
—— (2003) *Installation Art in the New Millennium: The Empire of the Senses*, London: Thames and Hudson.
Reiss, Julie H. (1999) *From Margin to Center: The Spaces of Installation Art*, Cambridge, MA: MIT Press.

INTERCULTURALISM

The term 'interculturalism' describes cultural interaction which confronts and/or combines the practices of one culture with those of one or more others. Intercultural theatre and performance can thus be understood as referring more accurately to hybrid activities rather than to specific genres of performance. Intercultural performance is visible in the assimilation of Asian and African aesthetics by such Western **directors** as **Antonin Artaud**, **Bertold Brecht**, Ariane Mnouchkine, **Peter Brook**, **Robert Wilson**, **Robert Lepage** and Julie Taymor. It is also visible in the pre-performance work of such Western directors as **Richard Schechner**, **Jerzy Grotowski** and **Eugenio Barba**, who have used Asian forms of psycho-physical preparation such as yoga to inform their methods of both **training** and **devising**. As these examples indicate, the term 'intercultural' is used more commonly to describe the influence of practices from the South, East or third world on those of the North, West or first world. But it can also be used to describe movement in the other direction, as in the cases of Nigerian playwright **Wole Soyinka**, who combines narrative forms from classical Greek and Shakespearean drama with local Yoruba myths, and of **Tadashi Suzuki**, who directs Western plays using **Asian performance** practices and traditions. It can also describe the hybrid 'border art' of **Guillermo Gómez-Peña**.

Following the sympathy for multicultural integration that was characteristic of much Western culture in the 1960s and 1970s, interculturalism partly arose in response to an increased desire – fuelled by **postmodernism** – to articulate cultural differences. As its widespread and longstanding practice indicates, intercultural performance has a number of irrefutable attractions. It can develop indigenous practices; it can lead to the creation of hybrid new forms of performance and expression; and it can help facilitate the understanding of different cultures. However, it has also been the subject of intense criticism. Because intercultural exchange often occurs between cultures with different levels of privilege and power, it can be exploitative, lacking respect or reciprocity or treating culture as commodity. And because intercultural performance is a form of cultural representation, it can be susceptible to misrepresentation, often trivializing and denigrating source cultures as cliché or stereotype, as when Western performance represents Asian and African forms as primitive. Such arguments have been made most boldly by **Rustom Bharucha** in his criticism of Brook's *Mahabharata* (1985).

Patrice Pavis has argued that interculturalism's arguments have become reductive, circular and outmoded. However, its practice and analysis usefully demand attention to the ethics of exchange and difference, to relationships of power, and to ideas of cultural autonomy. And such attention may be especially important as intercultural practices continue to spread within the contexts of globalization and the ongoing expansion of international theatre **festival** circuits.

Bibliography

Fischer-Lichte *et al.* provide geographic spread, Gainor provides historical depth, Holledge and Tompkins focus on women's performance, and Marranca and Dasgupta collect a strong range of critical articles and interviews. Martin's is a handbook for performance preparation. Pavis's analyses are seminal.

Bharucha, Rustom (1993) *Theatre and the World: Performance and the Politics of Culture*, London: Routledge.

Fischer-Lichte, Erika, Josephine Riley and Michael Gissenwehrer (eds) (1990) *The Dramatic Touch of Difference: Theatre, Own and Foreign*, Tübingen: Gunter Narr Verlag.

Gainor, J. Ellen (ed.) (1995) *Imperialism and Theatre: Essays on World Theatre, Drama and Performance 1795–1995*, London: Routledge.

Holledge, Julie, and Joanne Tompkins (2000) *Women's Intercultural Performance*, London: Routledge.

Marranca, Bonnie, and Gautam Dasgupta (eds) (1991) *Interculturalism and Performance: Writings from PAJ*, New York: PAJ Publications.

Martin, John (2004) *The Intercultural Performance Handbook*, London: Routledge.

Pavis, Patrice (1992) *Theatre at the Crossroads of Culture*, trans. Loren Kruger, London: Routledge.

—— (ed.) (1996) *The Intercultural Performance Reader*, London: Routledge.

INTERNET

The rapid growth in the use and potential applications of the internet in the last ten years of the twentieth century, an expansion that is continuing inexorably today, has had some notable impact on the field of performance. Although performance in 'cyberspace' can scarcely be considered 'live' in terms of direct **presence**, it can question this very **liveness** through online and remote interaction. The fine line between reality and what is merely a construct becomes more and more fragile in such works. Exponential improvements in the growth of computer memory and the development of webcams, digital video and streaming have enabled performances of all kinds (sadly much of this dominated and driven by pornography) to be transmitted immediately to millions worldwide, following Paul McCartney's landmark concert in December 1999 from the Beatles' venue The Cavern in Liverpool. As such, the internet can be considered another form for distributing performance material as well as an efficient and global marketing and information tool for artists interested in promoting their profile or networking possibilities. Many artists and performers have their own official websites for advertising and employment purposes such as casting, as well as for artistic ends.

The potential is far greater, though, than mere self-promotion, as **multimedia performance**, Net Art, experiments with online games, research into virtual reality, and the use of the internet directly in performance by, for example, **Guillermo Gómez-Peña** and **Stelarc**, have indicated. Gómez-Peña solicited

audience confessions online in response to his **installation** piece *The Temple of Confessions* (1994–97). Stelarc shifted his practice from total 'body suspensions', hanging from meat hooks in both public and private spaces, to virtual 'suspensions', linking himself to the internet through specially created Stimbod software. Such interactions are understandably costly, technologically extremely complex and even dangerous, so he performs them rarely. What these and other examples of internet-based performance proffer is a community for performance and the creation of interhuman networks that differ markedly from the live audience interacting in one shared space. These communities have an interesting political as well as social dimension too, protected as they can be by their technological and actual remoteness. The immersive world of virtual reality further extends the process of being a **spectator**, promoting interactivity rather than passivity.

The internet and related technology are also featuring more frequently within performances, as subject matter and as media for human interaction. An early influential example was in Patrick Marber's play *Closer* (1997), where two characters meet after an initial online chat, the content of which was projected on a screen. Companies like British group Blast Theory are increasingly exploring the internet in their multimodal artistic experiments, as in *Can You See Me Now?* (2001), a sort of interactive online game that also deployed satellite tracking. The full impact of the internet on and within performance has scarcely been felt yet, but it clearly suggests a range of practical possibilities. Theoretically, the internet is considered the epitome of a **postmodern** construct and opens up challenging questions about **performing**, spectatorship and site through electronic digital interaction. One typically postmodern attribute is the ever-expanding connectivity available through non-linear hyperlinking. Although not yet fully recognized as its own genre, 'internet performance' offers an interesting corollary to the recent growing interest in the embodied nature of performance.

Bibliography

Few books deal exclusively with the emerging interconnection between performance and the internet, but Giannachi gives a helpful introduction. The *Performance Research* issue collects together short pieces, some of which refer to internet-based practices. Birringer and Auslander focus on the broader issues that face performance in a highly mediatized society. The web addresses given below hint at the range of material available online.

AlienNation Company. Online. Available <http://www.aliennationcompany.com> (accessed 1 November 2004).

Allsopp, Ric and Scott deLahunta (eds) (1999) 'Online', a special issue of *Performance Research*, 4.2, London: Routledge.

Auslander, Philip (1999) *Liveness: Performance in a Mediatized Culture*, London and New York: Routledge.

Birringer, Johannes (1998) *Media and Performance: Along the Border*, Baltimore: Johns Hopkins University Press.

Fura dels Baus, La. Online. Available <http://www.lafura.com> (accessed 1 November 2004).

Giannachi, Gabriella (2004) *Virtual Theatres: An Introduction*, London: Routledge.

Kunstwerk-blend. Online. Available <http://www.kunstwerk-blend.co.uk> (accessed 1 November 2004).

Live Art Archives. Online. Available <http://www.art.ntu.ac.uk.liveart/indez.htm> (accessed 20 November 2002).

Stelarc. Online. Available <http://www.stelarc.va.com.au> (accessed 1 November 2004).

LIGHTING AND SOUND

Lighting and sound may be indispensable elements of performance events but they are often overlooked by the public, critics and academics alike. An explanation for this invisibility is the fact that they usually have supplementary or supporting rather than dominant roles. Used often to provoke emotional responses or create mood in a subliminal rather than overt way, they are mostly employed non-figuratively. They thus need to be considered in relation to other aspects of the **mise en scène** or production rather than just by themselves. If they are conspicuous, this may mitigate against the believability of a scene, as is fundamental to **naturalist** theatre, where the **spectator** needs to focus on the stage and the actors rather than the surrounding theatre technologies.

Lighting and sound are a vital part of **scenography**, though their primacy has often been disputed. **Konstantin Stanislavsky** and Anton Chekhov disagreed about the **director**'s inclusion of so many sound effects in production, which the writer thought shifted his plays away from the more symbolic register he desired. With quite another stylistic intention from Stanislavsky, designers like **Edward Gordon Craig** have emphasized and advocated the role of lighting, working with swathes of light and shadows rather than three-dimensional materials to create location, volume and mood on stage. **Bertold Brecht** revealed the mechanisms at work in the theatre to the spectator, whereas **Antonin Artaud** called for the use of all stage technology as part of his manifesto for a total theatre.

Yet, however unaware of lighting and sound the spectator or critic is, there is no denying their significance for: defining place (a room indoors as opposed to an open field outside); indicating the passage of time (lights rising to suggest dawn, reinforced by the sound of a chorus of birds); creating mood through colour or through suggestive sounds; establishing links or motifs that might close or open a piece, as in blackouts or introductory fanfares; and deliberately illuminating or obscuring what the **audience** can see and hear, so prompting them to reflect on the act of spectatorship and witnessing.

The introduction of electricity into theatres in the West at the beginning of the twentieth century greatly enhanced lighting's functionality as well as its creative potential. As electricity became established, and with the arrival much later of computers and digital technology, so have lighting and sound technologies become extremely advanced. Intensity, colour, size, speed, volume, range and complexity of cues are all possible with extensive variables, making lighting and sound design sophisticated art forms in their own right. Many directors exploit the potential of these technologies as autonomous elements in themselves. **Robert Wilson** uses light bars or washes on the cyclorama as a central part of his stage action. Battersea Arts Centre, one of the foremost experimental producing venues in London, ran a 'Playing in the Dark' season in 1998 without any lighting, bringing techniques familiar from radio into a three-dimensional public shared **space**.

Postmodern performance practitioners have shown ongoing interest in **playing** with light and sound as well as media like television, video and the **internet**. The replaying of sound bites from popular culture in British group Forced Entertainment's work, or the relaying of video extracts of previous **rehearsals** of the **Wooster Group**, are just two examples. Such interaction with stage technologies questions the actuality and **liveness** of the performance event through the use of prerecorded narration, voices off, **multimedia** focal points, or perhaps illogical shifts in time and space. The ability of sound and lighting to make an impact on the spectator or auditor, evident especially in large-scale concerts, **raves**, or events like the **Olympic** ceremonies and **parades**, seems inversely proportional to the interest they attract within theatre and performance studies.

Bibliography

The extensive chapter in the Brockett and Ball book sketches in recent histories of these technologies and highlights practical issues. There are many handbooks like Reid's and Fineli's, but few theoretical texts in this area. Pavis offers a short but useful introduction to analysis of these technologies in performance.

Brockett, Oscar G. and Robert J. Ball (2004) *The Essential Theatre*, 8th edition, Belmont CA: Wadsworth/Thomson Learning.
Fineli, Patrick (2002) *Sound for the Stage*, Cambridge: Entertainment Technology Press.
Pavis, Patrice (2003) *Analyzing Performance: Theater, Dance and Film*, trans. David Williams, Ann Arbor: University of Michigan Press.
Reid, Francis (2001) *Lighting the Stage*, Cambridge: Entertainment Technology Press.

LIVENESS

Liveness describes a quality of live performance – the sense that it is happening here and now. It is an important idea because it apparently distinguishes live performance from recorded performance-based media such as film and television, indicating that live performance has some intrinsic qualitative and even political difference from other forms of performance. It is an especially important idea because the nature, effects and even existence of this qualitative difference are the subject of considerable debate.

For many, performance's liveness gives it its distinctive energy, interest and social significance. It is in live performance that people – performers and **audiences** – encounter and potentially interact with one another in real time, **space** and social process. Performance's liveness is exciting because it cultivates a sense of **presence**, and because risk is unavoidable where accident cannot be edited out (as it can in recorded media). Performance's liveness is social because it produces meaning in a dynamic process, rather than in the fixed and passive form that recorded media seem to present. It gives live performance the potential to be a context where social change can be produced. And it is a quality that has been directly explored and exploited in theatre, stand-up comedy, speech-making, **body art**, **happenings** and **performance art**.

For performance theorist **Peggy Phelan**, what distinguishes live performance is the fact that it is live; the archive and the record of performance are not performance because they are set. For her, this ephemeral quality gives performance a particular political potential. Because it cannot be captured, performance is 'nonreproductive'; it resists becoming commodified, objectified and appropriated, and it maintains instead the dynamic possibility of being continuously creative. For Phelan, what makes performance exciting and gives it social value is not so much its sense of presence as its sense of absence – the sense that performance is forever escaping and cannot be reproduced. Phelan argues that performance theorists need to seek a 'live', **performative**, creative and critical discourse for analysing performance that enhances its ephemeral qualities, instead of trying to pin it down in conventional academic or journalistic prose.

Philip Auslander directly challenges Phelan's specific arguments as well as more conventional wisdom on liveness, arguing against seeing live performance as distinctive from other recorded media and proposing that seemingly live performance is pervasively mediatized. He demonstrates that early television was modelled on theatrical forms and that recent live performance is frequently adapted from films and television shows and is often **multimedia**, incorporating recorded images and sounds. Auslander concludes that the live and the recorded are deeply interlinked and that it is inaccurate to set them up as binary opposites. He disputes the idea that apparently live performance offers better opportunities for social exchange than recorded media do, arguing that live performance is premised not on an intrinsic connection between audience and performer but on their necessary separation. And by refusing to disconnect live and mediatized performance, he refutes Phelan's location of performance outside of an economy of reproducible commodities. Auslander's arguments can come across as intentionally provocative and contrary. Usefully, however, they aim to get beyond some of the mystifying, vague language that gathers around live performance, they question idealized notions of the performer–audience relationship, and they challenge the very idea that performance can escape commodity culture. They also provoke consideration of not only what distinguishes live performance from recorded media, but importantly the many things it now shares with those media. As technology like the **internet** becomes ever more interactive, and recorded media like reality television increasingly incorporate live sequences, the complex relationship between the live and the recorded requires continued critical scrutiny and articulation. Liveness is not a resolved term; it is at the centre of what does or does not make live performance unique and particularly meaningful.

Bibliography

Auslander, Philip (1999) *Liveness: Performance in a Mediatized Culture*, London and New York: Routledge.
Phelan, Peggy (1993) 'The Ontology of Performance', in *Unmarked: The Politics of Performance*, London: Routledge, pp.146–66.

MASKING/BODY ADORNMENT

In performance, ways of masking or decorating the body have been used repeatedly to transform, enlarge, disguise or separate performers off from the **everyday**, from ancient **rituals** to the make-up that turns West End or Broadway performers into cats. Archaeologists have provided evidence of such practices from prehistoric days onwards, unearthing pictures of the large headdress masks of ancient Greek theatre, for example. **Popular theatre** forms have often used masks from the red nose of the **circus** clown to the stock characters of commedia dell'arte. But such traditional practices have also become experimental when translated from their original context. Inspired by **circus** and commedia, **Vsevolod Meyerhold** used mask-like make-up to establish a grotesque idiom, **Bertold Brecht** made his *Caucasian Chalk Circle* (1954) characters representative beings through masking them, and **Jerzy Grotowski**'s actors adopted 'facial masks' in *Akropolis* (1962), based in part on **Asian performance** practices and Kathakali. Facial transformation is needed to play a character or role even in **naturalist** theatre, although in this genre the process is one of imitation within believable realms rather than exaggeration, distortion or the invention of a heightened stylized idiom.

Whatever their form, masking always has a double function. As make-up might cover a face, a 'mask' hides the performer's body. This reflects the common usage of the word outside theatrical contexts. But masks also create a new identity. In the theatre, masks project significant and complex meanings, depending on their materials, design, and the context in which they are worn.

As well as having a strong visual impact, the power of masks to transport the performer has frequently been articulated. In Asian performance, for example, where masks occur in numerous forms and have religious, aesthetic and historical importance, the Japanese noh *shite* actor meditates on his mask in the green room before turning into one of the gods or dead beings that people the noh stage. **Jacques Copeau**'s mask **training** and **Jacques Lecoq**'s neutral masks have proved how effective some sort of masking process can be for performers, not just in **rehearsal** of a role but also for the performer's self-development, to rid him or her of habits or clichés. Explorations of different styles of mask-based performance also stretch the performer's expressive abilities.

Such process-based explorations of what it is to perform and to metamorphose oneself correspond to the body adornment, piercings and tattoos that permeate daily behaviour. These are a continuation of ritually derived activities in secular contexts. **Stelarc** and **Orlan**, with her attempted *Reincarnation of Saint Orlan* (1990–93) as St Orlan to be brought about by radical cosmetic surgery, have further explored this crossover between everyday life and performance, as have many others involved in **body art** or **performance art**. Both these artists have examined how one can employ both simple and sophisticated technologies to test, alter or transform the body. Through her ongoing reconstruction, Orlan is interrogating how our identity is constructed and how we perform ourselves, ideas explored theoretically by **Judith Butler**. Masks and masking still make a significant contribution to contemporary performance exploration, even if technological advances and recent theories have shifted us well beyond the mythical awe inspired by ancient totemic face masks.

Bibliography

Emigh and Lommel have both discussed masks from an anthropological perspective. Schechter's collection explores masks in a range of performance forms from diverse cultural perspectives. Bell's edited collection was originally published in the journal *The Drama Review* and considers **puppets** as well as some mask-related theatre forms and practices.

Bell, John (ed.) (2001) *Puppets, Masks and Performing Objects*, Cambridge, MA.: MIT Press.

Brockett, Oscar G. and Robert J. Ball (2004) *The Essential Theatre*, 8th edition, Belmont, CA: Wadsworth/Thomson Learning.

Emigh, John (1996) *Masked Performance: The Play of Self and Other in Ritual and Theatre*, Philadelphia: University of Pennsylvania.

Lommel, Andreas (1981) *Masks: Their Meaning and Function*, New York: Excalibur Books.

Schechter, Joel (2003) *Popular Theatre: A Sourcebook*, London and New York: Routledge.

MISE EN SCÈNE

This is a term from French which literally denotes the act of putting something on stage. In the nineteenth century it was used to describe the staging of the text and specifically the text's **direction**. This is partly because its original use coincided with the rise of the director or, in French, the *metteur en scène*. However, an awareness of theatre as a total act which was more than the sum of its various parts began to coalesce in the late nineteenth century, was furthered by artists and critics like **Antonin Artaud** in the early twentieth century, and was secured by the rise of **semiotic** analysis from the early 1980s on. In these contexts, 'mise en scène' has increasingly been used in both theatre and film to articulate the total multidisciplinary act of staging the performance or film. It is thus understood to include the performance's direction, but also its **acting, scenography, lighting and sound**, costumes, use of **multimedia**, organization of time and **space**, and so on. Further, the term 'mise en scène' has emphasized how performance's meanings are produced not only in the performance product – the show – but also through the processes of both production and **audience** reception. A concept of mise en scène helps the critic to differentiate between different stagings – or mises en scène – of the same text and to designate them as, effectively, different theatrical texts. The term 'mise en scène' has been widely adopted in English theatre vocabularies especially, because it conveys these expanded senses of theatre as a multidisciplinary process and product that is the creative outcome of many contributors.

Bibliography

Pavis defines the term and its history in detail.

Pavis, Patrice (1998) *Dictionary of the Theatre: Terms, Concepts, and Analysis*, trans. Christine Shantz, Toronto: University of Toronto Press.

MOVEMENT

Movement is as intrinsic to performance and the theatre as it is to life. We recognize death by the absence of movement just as we identify performance as the movement of bodies in **space** through time – whether this passage is tortuously slow, as in **butoh**; aims at stillness, as in some of **Tadashi Suzuki**'s work; or is based on a familiar repertoire of daily gestures or means of locomotion, as in **naturalist** theatre. Whatever the stylistic end point, movement **training** or the aestheticized enactment of movements in performance requires discipline and **rehearsal** practice. It also necessitates more heightened attention than we give our body in **everyday** life. Our bodies are constantly in animation, be it through breathing, the circulation of blood, or the shifting of muscles as we negotiate the battle against gravity that a seemingly simple action like standing demands of us. We usually only pay attention to such movements if we are ill, injured or operating dysfunctionally for whatever reason, or if it is intrinsic to our vocation, as it is with **sports**. But performance frames and thus draws attention to movement. In performance, everyday functions need to be harnessed and exaggerated, repeated or isolated, coordinated or relaxed, in order for the body to engage with a different range and repertoire of movements than the habitual. One extreme is choreography in **dance**, where set movements are learned so that they can be precisely executed and become second nature.

All **directors**, teachers and performers inevitably explore movement in their work, but some do so more deliberately than others. As a teacher of actors, **Jacques Lecoq** developed a systematic pedagogical structure and training exercises for evolving performances and character from movement. **Konstantin Stanislavsky**'s approach to character and physical actions looked less at movement *per se* but rather for the psychological motivation for movement, arguing that all movements have a psychophysical purpose. But none have explored the potential of movement more than dancers. Choreographer/director **Pina Bausch** has prioritized *why* we move rather than *how*. **Rudolf von Laban** also used movement in performance for aesthetic purposes, as do all dancers, but he carried this interest over into everyday life. He observed, analysed and systematically annotated movement, seeing it as a way of knowing people. Many artists (and especially modernist ones) involved in the field of movement-based performance believe, as did dancer Martha Graham, that 'movement never lies'. They consider that it somehow shows us as we really are, an idea that **postmodern** theory has interrogated closely, arguing that ideas of reality, fixity and essence are highly questionable.

Some performance forms operate within a taxonomy of a daily repertoire of movements, to explore social relations, **performative** identities and connections with everyday life, while others are more abstract, exploring weight, velocity, patterns and shape, for example, as much dance does. There is general consensus that the daily gestures and range of movements of naturalist theatre do not need equivalent preparation or training time as do the codified gestures and ways of moving of **Asian performance** or ballet. Whether this is true is debatable, but codified movement forms are often very extreme, like being on pointe in ballet. Some even demand reshaping the body – to enable a particular bow-legged stance or way of walking in Kathakali, for example. Yet through an emphasis on duration, even daily or social movements can be given new purpose and significance; for example, Ulay and **Marina Abramović** walked towards each other along the Great Wall of China, one from each end, to meet in the middle in *The Lovers: Walk on the Great Wall* (1998). The movement might be everyday, but the spatial and temporal dynamics of the action make it extraordinary, a feature of much **performance art**. The **spectator**'s interest can be aroused as much by a demanding disciplined approach, which desocializes or reforms the body's mechanisms, as by the reframing of seemingly mundane movements.

Bibliography

Lecoq and Newlove each describe a particular approach to training. Fleshman includes introductory chapters on various aspects of movement systems, movement in therapy, and other applications, as well as covering practices worldwide. Goodridge focuses on rhythm in different cultures and across varying forms.

Fleshman, Bob (ed.) (1986) *Theatrical Movement: A Bibliographical Anthology*, Metuchen, NJ, and London: Scarecrow Press, Inc.
Goodridge, Janet (1999) *Rhythm and Timing of Movement in Performance: Drama, Dance and Ceremony*, London: Jessica Kingsley Publishers.
Lecoq, Jacques with Jean-Gabriel Carasso and Jean-Claude Lallias (2000) *The Moving Body, Teaching Creative Theatre*, trans. David Bradby, foreword by Simon McBurney, London: Methuen.
Newlove, Jean (1993) *Laban for Actors and Dancers*, London: Nick Hern Books.

MULTIMEDIA PERFORMANCE

Broadly speaking, this is any performance that combines different media. While it can therefore describe theatre that incorporates **dance** and **music**, it more commonly specifies work that mixes live performance with machines and/or mediated forms, such as computer technology, television, video, film and slide projection. As in **Antonin Artaud**'s total theatre and in **postmodern** forms of

visual theatre, multimedia performance aims to extend and enhance performance by exploring the full range of expressive media available. By juxtaposing the live and the mechanical or mediated, it also raises issues of **liveness** and **presence** and interrogates the aesthetic and social potentials of contemporary technology and media culture as well as live performance.

Multimedia performance was pioneered by **futurism**'s incorporation of machines and films into performance and by **Bertold Brecht**'s important predecessor, **director** Erwin Piscator, who put staged fictions in the context of real historical events by using large-scale documentary film projections as **scenographic** backdrops for live performance. It has proliferated since the 1960s and the rise of **performance and body art**, both as technological equipment and expertise have become more pervasive, but more importantly as questions about the relationships and boundaries between humans, our identities, our bodies, media and technologies have become more pressing. It questions our changing relationships to time and **space** by placing the 'there and then' of recorded performance within the 'here and now' of live performance. Exploring relationships between the performer's body and medical, computer and audio technologies, artists including **Orlan**, **Stelarc** and **Laurie Anderson** question where, how and by whom our identities, bodies, voices and realities are **performatively** produced in a technologically developed culture. By presenting multiple perspectives simultaneously, multimedia performance examines how electronic surveillance is increasingly infiltrating our lives and our privacy. In **Robert Lepage**'s *Seven Streams of the River Ota* (1994), for example, a character disappears into the private space of an on-stage photo booth but his fantasies are simultaneously broadcast in large-scale projection. As performance at the interface of the live and the mediated expands, it is developing into the virtual theatre of live **internet** performance and cyber-performance, where artists like Stelarc become part man and part computer, and can be controlled by a near or remote audience. Such performance not only draws the performer increasingly into cyberspace; it leads the audience there too.

Bibliography

Auslander's volume includes important articles on media and technology. Giannachi introduces key issues in, and practitioners of, different forms of virtual theatre. Lavender describes some multimedia performances and provides a brief analysis of the form's genealogies and effects.

Auslander, Philip (ed.) (2003) *Performance: Critical Concepts in Literary and Cultural Studies*, vol. 4, London: Routledge.
Giannachi, Gabriella (2004) *Virtual Theatres: An Introduction*, London: Routledge.
Lavender, Andy (2002) 'The Moment of Realized Actuality', in *Theatre in Crisis? Performance Manifestos for a New Century*, Maria M. Delgado and Caridad Svich (eds), Manchester: Manchester University Press, pp.183–90.

MUSEUM DISPLAY

Museum display has attracted the interest of performance studies scholars because it forces engagement with important issues about representing cultures and identities and the social production of meaning in time and **space**. Like other contexts of performance, museums are spaces in which **audiences** encounter and engage with selected and displayed objects and sometimes also **sounds**, moving images, **multimedia installations**, performers, and so on. As in other forms of performance, museum display aims to achieve a variety of effects, from instructing its audiences, to persuading them to a particular point of view, to producing a strong aesthetic effect, even one of charismatic **presence**. Influential performance studies scholar Barbara Kirshenblatt-Gimblett argues that museums are fundamentally **performative**, creating and repeating their own practices, their contents, the behaviour of audiences and ultimately the identities of audiences.

Following the influence of **historiographers** and **postmodern** theorists in the late twentieth century, museums have increasingly been recognized as contexts where knowledge is not objectively presented but is subjectively made. This recognition has provoked analysis of how museums produce meanings through processes of selection, omission, display and (re)contextualization. Despite their common best intentions to preserve and instruct, museums risk succumbing to familiar limitations of **intercultural** practice, potentially appropriating, decontextualizing and disrespecting the source cultures they represent. **Performance artists** and writers **Guillermo Gómez-Peña** and Coco Fusco make this point in their 'living dioramas', which challenge conventional, patronizing practices of ethnographic display. The point is also increasingly made by museums themselves, as they acknowledge the impossibility of achieving either comprehensive representation or complete objectivity and try to invoke broader contexts for understanding selected display materials. As discussed in the entry on **Holocaust memorials and museums**, architect Daniel Libeskind's Jewish Museum in Berlin, for example, demonstrates its subjective selectivity by focusing on a clearly limited choice of material that often relates to particular individuals' stories. The museum nevertheless aims to put these stories into a larger context beyond its own physical and temporal limits; it is marked externally with lines that, if extrapolated, 'join' the museum to important sites in Berlin's Jewish history. In a bid explicitly to share their subjective creation of meanings with their audiences, many museums have developed interactive multimedia installations. As with other experiments with audience interaction, however, it is worth asking whether the control these innovations seem to cede to their audiences is actually more apparent than real.

Museum practices of curatorship and display raise issues that are important well beyond the museum – in theatre programming; tourist attractions like Shakespeare's Globe in London; heritage sites; and historical recreations, perhaps especially those which incorporate performers, as at Plymouth Plantation in the USA. Like **site-specific performance**, heritage sites invoke the site constructively as a memory trigger for events that happened there; more problematically, they suggest that the sites' meanings transcend both time and change. A performance studies concept that might usefully challenge and develop museum practices is that of **liveness**, since it acknowledges the evanescence of the live event and raises fundamental issues about how to represent that event for future consideration.

Bibliography

Coming out of the field of museum studies, Karp and Lavine's book gathers excellent essays, which engage in detail with specific exhibitions and address a wide range of issues. Kirshenblatt-Gimblett is probably the most influential analyst of museums within performance studies.

Karp, Ivan and Steven D. Lavine (eds) (1991) *Exhibiting Cultures: The Poetics and Politics of Museum Display*, Washington, DC: Smithsonian Institution Press.
Kirshenblatt-Gimblett, Barbara (1998) *Destination Culture: Tourism, Museums, and Heritage*, Berkeley: University of California Press.

MUSIC, THEATRE AND PERFORMANCE

As Philip Auslander has pointed out, many theatre and performance academics have all but ignored music. This may be because of the commercial or conservative nature of many musicals and opera, which as a body of practice are not known for their radical form or content, and thus perhaps do not accord with the political or artistic interests of many scholars. Equally it may be that musical performance's focus on rhythm, **sound**, tone, pitch and voice requires expertise other than that demanded by the text–meaning–interpretation axis of conventional studies of the theatre. But music is a part of performance and the links between the disciplines are extensive, as even this fleeting survey suggests. We do not want to further perpetuate the omission Auslander has identified, but are concerned here not so much with music for its own sake but with how music relates to our specific focus on theatre and live performance.

Spectacular events accompanied musical concerts played in European courts in the seventeenth and eighteenth centuries, but the nineteenth century saw more considered theatrical experiments in musical performance in the West. Richard Wagner's idea of a *Gesamtkunstwerk* advocated a total theatre in which music was one of several indispensable strands. Melodrama was a **popular theatre** form in which all action was underscored and accompanied by music, often to heighten feeling or support the stylistic exaggeration. More recent music/performance interactions include the avant-garde experimentation of **John Cage** and Harrison Birtwhistle, with pieces like the latter's 'punk' opera *Punch and Judy* (1967). In some ways these have been no less influential than global commercial successes like *Miss Saigon* (1988), even if their **audiences** have been considerably smaller. Music can be, and has been, used for various ends in live performance: to expose characters' feelings; to create mood or a setting; or to comment through songs on plot, as in **Bertold Brecht**'s work. These are just some applications.

Some of the world's foremost **directors** have repeatedly returned to the potential of musical performance. **Robert Wilson** has collaborated frequently with singer-songwriter Tom Waits, **Peter Brook** has directed many operas, and Peter Sellars has presented several experimental operas based on real political events in a **postmodern** vein. As well as pointing to the precision demanded of his actors, **Jerzy Grotowski**'s use of the term 'score' shows the proximity between the fields, a gap which narrows further when a performance is based on **movement** and song as much as text, as in his own work. The idea of a score also reiterates the point that it is the **playing** or **acting** that makes a performance rather than the structure or content alone – just as notes written on paper do not make a piece of music.

Unlike the theatre, music travels easily, does not depend on live performance, and has therefore easily absorbed **intercultural** influences. Most traditional African and **Asian performance** forms are based on **dance** and are thus rooted in music and rhythm, the participants being performers rather than actors in the mimetic Aristotelian sense. They utilize stylized modes of representation that lie outside the familiar tropes of **realism**, an approach that has influenced artists like **Vsevolod Meyerhold** and **Eugenio Barba**. Music's prolific cross-cultural hybridization has helped shape Western theatre.

Music is also infinitely reproducible, operating in a realm of commercial possibilities of which live performance can only dream, and eschewing the difficulties of documentation and longevity which trouble the theatre and dance. But, whatever the scale of its appeal, live theatre-related music suffers from charges of narrow elitism, especially in relation to opera and classical works. The accusations against producers of opera have been slightly allayed by the popularization of the form through productions like Britain's National Theatre's *Jerry Springer the Opera* (2003), based on the TV chat show host. The tide might be turning, with rapid advances in digital technology opening up potential for further interaction between acoustic and musical technologies and the sort of conceptual investigations that have sustained much **performance art**, from Cage and **happenings** onwards, up to **Laurie Anderson**. This may help bring music and theatre closer together for mixed audiences, integrating the popular and the traditional with the sophisticated and the innovative.

Bibliography

Auslander has been a persuasive and almost isolated proponent, arguing for the inclusion of more music within performance analysis, as his book and his article in the diverse Little collection demonstrate. Frith writes from a cultural studies perspective but has a clear grasp of music as performance. *Theaterschrift* brings together interviews and reflections in English, German, Flemish and French.

Auslander, Philip (1999) *Liveness: Performance in a Mediatized Culture*, London and New York: Routledge.
Frith, Simon (1998) *Performing Rites: Evaluating Popular Music*, Oxford: Oxford University Press.

Little, Henry (consultant ed.) (2004) 'Adventures in Music Theatre', a special issue of *Contemporary Theatre Review*, 14.1, London: Routledge.

Van Kerkhoven, Marianne (ed.) (1995) 'Theatre and Music', a special issue of *Theaterschrift*, 9, Brussels: Kaaitheater.

NATURALISM AND REALISM

Naturalism and realism are aesthetic and literary categories, but in the theatre they refer specifically to artistic movements that represent real life on stage, using what now seem the overly familiar devices of believable characters, narrative action and plot. The two terms can be used with reference to most art forms, but in the theatre they are almost interchangeable, with only nuances of difference between them. Some theorists suggest that naturalism pays more attention than realism to social environment as an influence on character, and that realism tends to proffer a more critical and less imitative or illusionistic aesthetic, but these distinctions are too subtle and contentious to be of much use today and it is difficult to achieve consensus on this subject. What is important is that realism and naturalism are both founded on the premise that art should hold up a mirror to nature, a once revolutionary concept. This demands a mimetic mode of representation, drawing in part on the logic of narrative structures and staging implied by Aristotle's unities of time, **space** and action.

Whatever the word hints at etymologically, naturalism in the theatre has nothing directly to do with the 'natural', just as realism only implies the real through its manipulated reconstruction or reproduction. These genres are highly artificial conventions. Their well-established techniques and processes enable the suspension of belief that they ask of **audiences**, and create the imitation that is at their heart. Interestingly, naturalist theatre was initially a response to the even more artificial and exaggerated devices of melodrama and other 'pictorial' styles that dominated the theatre up to the middle part of the nineteenth century. As such, it was an innovative avant-garde form that challenged the aesthetic status quo.

Developments in the theatre followed the lead of fiction and novels by writers including Emile Zola. Zola was one of the key early proponents of naturalism, as demonstrated by his 1867 novel and eponymous play *Thérèse Raquin* (1873), and his 1881 manifesto advocating naturalism in the theatre. Although *Thérèse Raquin* has naturalist elements, it reveals an immature genre in development, leaning as it does frequently towards melodrama. Naturalism in the theatre took hold more firmly in the late 1880s and 1890s, cultivated by André Antoine of the Théâtre Libre, the first naturalist **director** of note, and groups like the Meiningen Company (from the south of Germany). It was then fostered by **Konstantin Stanislavsky**, whose system for actors and detailed directorial vision are almost considered templates for the creation of naturalist theatre.

One of the priorities of naturalist artists and writers was to expose on stage the minutiae of social life, depicting families in real contemporary situations, as in Anton Chekhov's play ***The Cherry Orchard*** (1904). Naturalism and realism were informed by Karl Marx's political theories, scientific advances and growing interest in classification, medical progress and increased knowledge about diseases and the body, and Charles Darwin's *On the Origin of Species* (first published in 1859). Darwin's evolutionary theory inspired naturalism's constructions of socially determined beings located in and reacting to specific environments, like Nora in Henrik Ibsen's *A Doll's House* (1879). His *Ghosts* (1881) introduced the issue of genetics that was coming to the fore in fervent debates about the environment and heredity. Under such influences, theatre moved on from melodrama and nineteenth-century Romanticism. Naturalism and realism heralded modern drama and all the artistic, social, cultural and scientific innovations that followed in the twentieth century.

However revolutionary it was in the beginning, naturalism's subsequent mainstream positioning has fuelled many counteractive revolts and experiments, from **Dada** through **Bertold Brecht**'s epic theatre to **performance art**. These have all questioned the social function of art and its forms by focusing on the presentational aesthetics of performance and its processes, as opposed to the supposedly realist representation of **everyday life**. It has repeatedly been argued that representation through naturalist aesthetics reinforces rather than challenges the status quo, and is therefore considered politically (as well as artistically) ideologically conservative. But naturalism and its history are complex and cannot be set against more experimental forms in an easy oppositional binary. The work of playwrights with explicit or implicit political or social messages – ranging from the 'kitchen-sink' drama of post-Second World War Britain, through Arthur Miller or Tennessee Williams's writings, to the plays of David Hare – contests such a view.

One question that refuses to go away is whether the role of naturalism in the theatre has been superseded by television and film, which can replicate reality so precisely. Yet, however much it might be considered the rather tired or conservative norm today, and in spite of such doubts about its current function or value, naturalism has shown extraordinary resilience, popularity and longevity and still remains the dominant theatre form in the Western world today.

Bibliography

Innes offers an introduction to naturalism, with a focus on and extracts from works by Ibsen, Chekhov and Bernard Shaw as well as Zola's manifesto. Styan takes a longer view of naturalist/realist playwrighting throughout the twentieth century. Williams' text is influential for its contextualization of naturalist theatre as an experimental form. Diamond analyses mimesis and realism from a **feminist** perspective.

Diamond, Elin (1997) *Unmaking Mimesis: Essays on Feminism and Theatre*, London: Routledge.
Innes, Christopher (ed.) (2000) *A Sourcebook on Naturalist Theatre*, London: Routledge.
Styan, J. L. (1981) *Modern Drama in Theory and Practice*, vol.1, *Realism and Naturalism*, Cambridge: Cambridge University Press.
Williams, Raymond (1989) 'Theatre as a Political Forum', in *The Politics of Modernism*, London: Verso.

PARATHEATRE

Para literally means 'beyond'. In practice, paratheatre therefore lies outside and beyond the **spatial**, temporal and structural forms of the theatre, denoting instead related practices such as workshops, **rituals**, **training** programmes, drama therapy or even **Augusto Boal**'s 'invisible theatre' with its unwitting **spectatorship**. **Jerzy Grotowski**, in relation to whose practice the term is frequently applied, conducted his paratheatrical work in the 1970s, after and beyond his successes in the theatre. He removed the spectator from the performance equation to encourage wider participation in what was termed 'active culture', centred on the non-professional performer as maker in a series of workshop-type activities rather than as passive recipient of events made for them. With no paying spectators, paratheatre operates according to very different economic criteria from aesthetic performance, although it can be commercially lucrative, as business training or personal development programmes prove.

Paratheatrical activities often draw on skills, techniques, strategies and even personnel that are deployed in the theatre. As in much paratheatre, Grotowski focused on the participant actor rather than the spectator, if indeed there is one. This emphasis can be seen in dramatherapy sessions, **acting** workshops and business team-building courses. In these contexts, 'performance' is not integral or an immediate corollary to the process, even if it may be the future longer-term aim or the motivation behind these practices. The participants are aware of being observed, judged, led or coached, but the role of observer is inside the process rather than the familiar more passive role of the external theatre spectator.

Paratheatre also refers to non-theatrical processes or activities that might be construed as theatre or defined as performance. The way of framing an event might draw it within the parameters of what can be considered theatre, as Banes's book on subversive art demonstrates. 'Paratheatre' is a fluid term that encompasses many aspects of performance beyond the familiar spectator–actor binary.

Bibliography

Literature related to paratheatre is extensive even if it does not use this specific term. It ranges from self-help books to theoretical texts that explore performance outside artistic frames, as in McKenzie's challenging theoretical exposition. Banes's collection of performance reviews scarcely defines paratheatre, but the term allows her to include 'cat' shows and the Japanese tea ceremony.

Banes, Sally (1998) *Subversive Expectations: Performance Art and Paratheater in New York, 1976–85*, Ann Arbor: University of Michigan Press.
Kumiega, Jennifer (1985) *The Theatre of Grotowski*, London: Methuen.
McKenzie, Jon (2001) *Perform or Else: From Discipline to Performance*, London: Routledge.

PERFORMANCE/PERFORMING

'Performance' has at least five relevant meanings in this context, indicating its importance but also its semantic instability and dynamism. First, it is used to identify the live event of presenting something usually pre-prepared before an **audience**. This can be the presentation of any performing art, including theatre, **music**, **dance**, **circus** or martial arts skills, **happenings**, **improvised** performance, and so on. Important features of this definition are the performance's **liveness** and usually an expectation that the performer will produce a sense of **presence**. This use of the term can also denote a particular performer's execution of a piece of music or a role, such as Ellen Terry's performance of Ophelia.

Secondly, and more broadly, performance describes all social behaviour including, as **Erving Goffman** argued, **everyday** behaviour. This understanding gained currency in the mid- to late twentieth century as scholars from philosophy to anthropology and sociology identified in social behaviour and **ritual** the repetitive or restored behaviour that **Richard Schechner** saw as essential to performance. For scholars in other disciplines, including **Judith Butler** in **feminist** philosophy, this association of behaviour with performance helped to pioneer a theory of behaviour as **performative** and constitutive of identity. It thus helped to theorize a political response to oppression by enabling the argument that inter-ruptions and variations in repeated behaviours could help to transform that oppression. Initially, this widespread theoretical use of the term 'performance' from the 1980s on made little direct reference to theatre or performance studies, seeming to deploy 'performance' more as a metaphor than a term with its own disciplinary genealogy, tools of critical thinking, or practices (as discussed by States). This decontextualized application of the word partly inspired performance studies' development as a discipline by challenging it to demonstrate how it could help to enhance understandings of performance's practices and effects through its own conception of the relationships between activities and audiences, **space** and time, process and product, activity and effect, and so on.

A third and growing use of the term denotes success or achievement, as we might talk of sexual performance, or the performance of a car, a company, the global economy, or a **sports** or **Olympic** athlete. While this particular deployment of the term might seem to have little direct relevance to performance in the context of this *Companion*, it is important to consider how its expansion and impact on ideas of power and knowledge might relate to other deployments, as Jon McKenzie does in his influential book *Perform or Else*. For example, this use shifts focus from the process of performance to the outcome or product, making not only a semantic shift but also an ideological one, for example, towards the values of capitalism.

Fourth, performance often is and has been used as a synonym for **performance art** and **body art**, coming out of a history of fine art practices. These forms of performance achieved prominence in the 1980s and have often exploited the liveness, presence and embodiment associated with the first use of the term to advocate for the rights of particular identity groups, such as women or lesbians and gay men.

While performance art is sometimes deconstructive, it can also intentionally reinforce ideas of coherent identity, narrative and representation in order to make political claims for the identities it represents. This sets it somewhat apart from the fifth and final form of performance to be discussed here, the form of deconstructive performance distinguished primarily by its distinction from **acting** in theatre. Where most acting aims to achieve mimetic representation, this form of performance is usually at least partly presentational, working to challenge **naturalistic** characterization and narration in order to question the apparent truths 'shown' by representational forms. This mode of performance has a long history, for example in avant-garde practices like **Dada**, **futurism**, **expressionism** and **Bertold Brecht**'s epic theatre. But it has been developed most extensively in **postmodern** performance, where the will to challenge the assumptions of received representational forms has produced a host of deconstructive and metatheatrical performance strategies that foreground process over product, interrogate theatrical illusionism and resist offering stable, conclusive meanings.

Bibliography

Carlson's study of performance's recent meanings and practices is informative and comprehensive. The other suggested sources each concentrate on one or two of the above definitions.

Auslander, Philip (1997) *From Acting to Performance: Essays in Modernism and Postmodernism*, London: Routledge.

Carlson, Marvin (2004) *Performance: A Critical Introduction*, 2nd edition, London: Routledge.

Kershaw, Baz (1999) *The Radical in Performance: Between Brecht and Baudrillard*, London: Routledge.

McKenzie, Jon (2001) *Perform or Else: From Discipline to Performance*, London: Routledge.

States, Bert O. (1996) 'Performance as Metaphor', *Theatre Journal* 48.1: 1–26. Reprinted in Philip Auslander (ed.) (2003) *Performance: Critical Concepts in Literary and Cultural Studies*, vol. 1, London: Routledge, pp.108–37.

PERFORMANCE ART/LIVE ART

Performance art (often called live art, especially in the UK) is a live artistic practice that evolved chiefly out of fine art – as differentiated from theatre. It developed as artists sought to extend art beyond the conventional media and practices of painting and sculpture. Much performance art was (and is) explicitly politically motivated, aiming to challenge dominant values and practices and to respond to social crises. Thus, though its roots reach back to performance in the 1910s, including **Dada** and the **Cabaret Voltaire**, it came of age in the era of second wave **feminism**, Vietnam **protests** and **happenings** in the 1960s and 1970s, continued throughout the 1980s during the right-wing leaderships of President Reagan and Prime Minister Thatcher and the rise of AIDS, and continues still. Performance art is difficult to define because it potentially combines so many media – including performance, text, **music**, **dance**, architecture, sculpture, video, film and **multimedia** – but also because it often aims to challenge categorization, exploring the expressive possibilities of combining diverse elements to produce new hybrids.

Performance art's initial rejection of traditional painting and sculpture reflected a widespread feeling in Western art practice from the 1950s onwards that these forms were limited by the piety and burden of their fine art histories. Performance art rejected their focus on representation, exploring the more direct possibilities of presentation. It displaced a conventional emphasis on the commodified art object, concentrating instead on the transient artistic process. Performance art shifted the emphasis from the object to the event, simultaneously refocusing on the artist as creator, the relationship of art to **everyday life**, the ephemeral event as art, and the very difficulty of documenting (or rendering as commodified object) artistic practice.

This focus on the artist meant that much performance art was and is concerned with identity and is frequently performed solo or by pairs rather than groups. **Laurie Anderson**, Bobby Baker, **Guillermo Gómez-Peña**, Spalding Gray, Karen Finley, and many others, have performed autobiographical monologues, exploring issues of memory, the social construction of the subject through everyday life activities, and – especially for **feminist** artists – women's limited access to the public sphere and the right to speak in it. Partly through the influence of 1970s **improvisational** dance techniques that used everyday movement, performance art also presents and self-consciously frames everyday actions. Thus, it recuperates activities often seen as banal, valuing them instead as worthy of artistic exploration and crucially **performative**, in the sense that their very repetitiveness contributes to identity formation (see **Judith Butler**). Such everyday activities include cleaning, as in **Marina Abramović**'s *Balkan Baroque* (1997); food preparation, as in Bobby Baker's *Kitchen Show* (1991); and masturbation, as in Vito Acconci's infamous *Seedbed* (1971), where he reportedly masturbated under a ramp built into the gallery floor while visitors walked above him, unable to see him. Like its close relation **body art**, much performance art also deliberately explores the materiality of the performer's body as an artistic medium – its physical limitations, fluids and social significations.

Performance art's interest in the **liveness** and ephemerality of the performance event indicates its broader interest in time. This is reflected in its more common British name, live art, and also in the names 'durational art' and 'time-based art'. As part of a widespread **postmodern** refusal of dominant representational conventions including 'grand narratives', performance art often rejects conventional linear narrative, using rules of duration instead to produce new patterns of sequencing and structure. Joseph Beuys spent a week with a coyote in a New York gallery in *Coyote: I Like America and America Likes Me* (1974). Linda Montana and Tehching Hsieh tied themselves together with a 2.5m rope in New

York for a year in *Art/Life One Year Performance 1983–84*. Such work draws attention to time partly to *show* the making – or processes – of art, even when the activity of making is precisely not very physically active or creative, according to conventional criteria. In Ulay and Abramović's *Night Sea Crossing* (1981), the artists sat and stared at each other over a table daily for up to twelve hours at a time, making an emotional crossing if not a physical one. Such durational work also draws attention to the effects of endurance, such as exhaustion and euphoria; the ironic ephemerality of the event – even if the event is a year long, ultimately, it will endure only in images and memories, which **Peggy Phelan** has discussed; and the resulting resistance to commodification of this artwork in an era that is witnessing the ongoing rise of consumer culture. Running parallel to performance art's concern with time is an interest in **space**, which it shares with **installation art**. Artists including Baker and Anderson have performed their **site-specific** work in such everyday spaces as homes and streets, again framing and drawing attention to conventional ideas of how to behave in these contexts.

Performance art is often ridiculed by popular culture as self-indulgent, esoteric, or even downright ridiculous, potentially compromising its counter-cultural ambitions but also indicating important questions about its possible elitism, solipsism and emphasis on individual over community. Despite this ridicule, artists continue to use performance art's hybrid possibilities and fundamental concern with identity to explore 'othered' identities such as queer identity. They also continue to hybridize its forms, increasingly by introducing techniques from multimedia and **visual theatre**. An innovation of the twentieth century, performance art continues in the twenty-first not least because it is effective in responding to political issues – especially to do with identity and commodity culture.

Bibliography

See also the entry on **performance**. Stiles *et al.* and Goldberg's two books provide a history of the form and excellent photographic illustrations. Banes and Carr collate their New York newspaper criticism on performance art. Shank describes many American examples. Kaye and Carlson place performance art in a more developed critical and historical framework. Hill and Paris's collection of interviews offers practical advice on making performance art.

Banes, Sally (1998) *Subversive Expectations: Performance Art and Paratheater in New York 1976–85*, Ann Arbor: University of Michigan Press.
Carlson, Marvin (2004) *Performance: A Critical Introduction*, 2nd edition, London: Routledge.
Carr, C. (1993) *On Edge: Performance at the End of the Twentieth Century*, Hanover, NH: Wesleyan University Press.
Goldberg, RoseLee (1998) *Performance: Live Art since the 60s*, London: Thames and Hudson.
—— (2001) *Performance Art: From Futurism to the Present*, revised and expanded edition, London: Thames and Hudson.
Hill, Leslie and Helen Paris (2001) *Guerilla Performance and Multimedia*, London: Continuum.

Kaye, Nick (1994) 'Live Art: Definition and Documentation', *Contemporary Theatre Review* 2.2: 1–7.

Shank, Theodore (2002) *Beyond the Boundaries: American Alternative Theatre*, revised and updated edition, Ann Arbor: University of Michigan Press.

Stiles, Kristine *et al.* (1998) *Out of Actions: Between Performance and the Object, 1949–1979*, London: Thames and Hudson.

PERFORMATIVE/PERFORMATIVITY

'Performative' (as both noun and adjective) and 'performativity' have become key terms in performance studies, even though they are often used rather generally (like the term 'theatricality') to include anything that has a theatrical or performance-like quality. As an adjective, 'performative' was coined by John Austin, Professor of Philosophy at the University of Oxford, in his William James Lectures delivered at Harvard University in 1955. Austin argued that words are not just for naming or describing things but can also *do* things, effecting change. Utterances, or 'speech acts' as he called them, can be performative and causal, pronounced in order to make something happen, as in the two simple but powerful words 'I do' at a wedding. This focus on action is what links the idea to performance, a connection that was promulgated by performance studies departments like that at Northwestern University in Chicago, Illinois, which emerged partly from the field of communication studies. In the theatre, words are carefully and intentionally selected either by an author or by the **devising** performer, to develop a character or plot, to evoke a feeling or to indicate something to an **audience**. Their causal effect is thus more manifest than words spoken in a daily context. Focus on the performative within performance has developed Austin's initial theoretical treatise to consider in detail *how*, as well as why, words are actively stated or brought alive through their utterance.

Discussions responding to Austin and attempting to define performativity multiplied with the rise of poststructuralist and **postmodern** thinking in the 1970s, spurred on by questions about how reality and actions are constructed. In the 1980s, **Judith Butler** developed Austin's theories to suggest that identities are performed, that they are not necessarily biologically predetermined but are constructed through a 'stylized repetition of acts'. If this is so and identity is not something that is fixed, hegemonic understandings of identity (gender, sex, sexuality, etc.) can then be undermined through variations and disturbances in these. Butler argued that, as performance is constructed through its iteration (in **rehearsals** and through repeated showings), so can behaviour be. The performative as both a practice and an idea therefore has a radical potential, as **Orlan**'s performances have forcibly demonstrated.

The term 'performative' has been co-opted by a range of disciplines, from philosophy (where it began), through sociology, to theatre and performance studies. Its nuances vary greatly according to the context in which it is used. Debates about performativity rage on, as they do with its sister 'theatricality', a term equally open to interpretation and misunderstanding, as Davis and Postlewait have suggested in their tracing of that term's lineage and complexities.

Bibliography

Austin's book reads in an informal oral style, as it comprises posthumously annotated lectures. Butler's range of texts develops her views on the performative nature of gender, whereas the Parker and Sedgwick collection (which includes another text by Butler) focuses on catharsis in the theatre but also performativity in non-theatrical contexts.

Austin, John L. (1962) *How to Do Things with Words*, London: Oxford University Press.

Butler, Judith (1990) 'Performative Acts and Gender Constitution: An Essay in Phenomenology and Feminist Theory', in *Performing Feminisms: Feminist Critical Theory and Theatre*, Sue-Ellen Case (ed.), Baltimore: Johns Hopkins University Press.

—— ([1990] 1999) *Gender Trouble: Feminism and the Subversion of Identity*, London: Routledge.

—— (1997) *Excitable Speech: A Politics of the Performative*, London: Routledge.

Davis, Tracy C. and Thomas Postlewait (eds) (2003) *Theatricality*, Cambridge: Cambridge University Press.

Parker, Andrew and Eve Kosofsky Sedgwick (eds) (1995) *Performativity and Performance*, London: Routledge.

PHENOMENOLOGY

As enquiries into what consciousness is and how it is constructed have become dominant in the sciences, phenomenology, with its emphasis on the experience of the **spectator** and the performer, has attracted growing interest as a philosophical framework for analysing performance. It challenges **semiotics** and other meaning-based systems of performance analysis, whose attempts to rationalize and explain communication in the theatre purely as a system of codes have proved limiting. Phenomenology emphasizes the role of the senses in reception, prioritizing sensations, feelings and other emotional phenomena and consequently valuing descriptive modes. It implies a form of enquiry that penetrates the specific and local context, what Clifford Geertz has called 'thick description' in relation to anthropological observations. Such evaluation centres on the perspective of the person perceiving and their physical **presence** within the work being observed. The very active responsiveness that this implies is diametrically opposed to the idea of cool, objective analysis. Phenomenology also resists the segmentation that is intrinsic to semiotic analysis. Consideration of units of meaning is replaced by an emphasis on the total embodied experience and flow. As activities in **dance** and physical theatre have expanded, so has phenomenology gained ground, often operating in conjunction with theories that place performance work in a wider sociological or cultural context, balancing the personal response with a more social or public framework. Phenomenology has also been useful for studies of the work of the performer and process-based accounts where personal and individual development take priority over the encounter or interaction with an **audience**, which are usually founded on reception theories.

Maurice Merleau-Ponty, one of the main exponents of phenomenology as a philosophical theory, has had a central influence on performance analysis because of his interest in the body. He developed the earlier ideas of Martin Heidegger and phenomenology's founder, Edmund Husserl, and notably challenged Jean-Paul Sartre's existentially based theories, that he considered were predicated on a problematic Cartesian dualism that separated mind and body. Much of the pioneering work in applying phenomenological approaches to performance that drew on Merleau-Ponty's groundbreaking writings has originated in dance studies. Proxemics, kinaesthetics and **sound**, aspects of performance to which **Antonin Artaud** paid special attention and which resist the closure or fixity that a more semiotic approach might produce, are primary focuses for phenomenological analysis. In the theatre, Bert States's writing and Stanton B. Garner's work on Beckett have been influential, for Beckett's plays, like dance, rely as much on **movement**, rhythm and **space** as they do on text. **Judith Butler** has extended such considerations of performance into her work on gender, where she has argued that identities and even gender are constructed and performed rather than being predetermined or given. Although critics have decried phenomenology for being essentialist and individualized, or too detached from political, cultural or social mechanisms, there is no doubting its important place within a range of potential theoretical systems for the analysis of performance and performance processes.

Bibliography

Merleau-Ponty's book and other philosophical texts are significant primary sources but are inevitably dense. Much insight into this difficult area can be gained by reading their theories through examples of performance in the more directly relevant books of Garner, States and Sheets-Johnstone, for example.

Garner, Stanton B. (1994) *Bodied Spaces: Phenomenology and Performance in Contemporary Drama*, Ithaca, NY: Cornell University Press.
Geertz, Clifford (1973) *The Interpretation of Cultures*, New York: Basic Books.
Merleau-Ponty, Maurice ([1945] 1962) *Phenomenology of Perception*, trans. Colin Smith, London: Routledge & Kegan Paul.
Sheets-Johnstone, Maxine (1966) *The Phenomenology of Dance*, Madison: University of Wisconsin Press.
States, Bert O. (1985) *Great Reckonings in Little Rooms: On the Phenomenology of Theater*, Berkeley and Los Angeles: University of California Press.

PLAY

Play is a huge area for investigation and an activity that touches on folklore, anthropology, philosophy, psychology and ethnology, as well as being central to theatre and performance in general. It is also something that is practised by cultures and societies globally, even if each of them describes it differently. Play is ubiquitous – we all play – yet it is hard to pin down what we are doing when we do it, let alone to discover why we do it.

Analyses of play have ranged from British **psychoanalyst** Donald Woods Winnicott's case studies of child behaviour to the broader influential work of French sociologist Roger Caillois and Dutch historian Johan Huizinga. These last two have been central in assessing what play is from the perspective of their own disciplines. Attempts by Caillois and others to systematize and categorize types of play have been interesting, but ultimately they merely reinforce how both fluidity and an absence of boundaries are endemic to play and games. Mihaly Csikszentmihalyi referred to such a capacity – the state of being inside an experience and of losing oneself in it – as 'flow', with the recognition that this mode is somehow outside the daily weft of life or, as **Victor Turner** put it, 'sub-junctive'. As such, through proposing 'What if?', play has the power to subvert or undermine authority through parody, critique or mere laughter, as indicated in studies of clowning and **carnival**, and as evidenced by the appearance of the trickster figure in many cultures, as in **Augusto Boal**'s joker, to name one specific theatre-related example. It is naive, though, to believe that games are not serious, as Clifford Geertz has shown in his analysis of 'deep play', which emphasizes the potential risks and serious consequences of playing. Play easily crosses over from being a discrete and safe activity to one that is consequential – the phrase 'We were only pretending' has been uttered countless times by children to cover up a more serious transgression when play has got out of hand. Play transports its participants, altering biological patterns and mental states, speeding up the heartbeat, making participants alert and sending adrenalin coursing through the veins.

Within performance studies, **Richard Schechner** has been central in analysing the role of play in performance or play as performance, addressing the vexed question of what the function of play might be. His enquiry is inevitably limited and he openly admits that any analysis of play postulates more questions than it can answer. His work draws on myriad theories and a vast range of exemplars, from **sports** to children's games, through the theatre's formal structures, to **animal** behaviour, all of which fall within play's auspices. Animal play is striking for its similarity to human games, which suggests a biologically driven need for play. This can be set against the idea that play has evolved as a cultural form, part of civilizing progress linked to aesthetic expression. Certainly, both aspects pertain to play, though to what extent depends on the form the playing adopts. Rugby, for example, is animalistically territorial and violent, yet (as the **haka** and rugby's rules and tactical skills all demonstrate) it is also sophisticated, formal and aesthetically pleasing to watch. Such complex possibilities arise because playing is a fundamental human activity and as such varies from individual to individual and across cultures in its form, function and articulation. It spans an individual's trivial inconsequential prank or joke to part of a community's calendrical **ritual**, the practice of which is deemed vital in order for plants to grow. It is thus culturally specific and yet also enacted by animals, and so eludes easy definitions.

The other difficulty with defining what play is, as some theorists like **Erving Goffman** have argued, is that we continually play by adopting roles in our **everyday lives** according to differing social situations and their needs or assumed hierarchies. We **improvise** continually in our interactions. **Postmodern** thinking has extended this idea that there is no such thing as a stable or fixed identity, for if even gender is a construct, as **Judith Butler** has suggested, then playing with representations of who we are is central to our being.

The kind of play practised in performance forms like the theatre, to which **Peter Brook** alluded when he wrote in *The Empty Space* (1968) that 'a play is play', has much clearer parameters. In such play or plays a specific **space** for the event is chosen and there is mutual agreement between all participants about the rules of the game. If **naturalist** in style, this depends on imitation and an accepted lie, recognizing that the character should somehow **mask** the actor, though both co-exist simultaneously and cross-refer. In **devised** work, the role of play is more experimental and encourages risk-taking, not just for the performers. The devising process might extend into a show, so that the **spectator** is unaware of what is scripted and what improvised in the present, reinforcing the sense of **liveness** in performance. Playing reveals and hides, it separates and integrates. It is the sheer complexity and range of such multiple understandings and practices of play that makes the term fascinating yet also all but meaningless unless precisely contextualized.

Bibliography

Schechner has written extensively on play and performance. Other key texts more generally on play are listed below, a tiny selection of the vast amount of material available.

Caillois, Roger (1979) *Man, Play and Games*, New York: Shocken Books.
Geertz, Clifford (1973) *The Interpretation of Cultures*, New York: Basic Books.
Huizinga, Johan (1970) *Homo Ludens*, New York: Harper.
Schechner, Richard ([1977] 1988) *Performance Theory*, London: Routledge.
—— (2002) 'Play', in *Performance Studies: An Introduction*, London: Routledge, pp. 79–109.
Winnicott, Donald Woods (1982) *Playing and Reality*, London: Routledge.

POPULAR THEATRE

Popular theatre is a broad category for defining performance whose forms range across melodrama, street theatre, **circus**, vaudeville, clowning, mime and musicals. Historically and culturally, it encompasses ancient Greek theatre in the West and kabuki and Kathakali in **Asian performance**, as well as many types of contemporary and twentieth-century performance practices. It immediately becomes evident that the term means little if separated from the ideologies that inform it, the forms in which it is manifest and the context in which it happens. What is popular in Britain might not be so in **Augusto Boal**'s Brazil. Beyond cultural specificity, though, there have recently been a number of productions that have mass popular appeal worldwide, like the commercial circus work of Cirque du Soleil, or the Abba tribute musical *Mamma Mia* (1999), which has been presented in at least eighty countries. These examples point to the need to make a distinction (even if this formula is not rigid and the gap is sometimes bridged) between popular commercial theatre and, at the opposite end of the spectrum, popular theatre that has an overt political agenda.

Outside commercial contexts, popular theatre refers more frequently to a politically and socially minded approach to making theatre, as **Bertold Brecht**, Boal or **Vsevolod Meyerhold** practised, that aimed to bring working-class **audiences** into theatres or take the theatre out to them. At its most extreme, this impulse materializes as **demonstrations**, like the street performances of America's **Bread and Puppet Theatre**. Popular theatres often share similar priorities. They want to be accessible, cheap to make and participate in, are often large-scale and rough-and-ready in their format, use vernacular materials or sources, and provide entertainment as much as education or instruction. Popular theatre also draws readily on structures like **carnival**, **sports**, **happenings** and the circus, and familiar forms like **puppetry** or **masks**, to broaden its appeal and encourage access. Throughout twentieth-century theatre history, numerous artists and **directors** have consciously modelled their work on older popular theatre models in order to increase and broaden the currency and impact of their own practices. **Peter Brook** favours the immediate and rough Elizabethan theatre, whereas **Jacques Copeau** toured French villages with models based on Greek theatre and commedia dell'arte.

Inevitably, popular theatre often occurs in non-theatre **spaces** and is **site-specific**. Italian performer/playwright Dario Fo has shown his *Mistero Buffo* (1969) in football stadia and factories, and the San Francisco Mime Troupe toured to targeted community venues, just as John McGrath took his company 7:84 to the remote Scottish Highlands in the 1970s. Those who have continued to work predominantly within theatre architecture, like Meyerhold and Brecht, have attempted to change its atmosphere, its **scenography** and even its construction, with cigar smoke, constructivist sets or theatres in the round.

Even if in practice it already existed for thousands of years, the idea of formalizing popular theatre as an institution or recognized term began most evidently in mid-eighteenth-century France with Jean-Jacques Rousseau's call for a '*théâtre populaire*'. In the following centuries and in a range of countries, such aspirations materialized in diverse forms, from transitory **festivals** to the establishment of culture centres to receive work as well as promote artistic involvement. Such multi-purpose buildings multiplied throughout Communist Eastern Europe and Russia. Britain's creation of a single national theatre in London in 1976 diminishes next to the establishment of five regional national theatres in France, which began with the founding of the Comédie-Française in 1680. Arguments continue to rage about how these institutions are or are not elitist, and numerous strategies have been tested to bring in a wider audience base. But the popularizing of theatre is complex and needs to encompass many sociological as well as aesthetic considerations: about the space in which the events happen, the form it takes, its content, the economics of the artistic exchange, cultural diversity (of which **intercultural** practice and theory have made us acutely aware) and the message or import of the work and its life after the performance. To sustain a popular theatre it is vital to build audiences while challenging them – no mean feat! Audiences are unpredictable and often fickle. Most artists might want their work to be popular, but how is such esteem achieved without compromising artistic values? And how does one innovate with traditions, while maintaining their essential qualities? In such conundra lie the complexities that make the very idea of popular theatre an ideology that is hard to attain in practice.

Bibliography

There are as many books as there are types of theatre within this broad category. The two edited collections below exhibit this range and introduce key practices and issues, most usefully in the up-to-date Schechter collection. McGrath's is a classic and influential practitioner's manifesto.

McGrath, John (1981) *A Good Night Out: Popular Theatre: Audience, Class and Form*, London: Eyre Methuen.

Mayer, David and Kenneth Richards (eds) (1977) *Western Popular Theatre*, London: Methuen.

Schechter, Joel (2003) *Popular Theatre: A Sourcebook*, London and New York: Routledge.

POSTMODERNISM

Postmodernism is a range of cultural practices and sensibilities that have developed especially from the 1980s on and that reject some of the apparent certainties, or 'grand narratives', of modern paradigms of thought. Challenging ideas of coherent identity and universal value and truth as not only impossible but also duplicitous, it proposes that these 'grand narratives' only pretend to represent everyone's interests and actually represent dominant class interests. Having discarded universalism, postmodernism explores how meaning is always multiple and contingent on contexts, **audiences** and makers. Roland Barthes influentially proclaimed 'The Death of the Author' (1977) and advocated a more democratic understanding of the production of meaning by emphasizing meaning's contingency even in a written text and attributing its production to the reader/audience. Jean Baudrillard argued that the media saturation of contemporary consumer culture made it impossible to distinguish between the real, or truth, and the representation: everything is simulation. Because it is concerned with meaning's representation – however compromised – postmodern art practice is often conspicuously self-conscious or meta-representational. Thus it is interested not only in what meanings it is making, but also in how it is making them, often emphasizing process over product.

In performance, postmodernism's rejection of apparent certainties takes numerous forms. It is visible in movements away from text-based theatre towards the potentially more democratic **devising** techniques practised by **Split Britches** and **Robert Lepage** and the **playful** and destabilizing approaches to identity characteristic of much **performance art**. It is there in the hybridization of performance disciplines epitomized by **Pina Bausch**'s dance theatre, **Guillermo Gómez-Peña**'s and **Annie Sprinkle**'s activist performance/**protest** interventions, and in the diversification of the disciplines of theatre and performance studies. Postmodernism's media saturation is explored in the **multimedia** work of **Orlan**, **Stelarc** and **Laurie Anderson**. And such **visual theatre** as **Robert Wilson**'s or **Tadeusz Kantor**'s pursues postmodernism's interrogation of the image as truth or simulation. For many critics, postmodern performance is epitomized in the work of the **Wooster Group**. This queries the truth of **naturalist** theatre through different approaches to: **acting/performing**, which aims less to represent character than to acknowledge that it presents the performer; text, which appropriates and mixes high and low cultural source material; and style, for example in the Group's use of violently non-linear composition and multimedia. For many critics, performance's **liveness** makes it the ideal medium through which to test postmodernism – but for two different reasons. For some, this liveness seems to insist on performance's authenticity, authority and truth, presenting a useful challenge to postmodernism. For others, performance's liveness insists on the material presence of the body and resists the abstraction of universalist thinking.

While postmodern performance is often easy to recognize, its effects are widely debated. For its supporters, it is democratizing because it challenges elitist, universalist assumptions, and it is often thrillingly pleasurable in its playful abandon of the familiar, its renegade engagement with diverse source materials, its exuberance and its humour. For its detractors, these same qualities can make it descriptive of too broad a range of practices to be critically useful. Worse, they can make it deliberately obscure, elitist and – while spectacular – emotionally and politically empty. Its critics also point out that postmodernism's aim to challenge racist or sexist cultural assumptions by presenting controversial material is fundamentally compromised by its simultaneous interrogation of the possibility of representing anything truthfully. For example, the Wooster Group's refusal to provide explicit rationale for including taboo material risks allowing that material to be read as condoned by the performance rather than as the object of the performance's critique. Similarly, postmodernism's radical contingency can seem to place it outside of history, beyond the possibility of commenting on the past, the present or the future. In other words, postmodern performance risks a dangerous ethical relativism.

In response to such criticisms, Philip Auslander has argued that postmodern performance does not aspire to be a political theatre; rather, he argues, it is a 'resistant' theatre *with* politics, aware of its political and ideological effects but not necessarily making an explicit argument because it does not assume this is possible. Baz Kershaw regrets the way Auslander's model casts postmodern performance as politically passive rather than active. He proposes that we look to a greater range of performance practices (from prison theatre to protest) to see how they make interventions in much broader contexts that are less compromised by the theatre's commodification, and to appreciate how their political radicalism is enhanced by their contexts and reception. As the scale of debate around postmodern performance's effects makes clear, it challenges representational practices but has by no means resolved them.

Bibliography

Seminal postmodern theory texts include those by Barthes, Baudrillard and Jameson. Auslander, Kaye and Kershaw explore at length the relationships between postmodernism and performance. Bertens and Natoli's collection includes articles on Chinese-American performance-maker Ping Chong, Robert Lepage and the Wooster Group. Birringer makes reference to (among others) Laurie Anderson, Pina Bausch and Robert Wilson.

Auslander, Philip (1997) *From Acting to Performance: Essays in Modernism and Postmodernism*, London: Routledge.

Barthes, Roland (1977) 'The Death of the Author', in *Image Music Text*, ed. and trans. Stephen Heath, London: Fontana.

Baudrillard, Jean (1994) *Simulacra and Simulation*, trans. Sheila Faria Glaser, Ann Arbor: University of Michigan Press.

Bertens, Hans and Joseph Natoli (eds) (2002) *Postmodernism: The Key Figures*, Oxford: Blackwell.

Birringer, Johannes (1991) *Theatre, Theory, Postmodernism*, Bloomington and Indianapolis: Indiana University Press.

Jameson, Fredric (1991) *Postmodernism, or, The Cultural Logic of Late Capitalism*, London: Verso.

Kaye, Nick (1994) *Postmodernism and Performance*, London: Macmillan.

Kershaw, Baz (1999) *The Radical in Performance: Between Brecht and Baudrillard*, London: Routledge.

PRESENCE

In the context of performance, 'presence' is used to describe a perceived quality of performance – that is usually live but is sometimes recorded – where the performer appears to be notably focused or 'in the moment'. What these tautologies mean is that performers convey charisma, strong engagement with themselves, their roles and/or their work, a particular quality of concentration, and a special 'aura', to use Walter Benjamin's term from a different but related context. The performer's presence strongly engages the **audience**'s attention and cultivates the audience's own sense of presence – a sense of the importance of being in that moment at that event. Some performance traditions such as Method **acting** seek to maximize this sense of presence because they perceive it as consonant with focused performers and an audience that is engaged, responsive and even enthralled. Other performance traditions, including **postmodern** ones, often seek to challenge performance's apparent reliance on presence. This is because they see it as potentially manipulative – as in the seductive, charismatic performance of state leaders such as Hitler – and exclusive, since it is only available to those audience members privileged enough to witness the performer's ecstatic moment here and now, and it is often perceived as introspective and self-indulgent. By drawing attention to a sense of selfhood, presence can facilitate critical engagement with ideas of subjectivity, be that the psychologically coherent subjectivity cultivated by the presence of **naturalism**'s characters or the fractured subjectivity often explored through the qualified presence of postmodernism's performers. Because of its reliance on a sense of immediacy, it shares with the concept of **liveness** not only many features, but also many points of contention and debate. Benjamin's reflection on what happens to the aura of the unique painting now that mechanical reproduction has challenged the uniqueness of any artwork is useful to consider in relation to the fate of presence in an age of **multimedia** performance.

Bibliography

Auslander's discussion of presence identifies some of its potentials and problems. For a fuller discussion of related issues, see the **liveness** entry.

Auslander, Philip (1997) *From Acting to Performance: Essays in Modernism and Postmodernism*, London: Routledge.
Benjamin, Walter (1973) 'The Work of Art in the Age of Mechanical Reproduction', in *Illuminations*, London: Fontana Press.

PROTESTS, DEMONSTRATIONS AND PARADES

These are forms of mass group performance that generally take place in public **spaces** in order to influence public opinion by occupying and exploiting the power of those sites. While not strictly theatre, these forms often deploy its features – such as **music**, props, orchestrated **movement** and organized time – to harness its symbolic effects. While protests and demonstrations are broadly associated with counter-cultural activism, parades are often State-organized and State-supporting: consider, for example, **Olympic** ceremonies, Victory parades, Hitler's infamous Nazi Nuremberg rallies, and inaugural processions for State rulers. Parades can also support other forms of social authority – Christmas parades common in many Western cities, for example, can be seen to support capitalist consumerism.

Most commonly, though, protests and demonstrations occupy public space in ways intended to challenge authority, claim freedom of movement and expression, consolidate a sense of counter-cultural group identity, and reclaim a sense of democratic agency for the people rather than the State. As twentieth-century political theatre-makers grew dissatisfied **performing** for self-selecting **audiences** inside theatre buildings, they moved their work outside and adopted practices from protests and demonstrations. This is illustrated in **happenings**, the work of the **Bread and Puppet Theatre**, **performance art** and **installation art**. In complementary ways, political activism co-opted more and more performance techniques to enhance its symbolic and actual power. Thus, early **feminist** suffragettes used marches and other forms of visible public protest to insist on and occupy their literal and metaphorical space within a democratic society, and they often protested on sites associated with the State in order directly to challenge its authority. Many other civil rights protesters have done the same, including: African Americans in the 1950s; anti-war protesters in the 1960s, 1970s and early twenty-first century; **las Madres de la Plaza de Mayo** in Argentina from the late 1970s on; anti-nuclear protesters in the 1980s; gay, lesbian and queer rights activists in the Pride marches from the 1980s on; Greenpeace and other ecological protesters from the 1980s on; Chinese protesters in **Tiananmen Square** and East Berliners on the Berlin Wall in 1989; and anti-globalization protesters from the late 1990s on.

While the pervasiveness of twentieth-century protest and demonstration is not in dispute, its political efficacy has been questioned. **Richard Schechner** and others have argued that protests and demonstrations share with **Bakhtinian carnival** the potential to be both socially transgressive and – by acting as a short-term valve that releases social pressure – always only temporary and often supportive of the status quo. Baz Kershaw acknowledges that protests and demonstrations are at least partly conservative because they are always somewhat repetitive and familiar, but he argues that they nevertheless continue to take new forms and so they are not purely conservative. Responding to arguments that theatre has become less political in **postmodern** contexts, Kershaw also argues not only that culture has become more pervasively **performative**, but also that it has become more politically performative, the proliferation of protest offering a case in point.

Bibliography

Cohen-Cruz brings together a vast international selection of writings on the topic. Schechner's analysis of a range of events – including the fall of the Berlin Wall and the Tiananmen demonstrations – considers their political effects centrally in the terms of Bakhtinian carnival. Kershaw considers many of the same examples and argues for an analysis that goes beyond Bakhtin's liberating–oppressive binaries.

Cohen-Cruz, Jan (ed.) (1998) *Radical Street Performance: An International Anthology*, London: Routledge.
Kershaw, Baz (1999) 'Fighting in the Streets: Performance, Protest and Politics', in *The Radical in Performance: Between Brecht and Baudrillard*, London: Routledge.
Schechner, Richard (1993) 'The Street Is the Stage', in *The Future of Ritual: Writings on Culture and Performance*, London: Routledge.

PSYCHOANALYSIS

Psychoanalysis is the study of mental processes, especially unconscious ones. Pioneered by Sigmund Freud from the late nineteenth century into the 1930s as a therapeutic treatment for neurosis, it has become an important tool of cultural practice and analysis. Freud established that the self is made up of three parts: the id, composed of instinctual desires; the super-ego, the repressive social rules we internalize; and the ego, the social individual who partly reconciles the id and super-ego. Socialization requires the individual to repress many of the id's desires, but these do not vanish. Instead, they form the individual's unconscious – active mental processes that we may feel we have little knowledge of, let alone control over. The unconscious cannot be analysed directly because it is repressed. Therefore, it has to be studied through its indirect expression in jokes, slips of the tongue, repetitions, dreams, creative practices including performance and writing, and physical symptoms that have no apparent organic cause.

Freud linked psychoanalysis to theatre by using names of dramatic characters for psychoanalytic concepts including the Oedipal and Electra complexes, exploring subjectivity through characterization in dramatic literature and performance, and describing many formative events as acts of social **mise en scène**. The primal scene, for example, is the real or imagined scene where the child first witnesses parental sex and perceives his or her own origins. Theatre and psychoanalysis are further linked through many other shared concerns. Psychoanalytic paradigms for understanding identity, desire and relationships are visible in the family dramas of William Shakespeare, August Strindberg, Henrik Ibsen, Tennessee Williams, Edward Albee and Federico García Lorca, for example. Franz Wedekind's drama and the writing and theatre practice of **Antonin Artaud** share psychoanalysis' interest in repressed desires. Strindberg's *A Dream Play* (1902) and **Hélène Cixous**'s *Portrait of Dora* (1976) attempt to mimic the non-linear structure of the unconscious.

Psychoanalysis's greatest contributions to theatre and performance have been the tools it provides for critical analysis. **Feminist** theories of **audience** spectatorship, for example, have been influenced by psychoanalytic concepts of scopophilia (the love of looking), masochism (the drive to be controlled by another) and the mental processes that produce sexual identity. Performance itself has been understood as fantasy, the mise en scène of desire, and a safe way of enacting desire by displacing it through identification on to characters who stand in for ourselves. Relationships between the **actor**, **director** and audience, and within processes of **rehearsal**, **improvisation** and **devising**, have been informed by reflection on their psychodynamics. Analysis of the fetish – the object that stands in for something that is absent – provides a means of understanding the unconscious investment that audiences make in willingly suspending their disbelief. Theories of the abject – that which bodies expel and which we may find both repulsive and compelling – can inform understanding of the **body art** of Franko B, **Stelarc** and **Orlan**. As therapeutic psychoanalysis can help to work through trauma by staging it through the 'talking cure', performance can aim to do the same through a **performative** cure or enactment. Such a critical approach helps to explain the social function of many **Holocaust memorials and museums**, performances like Orlan's *Reincarnation of Saint Orlan* (1990–93), such repeated protest as that staged by **las Madres de Plaza de Mayo** and, for **Peggy Phelan**, all performance. Phelan argues that performance's **liveness**, evanescence and ensuing absence and loss make it a helpful form of rehearsal for experiencing loss elsewhere in life – for example, through bereavement. Freudian psychoanalysis has been widely criticized; for example, its theories of human development have been seen as falsely universalizing. But psychoanalysis' theorization of the unconscious remains crucial to current understandings of subjectivity and human behaviour, including performance.

Bibliography

Reinelt and Roach include a useful introduction to psychoanalysis and two essays focusing on identification. Campbell and Kear's collection addresses a broader range of topics, from rehearsal and therapeutic processes, to melancholy and homesickness, to social trauma. Murray focuses on the relationship of trauma to the production of racial and gender identities in theatre and film. Pellegrini explores intersections between psychoanalytic theory and gendered and racial identity in contemporary performance.

Campbell, Patrick and Adrian Kear (eds) (2001) *Psychoanalysis and Performance*, London: Routledge.
Murray, Timothy (1997) *Drama Trauma: Specters of Race and Sexuality in Performance, Video and Art*, London: Routledge.
Pellegrini, Ann (1997) *Performance Anxieties: Staging Psychoanalysis, Staging Race*, London: Routledge.
Reinelt, Janelle G. and Joseph R. Roach (eds) (1992) *Critical Theory and Performance*, Ann Arbor: University of Michigan Press.

PUPPETRY

What separates puppets in performance from art objects or anthropological curios hung on a domestic or art gallery wall is the puppeteer or performer's ability to manipulate the object and thus bring it to 'life'. This principle can be carried over to any object, from a crudely shaped piece of wood to a sophisticated **mask**, costume or other body adornment. **Tadeusz Kantor**'s mannequins shadow his actors, overtly exploring the dialectical dynamic between animate and inanimate beings and questioning how theatre uses artifice to bring events to life and **plays** with **liveness**. As children manipulate puppets or dolls to represent challenging real-life situations by safe proxy, so can puppets intimate other worlds. **Edward Gordon Craig** emphasized this potential in his writings on the *Übermarionette*, recalling how puppets evolved from **ritual** and totemic representations of another spiritual dimension. This is still seen in much **Asian performance**, where the use of puppets is common, as in Balinese shadow puppetry. They can possess great power and transport vital messages to a community through the puppeteer/medium, who is sometimes also a shaman. Craig's vision was shared by many modernist artists and groups such as the **surrealists**, **Dadaists** and **futurists** in the early part of the twentieth century, who believed puppets make striking metaphors, representing the human condition of subjugation and powerlessness in an often absurd but immediate way. Power play lies at the heart of puppetry's interactions with live performers.

Even detached from any religious or spiritual implications, puppets can carry authority because of their visual impact rather than their suggestions of a metaphysical realm. Julie Taymor's *Lion King* (1997) is one of the best-known examples. An inanimate object can provoke human sensitivities and diminish our self-importance through its vastness, exposing feelings of vulnerability or, alternatively, reinforcing them through placing the human body alongside miniatures. Such qualities have been utilized by **Bread and Puppet Theatre** for mass participatory events as well as for **protests, demonstrations and parades**. Puppets can also broach taboos and do the humanly impossible, like the moon-walking astronaut puppet of **Robert Lepage**'s *The Far Side of the Moon* (2000) or the wife- and child-beating violence of a Punch and Judy show illustrate. In such knock-about forms, puppets are frequently satirical, can carry topical and critical messages, and are a highly accessible style of **popular theatre**. Alfred Jarry's *Ubu Roi* (1896) exploited such popular but transgressive potential in its characterizations, as did the **Cabaret Voltaire**, with their inclusion of puppets and objects in their cabaret events.

Whatever form puppets possess, be it as shadow, rod, glove, marionette, body double or ritual totem, they have a powerful transformative ability in both popular and more esoteric modes of performance, linking ancient roots with up-to-date concerns and practices. With the advance of nano-technology and shrinking computers, it seems inevitable that we will become increasingly used to robots intervening in our lives and acclimatized to the **presence** of the 'puppet' object in our homes as well as in our theatres.

Bibliography

Segel considers some of the forms puppets (in the loosest meaning of the word) have adopted in the modern period. Schechter provides five articles on a range of puppet styles from different cultures, a project Bell's edited collection takes further, with numerous illustrations. His other book is a broad up-to-date historical introduction, while Tillis gives a more theoretical survey.

Bell, John (2000) *Strings, Hands, Shadows: A Modern Puppet History*, Detroit: Detroit Institute of Arts.
—— (ed.) (2001) *Puppets, Masks and Performing Objects*, Cambridge, MA: MIT Press.
Schechter, Joel (2003) *Popular Theatre: A Sourcebook*, London and New York: Routledge.
Segel, Harold B. (1995) *Pinocchio's Progeny: Puppets, Marionettes, Automatons, and Robots in Modernist and Avant-Garde Drama*, Baltimore: Johns Hopkins University Press.
Tillis, Steve (1992) *Toward an Aesthetics of the Puppet: Puppetry as a Theatrical Art*, Westport, CT: Greenwood Press.

REHEARSAL

The French call rehearsals *répétitions*, affirming the necessity that is central to most rehearsal processes to repeatedly go back over and practise material. In English-language usage, the word has entered into common parlance to indicate a draft run-through, implying that this is just a stand-in for the real thing, the event or performance itself. Yet, as all performance practitioners know, rehearsals are fundamental to the making of a performance, though there is no prescription that good rehearsals (whatever that implies) lead to successful performances. One primary role of rehearsals is to create an ensemble feeling as it is often described, though few critics or academics are ever specific about what this actually means. Feelings of ease, creativity, self-confidence and mutual trust, which are also central to **training** approaches, can and should carry over into performance once the job of rehearsals is finished. But some **directors** avoid constructing the rehearsal–performance continuum so linearly, calling actors back for rehearsals during runs of a production. Some theatres, like Britain's National Theatre, to name but one, also have the luxury of instituting previews before the official press night, when a work is presented to a paying public but is framed as still being in preparatory or rehearsal mode, not the 'real thing', and therefore not subject to critical scrutiny or review. Such a practice opens up the terms 'rehearsal' and 'performance'.

The substance of rehearsals is primarily contingent on the various requirements made of actors: to learn lines; to enter into their roles; to establish their **movements** and interactions (also known as blocking); to create a **mise en scène** or the integration of disparate parts of the staging and their related technologies; to create the 'world of a play' or its aesthetic, sometimes according to details like the period setting, unity of time and **space**, and variations in the mood. The director's timing of when to bring the disparate elements of a production together, or knowing when to run a play in rehearsal, is crucial – too late and the performance will look under-rehearsed and half-baked, the actors hesitant and lacking confidence. Too soon and they might become mechanical – the first night is just one of many repetitions, and there needs to be further enrichment as the performance is run in. The idea of a cohesive vision is fundamental, even if the style being worked on allows juxtaposition and rupture. Even chaos has its own rules, and staged chaos might need to look unplanned and as though it is happening every night for the first time, as in Forced Entertainment's *Bloody Mess* (2004, UK).

In British theatres where the focus is on producing plays quickly, rehearsals typically last for three or four weeks. In countries where there has historically been substantial state subsidy of the theatre, they might last a year or more. This was the case with **Konstantin Stanislavsky** and **Vsevolod Meyerhold**, and is even true today of an ensemble like Lev Dodin's Maly Theatre from St Petersburg. With recent growing interest in **devised** work, the nature of rehearsals has become more exploratory and they have subsequently needed to be longer. Rather than being for the purpose of interpreting and blocking a text, rehearsals have become more often a period of group-led creative exploration, though this still needs to be balanced with or subsumed within the director's vision and/or the requirement to deliver a 'show' by the opening date.

As well as fulfilling the crucial role of establishing the performers' work, the director also has to oversee the integration of the designer and their technical team, unless they also take charge of the **scenography**, like auteur-directors **Tadeusz Kantor**, **Robert Wilson**, **Robert Lepage** and Socíetas Rafaello Sanzio's Claudio Castellucci. In larger companies, rehearsals will be run by a stage manager and his or her team, who incrementally introduce production elements like props and costume or a floor plan of the set, culminating in the technical and dress rehearsals when **lighting and sound** are fully incorporated. On the European continent, dramaturgs either work on specific productions or are sometimes based permanently in a theatre. They occasionally take responsibility for script development and contextual materials that pertain to the background or translation of a play and might provide information on its other productions for research purposes.

Of course rehearsals cannot replicate the experience of performance, only prepare for it. They should provide a familiar structure within which the actors are more or less free to respond within a production's particular parameters. Rehearsals help make the unknown interaction of performance less daunting. Games, **play** and **improvisation** are useful for breaking down barriers between actors and for encouraging relaxation and creativity, but there are very few commonly recognized and utilized rehearsal systems. One that has recently come to prominence is the RSVP (Resources, Scores, Valuaction, Performance) cycles, developed by American **dancer**/choreographer Anna Halprin with her architect husband Lawrence, and utilized by Robert Lepage. RSVP offers a collaborative, affirmative model of group work, useful also for companies rehearsing without a director figure, who would normally be the outside eye and final authority. Anne Bogart's 'Viewpoints' is another dance-derived approach that provides both a vocabulary and a clear creative methodology for group work. Such methods help formalize the process of editing and eliminating discovered material. This leads seemingly to great waste but also, hopefully, to a concentrated distillation, and is a crucial function of rehearsals, especially if a work is devised.

Good documentation or even accounts of rehearsals are rare, in part because they are a time for 'private' exploration. Observers or outsiders might unsettle the atmosphere, making actors self-conscious. But the lack of documentation also indicates the difficulty of writing about an often serendipitous process where methods or systems may be inappropriate. A director's relationship to each performer has to be individually tailored to their needs and limitations. Rehearsal methods are as varied as the possibilities of performance they precede.

Bibliography

It is necessary to read widely to garner information about specific rehearsal approaches and strategies. Mitter's book is about four directors' theories of **acting** and their training ethos and exercises, rather than the rehearsal process *per se*, which Toporkov describes well.

Schechner provides a brief overview and introduces the RSVP cycles. Mitter and Shevtsova's broad collection offers good opportunities for comparing varied practices.

Bogart, Anne (2001) *A Director Prepares*, London: Routledge.

Delgado, Maria M. and Paul Heritage (eds) (1996) *In Contact with the Gods? Directors Talk Theatre*, Manchester: Manchester University Press.

Mitter, Shomit (1993) *Systems of Rehearsal: Stanislavsky, Brecht, Grotowski and Brook*, London: Routledge.

—— and Maria Shevtsova (eds) (2005) *Fifty Key Theatre Directors*, London: Routledge.

Schechner, Richard (2002) *Performance Studies: An Introduction*, London: Routledge.

Toporkov, Vasily Osipovich (1998) *Stanislavski in Rehearsal: The Final Years*, London: Routledge.

RITUAL

Ritual is impossible to encapsulate simply and briefly, ranging from ubiquitous **everyday** aspects of human behaviour, through specific cultural patterns of action much closer to formal performance, to a theoretical term that has multiple possible definitions and applications. Broadly, ritual denotes an action or series of actions that are done in order to have an effect – to alter the weather, to bring prosperity or to move a person from one phase of life to another in a rite of passage. This last function is frequently linked to difficult life events, of growing up, conjoining or separation, and in these contexts rituals function as a support and a means to enable transitions. With their emphasis on efficacy, rituals can be distinguished from much performance in that they have at their centre active participation, someone or a group doing rather than presenting something – for it is by this activity that a belief is confirmed or change is thought to be brought about. However many elements ritual and performance share, this shift away from the actor–**spectator** binary towards **paratheatre** and the actions of the performer is crucial for understanding the substance and significance of ritual activities.

In psychological terms, a ritual denotes repetitive behaviour that may be a sign of an individual's mental instability or disorder. Beyond the individual, rituals often have a social function, for example in encouraging group cohesion. This is very evident in youth culture and in **sports**. Supporters' songs, **movements**, chants and gestures all have ritual qualities, defining one community in relation to their opposition. The **haka** epitomizes this element of display within sports. A sense of group identity is involved on a much larger scale with regard to the religious aspects of rituals. Ritual ceremonies exist as forms of prayer and worship in most cultures. Rituals are not only part of human behaviour, however. Just as **animals play**, so do some animals practise what can only be called rituals. This is usually related to courtship challenges and demonstrations – peacocks flourishing their tails, for example. It appears that rituals have more than a purely cultural basis. **Victor Turner** explored this view and tentatively proposed that rituals have a biological basis and our participation in them is genetically conditioned.

Any serious study of what rituals are needs to begin with anthropology. However different his views at the end of his life, Turner began his research in anthropological fieldwork, which led later to his adoption of a process he called performing ethnography. Rituals were re-enacted in the classroom in order for students to learn about them through active participation rather than just observation, even if the ritual was decontextualized and performed. Similarly, **Richard Schechner**'s observation of **Yaqui Lent and Easter ceremonies** helped his research into possible sources of the theatre by looking at ancient but still extant practices. Such comparative present-day analysis differs from the more familiar historical trajectory that considers the theatre's evolution from Dionysian ritual into ancient Greek theatre and beyond. Investigation of current ritual practices has proved more fruitful than historically based analyses, partly because of the lack of information about pre-Dionysian rituals. They have been inspiration and offered practical materials for theatre artists like **Tadashi Suzuki** and **Jerzy Grotowski**. Grotowski pursued detailed research into 'objective' elements of practice informed by ancient crafts and knowledges embodied in ritual gestures, songs and ways of moving, often derived from Haitian voodoo.

An inseparable conjunction between religious ceremony and dramatic presentation lies behind many **Asian performance** forms such as **Balinese dance-theatre**, a factor **Antonin Artaud** clearly identified. This proximity has informed **interculturalism** and has bled into secular events otherwise framed as **performance art** or **happenings**. *Paradise Now* (1968) overtly used ritual structures in performance. **Marina Abramović**, **Guillermo Gómez-Peña** and Joseph Beuys – in his *Coyote: I Like America and America Likes Me* (1974) – have all adopted ritualistic elements as ways of structuring and framing their artworks, with Beuys operating almost as a shaman. Shamans are central to many rituals and, attributed by their community with special powers, they often guide initiates and control proceedings, much as a **director** might orchestrate a theatre event. Fruitful comparisons have been made between Western magicians, performers or theatre artists and the shaman's role as a conjuror or medicine man.

At the core of the numerous comparisons that exist between rituals and performance lies the fact that performance shares with rituals a non-daily and specialized use of time and **space**, often enacted in buildings that are set aside for that purpose, like churches and mosques, or at least temporarily transformed from their daily use. As such, rituals are not to be distinguished and separated from performance, but, as Schechner has pointed out, they should rather be placed alongside each other on a continuum, their practices, functions, aesthetics and characteristics often overlapping and shared.

Bibliography

Below is just a small sample of a mass of materials, especially if this includes anthropological fieldwork on rituals. Schechner devotes a useful summative chapter to ritual in *Performance Studies*.

Harvey, Graham (ed.) (2003) *Shamanism: A Reader*, London: Routledge.

Schechner, Richard ([1977] 1988) *Performance Theory*, London: Routledge.

——— (2002) *'Ritual,' in Performance Studies: An Introduction*, London: Routledge.

Turner, Victor (1969) *The Ritual Process*, Chicago: Aldine.

——— (1982) *From Ritual to Theatre: The Human Seriousness of Play*, New York: Performing Arts Journal Press.

SCENOGRAPHY

Even though the practice has existed for hundreds of years in various forms, as a term 'scenography' is relatively new and still unfamiliar. It has superseded the phrase 'theatre design', for 'scenography' denotes the integrated work on all elements of a production, from costumes through soundscapes to **masks**, a breadth which the expressions 'stage design', 'scenic design' and 'theatre design' cannot encompass. Although etymologically its roots in Greek refer to scenic painting, in a performance context it alludes to the three-dimensional construction of a visual, aural, material and spatial **mise en scène**, using a synthesis of different technologies, from the intangibles of **lighting and sound** through to the actuality of wood and cloth. It is, however, only in the interaction of these elements with living beings, the performer and (more tangentially) the **audience** that scenographers' plans become fully realized in a performance **space**. The idea that designers create backdrops or decorative environments to foreground the performers was central to Restoration theatre, for example, but was replaced by notions of total performance environments that surround the performer and even at times the spectator, as artists like **Antonin Artaud** championed. The term 'scenography' has evolved along this trajectory from image to **installation** and participation.

In practice, scenographers have to negotiate a fragile balance between the visual and imaginative dimensions of a stage design and its functionality for performers, technicians and a **director**. In order to realize a world represented in a text or to construct a space for performers to inhabit, scenographers need to share their vision with the director in a long process of research, consultation and negotiation. Traditionally, a design emerges initially on paper from textual and contextual research before appearing as a model box. It is then that the mechanics of a design become manifest and budgetary considerations start to make a direct impact, though they will always have been an important consideration. As well as responding to a director's interpretation or a **devising** team's desires, the scenographer liaises closely with production staff, who will build and handle a set or environment through various scene changes or in and out of a van if a production tours. In addition, the scenographer has to convince the performers about his or her designs – a third but equally vital relationship, for the performers have ultimate responsibility to bring the scenography to life before or in proximity to the spectator. The scenographer needs organizational and diplomatic as well as creative skills, in what is a truly collaborative art.

Some directors like **Robert Wilson** and **Tadeusz Kantor** eschew such collaboration. From visual arts backgrounds, these two director/designers are representative of auteur artists who take sole responsibility for designing the stage environment. Their success has, however, supported the emergence of the scenographer's role within performance-making, an idea championed especially by **Edward Gordon Craig** and Adolphe Appia at the beginning of the twentieth century, when scenic design mostly involved backdrops for **naturalist** dramas. A turn towards abstract and non-realist designs followed, enhanced by the harnessing of complex stage technologies – in the Constructivist scenography that **Vsevolod Meyerhold** developed and in the pioneering work of Czech designer Josef Svoboda with **multimedia** slide and film projection.

Today, visual aspects of performance are increasingly being foregrounded. The growing interest in devised work, installations and **performance art**, as well as **environmental** and **visual theatre**, has opened up notions and understanding of what a scenographer does and the place of his or her work in creating a total mise en scène. Emphasis has shifted away from designs that are finished months before **rehearsal**, towards the construction of a space together with the performers. Similarly, many artists are now more excited by pre-existing spaces, as in **site-specific performance**. These serve as a reminder that design is as much about what you leave out as what you put in. The design, architecture, architectonics and the location of theatre and performance spaces have all become the focus of many recent theoretical studies. The idea that these are inhabited passively by the spectator is long gone, with questions about interaction, participation, **phenomenological** experience and virtual space driving scenographic practices forward.

Bibliography

Howard's book is clear and accessible, drawing on her extensive experience as a scenographer, while Brockett and Ball present more traditional models of what they call scene design.

Brockett, Oscar G. and Robert J. Ball (2004) *The Essential Theatre*, 8th edition, Belmont CA: Wadsworth/Thomson Learning.
Howard, Pamela (2002) *What is Scenography?*, London: Routledge.
Thorne, Gary (1999) *Stage Design: A Practical Guide*, Ramsbury, Wiltshire: The Crowood Press.

SEMIOTICS

Semiotics provides a system of analysis of performance that emerged in the 1970s. Theatre semiotics evolved from semiological theories of communication and language that had been used to examine the way the arts impact on the **spectator/** reader. In the theatre, semiotic analyses like those of Keir Elam extended the linguistic studies of Charles S. Peirce and Ferdinand de Saussure, who were both

– broadly speaking – structuralists. This term describes theorists whose work is predicated on analysing how things are constructed rather than the context in which they operate or their history. Semiotics initially offered detailed and seemingly comprehensive models for analysing the minutiae of performance events. In the 1980s, though, even as some critics like Patrice Pavis were elaborating on its overarching concepts, its principles were repeatedly questioned. Criticism centred partly on the need for semiotics to isolate certain aspects of a performance such as costume, **lighting or sound** for analysis, before reassembling these elements. This fragmentation meant that semiotics was less able to deal with the temporal flow of theatre, as Pavis has pointed out. This approach also struggled with much experimental **postmodern** performance that deliberately played with the dis-junctures between signs, and which exploited the dense layering of different systems or codes. Semiotics was able readily to analyse **visual theatre** and **sceno-graphic** aspects of performance, such as a set, costume or the appearance of particular characters, but engaged inadequately with embodied actions. Critics also questioned the assumption that everything can be subsumed within a realm of legible understanding, recognizing instead that much of performance is ineffable, and certainly momentary. In focusing on coded systems of signs, semiotics perhaps overvalued intention, implying that there is a linear progression from authorial intent through the act of communication to reception, following the sign, signifier and signified model on which structuralist theories of language are broadly based. Roland Barthes countered such an emphasis on intention with his writings on 'The Death of the Author', and attempted also to look at the physicality of performance in 'The Grain of the Voice', for example, which examined timbre and tonality as much as language itself. Shifts away from the problematic closure inherent in the idea of reading and interpreting visual signs were vital developments in semiotic analysis.

With these reservations in mind, while we might consider ourselves to be in a post-semiotic age of performance analysis, the assiduousness, clarity and clinical rigour of semiotic approaches still serve an important function. Used in conjunction with other models, semiotics offers systematic ways of breaking the dense com-plexity of performance events into manageable elements, whatever the inadequacy of this segmentation. Semiotics has an indispensable role in the ongoing quest for comprehensive methodologies of dissecting performance, not just because of its historical importance.

Bibliography

There is a wealth of background material on semiotics and the structuralist approaches (mentioned above) that have been central to the development of semiological analysis. What follows is a small range of some of the main theorists who have engaged with this mode of study in the theatre, both approvingly and critically. Pavis's more recent book has a useful section on the limitations of semiotic analysis. Barthes's book contains his influential articles mentioned above.

Aston, Elaine and George Savona (1991) *Theatre as Sign System: A Semiotics of Text and Performance*, London: Routledge.

Barthes, Roland (1977) *Image Music Text*, ed. and trans. Stephen Heath, London: Fontana.

Elam, Keir (2002) *The Semiotics of Drama and Theatre*, 2nd edition, London: Routledge.

Pavis, Patrice (1982) *Languages of the Stage*, New York: PAJ Publications.

—— (2003) *Analyzing Performance: Theater, Dance and Film*, trans. David Williams, Ann Arbor: University of Michigan Press.

Ubersfeld, Anne (1999) *Reading Theatre*, trans. Frank Collins, Toronto: University of Toronto Press.

SPACE

In a very basic formulation, theatre and performance are both events which take place in time and space and in which performers and **audiences** participate, and therefore thinking about space is fundamental to understanding how theatre and performance make meaning. It has thus become a central critical practice since the late 1960s, with the rise of newly spatialized performance practices by the likes of **Tadeusz Kantor**, **Peter Brook**, numerous **performance artists**, **installation artists** and makers of **site-specific performance** and **happenings**, and the development of **semiotic**, anthropological, **phenomenological** and other materialist approaches to analysing performance.

Theorists commonly divide theatre space into three categories: the stage space, the theatre space and the theatre environment. Stage space usually refers to the on-stage scenic area and its **scenography**. Examining stage space in phenomenological or material terms, we might consider how it facilitates or limits **movement** for on-stage performers and objects and how it affects opportunities for interaction between performers. Analysing stage space in semiotic terms provokes consideration of its metaphorical and fictional significations, such as whether it represents a recognizable place like a drawing room, and/or whether it is abstract, invoking a mood of airy optimism or restricted oppression, for example. The theatre space is the architecture that encompasses stage and audience spaces. Thinking about this helps critics analyse the relationship between the performance and the audience by considering sightlines, acoustics, proximity, scale, furnishings, audience and performer amenities, and so on. Common Western theatre space configurations include the proscenium-arch or end-on arrangement, the thrust stage, the traverse and the theatre-in-the-round. In more abstract terms, reflecting on theatre space may help us consider the space's emotional effects, such as whether it feels open or closed, for whom, when, and so on. The theatre environment is the site of the theatre in its wider social geography – where it is located geographically and what the significances of that location are. For example, is the theatre in a marginal location off-Broadway or on the Fringe? Is it out of the way for many but still a site of 'pilgrimage' such as Stratford, England, or any city hosting the **Olympics**?

As these examples all suggest, space is social; it produces social effects and meanings that are, in turn, ideological. Thus, analyses of performance space must not stop short at phenomenological and semiotic analyses but press on to consider the social and ideological meanings of performance spaces. How, for example, does stage space configure relationships of power between characters? How does the theatre environment affect diverse audiences' accessibility to the theatre – through the expense of travelling there, or through the sense of safety or danger the site produces? How does theatre space produce relationships of power between audiences and performers, as well as between different performers and different audience members, for instance in the hierarchical location of backstage dressing rooms and seats in the auditorium? Why does theatre commonly **mask** its sites of labour – such as the **lighting** box – in order to enhance its sense of **naturalism**? And what did **Bertold Brecht** achieve in dismantling this kind of masking? These are all questions which much politicized performance practice – such as **protest**, **popular theatre** and the work of **Augusto Boal** – is acutely aware of. In his influential book, *The Empty Space*, Peter Brook argued, 'I can take any empty space and call it a bare stage', suggesting that a performance space is ideologically neutral until performers give it meaning. However, much recent politicized performance and critical analysis of space indicates instead that any space comes already ideologically loaded with meanings produced by shape, decor, location, history, relationship to other performance architectures, and so on. There are no empty spaces, only variably different spaces.

Although there is more extensive critical analysis of theatre space than performance space, many of these ideas are directly transferable to thinking about such things as **ritual**, **sport**, performance art, **rehearsal** and other forms of performance. And, although space is fundamental to all performance, it has been especially explored in the large-scale theatre work of such artists as **Robert Wilson** and **Laurie Anderson**. Many **directors**, including Brook, **Tadashi Suzuki**, **Robert Lepage** and Ariane Mnouchkine, director of Paris's Théâtre du Soleil, founded dedicated sites for producing their work in order to develop a sustained relationship with a particular social, geographical and architectural environment. Similarly, many companies produce site-specific theatre to foreground the spatial meanings of the site of production. David Wiles argues that recent theatre practice may be moving away from the modernist propensity to produce in 'containers' or supposedly 'abstract' dedicated theatre spaces, to produce in sites where physical and social specificities can be engaged with more productively and directly.

Bibliography

McAuley concentrates on stage space, the Leacrofts on theatre space and Carlson on the theatre environment. Wiles develops a sustained critical analysis of the first two aspects.

Brook, Peter (1968) *The Empty Space*, London: McGibbon and Kee.
Carlson, Marvin (1989) *Places of Performance: The Semiotics of Theatre Architecture*, Ithaca, New York: Cornell University Press.
Leacroft, Richard and Helen Leacroft (1984) *Theatre and Playhouse: An Illustrated Survey of Theatre Building from Ancient Greece to the Present Day*, London: Methuen.

McAuley, Gay (1999) *Space in Performance: Making Meaning in the Theatre*, Ann Arbor: University of Michigan Press.

Wiles, David (2003) *A Short History of Western Performance Space*, Cambridge: Cambridge University Press.

THEATRE

The word 'theatre' has interesting permutations in many languages and has encompassed a panoply of nuances since its etymological origins in the Greek word *theatron*, a place for viewing or seeing. It is even spelled differently in American and British usage. Intriguingly, it denotes the form itself, the repertoire of plays which are its constituent elements, as well as the buildings in which those events occur. In many dictionaries, the first definition listed is the building, undoubtedly the most straightforward aspect of this term. Further definitions show how widely the term ranges linguistically, from being the site where battles take place in wars (as in the **Gulf War**), to a place for medical operations – a corollary which has inspired several practitioners. This latter meaning reminds us how, rather than being the sealed, sterile **spaces** they are now, operating theatres used to be open for observation by medical students and even the public, a notion that **Jerzy Grotowski** explored in *The Constant Prince* (1965). Thus the word alludes to a form which is hard to pin down and very much defined according to its epoch and culture, as much as it refers to concrete spaces.

The theatre as a practice or form of artistic work is usually bound by the events or playtexts which it mainly comprises at any given time. Critics and theorists have often attempted to group these in broad categories linked to content and style, be it the Theatre of the Absurd, melodrama or the drama of Angry Young Men, to name but three. Numerous **directors** have been instrumental in this categorization. **Peter Brook** and Jerzy Grotowski stripped the theatre down to define it as an encounter between the actor and **audience**, with elements like **lighting and sound** having only peripheral significance. Directors like **Augusto Boal** and **Bertold Brecht** used **popular theatre** for political and social means, to educate and enlighten as much as to entertain. Groups like America's Living Theatre and **Bread and Puppet Theatre** have found theatre buildings limiting, restricted by the formal arrangements of the auditoria and the fact that in such a context their work is only for those who actually enter these buildings. They have therefore taken their practice out into public and community spaces, sometimes engaging in a kind of **paratheatre**, or performing in and as **demonstrations**. **Site-specific performance** is an extension of this desire, its **playing** with spatial boundaries calling into question the parameters of the nature of theatre and where it is located.

Theatre is one part of the broad spectrum that is known as performance. At the end of the twentieth century, there was increasing interest in this term 'performance'. The expansion of performance studies courses (particularly in the United States) and cross-disciplinary discussions about **performativity** have demonstrated this. Progressively, events like site-specific pieces and **happenings**, which do not take place within theatres, have been studied more as part of performance than of theatre. The growing study of the history and current manifestations of **performance art** have also clarified what theatre is and is not. The idea that it revolves around playtexts, mimetic representation or other modes of **acting**, and utilizes specific theatre technologies, has become more entrenched, although not definitively or unproblematically. Theatre depends on **rehearsals**, **training** and collaborative work, even if this is just a director and solo actor. It thus operates within an economic framework that supports groups or companies rather than individuals. Performance art (or **live art** as it is also known in Britain) tends to be more individual in its personnel, more able to adapt and respond to its environment, and is economically more independent. More significantly, it overtly plays with the modes of representation and the roles of performer and spectators that much theatre seems to take for granted. Its main technology has also often been the body, especially in body art practised by the likes of **Stelarc**, **Marina Abramović** and **Orlan**. This is not to say that theatre is necessarily conservative or reactionary; only that performance art has often experimented more radically than the theatre with the forms and theoretical positions that playing constructs.

At the heart of the theatre are its buildings, and these absorb much of the costs and energy of supporting this art form. Theatre buildings reflect the styles, interests and needs of an era. The Olivier auditorium at Britain's National Theatre (the theatre building opened in 1976) represents the idealism of a popular theatre and mass audiences, based as it is on ancient Greek amphitheatres. In the 1990s, the intimacy of the Cottesloe Studio became more appealing for directors, as it was hard to make work succeed in the 1,160-seat Olivier. The availability of small cheap rooms above pubs in London and other British cities, and of warehouse and loft spaces in New York and elsewhere, catered for this inclination and supported the vibrant growth of Fringe theatre and off-off-Broadway. At the other end of the spectrum, large venues have green rooms, dressing rooms, backstage and specialist technical areas – spaces that are closed to audiences – often with separate entrances from those used by the spectators. Ideologies of the theatre are embedded in the bricks and mortar and the structures into which these coalesce – a point illustrated by many nations' efforts to affirm their national identities by building national theatres. Some architects have tried to reconfigure such hierarchies, building theatres-in-the-round (as at Stoke-on-Trent in England), which have a democratic rather than hierarchical seating structure as well as increased intimacy.

'Theatre' is a problematic word that implies a vast range of forms, materials or spaces. It therefore always needs to be defined to reveal the innate assumptions its usage contains. These assumptions may say more about the person using the term and the context in which they operate than they do about the theatre itself.

Bibliography

Below is a selection of reference texts, as well as Mackintosh's book on theatre buildings and Carlson's semiotic analysis of theatre architecture and sites. The Pavis dictionary deals with more theoretical terms than the other reference sources.

Carlson, Marvin (1989) *Places of Performance: The Semiotics of Theatre Architecture*, Ithaca, New York: Cornell University Press.

Hartnoll, Phyllis (ed.) (1983) *The Concise Oxford Companion to the Theatre*, 4th edition, Oxford: Oxford University Press.

Mackintosh, Iain (1993) *Architecture, Actor and Audience*, London and New York: Routledge.

Pavis, Patrice (1998) *Dictionary of The Theatre: Terms, Concepts, and Analysis*, trans. Christine Shantz, Toronto: University of Toronto Press.

Stanton, Sarah and Martin Banham (eds) (1996) *The Cambridge Paperback Guide to the Theatre*, Cambridge: Cambridge University Press.

THEATRE ANTHROPOLOGY

It is not unrelated, but theatre anthropology should not be conflated with comparative explorations of the discipline of anthropology as a way of understanding what theatre and performance are. Anthropological concepts, and to a lesser extent practices, have proved central to the evolution of performance studies, as **Victor Turner**'s work has exemplified, linking performance with other aspects of human behaviour like **ritual** and **play**. Theatre anthropology, on the other hand, is a much more specific praxis developed by **Eugenio Barba** under the auspices of the International School for Theatre Anthropology, founded in 1979. His approach examines the differences and similarities between Western and **Asian performance** practices, looking at what common principles underlie performance cross-culturally. The analytical focus is more on the performer rather than performance as such, examining how roles are constructed and with what implicit assumptions. It thus considers performance processes outside cultural and social contexts. This has attracted criticism for its universalizing tendencies from the likes of **Rustom Bharucha**, as well as from **feminist** critics, who have asserted that Barba has ignored or sidelined issues of gender, especially in his analyses of female impersonators in Asian performance. Others have protested that he has excluded African performance from his research focus, which Barba counters by emphasizing the need to narrow down and select in order to make his research operable. These debates have helped crystallize issues regarding **intercultural** performance and the borrowing or application of non-Western or foreign techniques in Western theatre.

Focusing on what he terms 'pre-expressive behaviour', Barba has identified theatre anthropology's core principles as follows: the amplification and dilation of the body energetically and **spatially**, to create an energized and 'extended' performer; the use of extra-daily rather than daily techniques, pushing and enlarging the body's capabilities and balance beyond usage familiar to social situations; opposition as a guiding principle of **movement**, as in a counterbalance or in moving downwards to prepare for a jump upwards; and 'inconsistent consistency', the internal logic or consistency which coded extra-daily modes of performance possess. Ballet, mime or kabuki, for example, all have unique to them their own particular ways of moving the feet, which must be followed precisely and sustainedly. Barba has extended his research from **training**-based and theoretical enquiries into the creation of new performances with cross-cultural forms. On paper and in the theatre, his approach has made an original contribution to the study of performer processes and **acting**, though not without stirring controversy.

Bibliography

Barba's two texts lay out the fundamentals of this approach, with numerous illustrative examples in the large dictionary. Watson's book has a range of more critical positions on theatre anthropology in broad relation to intercultural theories.

Barba, Eugenio (1994) *The Paper Canoe – A Guide to Theatre Anthropology*, trans. Richard Fowler, London: Routledge.
—— and Nicola Savarese (eds) (1991) *A Dictionary of Theatre Anthropology: The Secret Art of the Performer*, London: Routledge.
Watson, Ian and colleagues (2002) *Negotiating Cultures – Eugenio Barba and the Intercultural Debates*, Manchester: Manchester University Press.

THEATRE OF THE OPPRESSED

The term 'theatre of the oppressed', coined by **Augusto Boal** after Paolo Freire's writings on oppression, has become recognized and adopted internationally for denoting a way of creating theatre and conducting **paratheatrical** work with a particular ideological framework. At its heart, this is the attempted liberation through performance techniques of a group or individuals from their own restriction or burden, be it social, cultural, financial, psychological or political. Boal has developed several techniques and modes of performance, often involving games, that can operate in theatre and non-theatre milieus to achieve his aims of social franchisement and support. As well as formulating new practices, these processes have resulted in the reconception of specific terminology within the theatre, like his idea of spectactors. Boal's combined theoretical and practical approach is meant to give people understanding and even, through **rehearsal**, experience of the possible means by which they can improve their oppressive situations. Even if these do not lead directly to change, they make the participants aware of their own potential to find other ways of living and being.

One technique often used within theatre of the oppressed, Forum Theatre, allows **audiences** to participate by halting the action of a piece, orchestrated by a go-between figure called a joker. Typically, these 'plays' or short dramas tackle a local or topical problem head-on. The audience members can then suggest alternative responses to the issue and act these out themselves, positing ways of solving real-life difficulties and oppressions and thereby empowering themselves and their communities. Boal considers this to be a 'rehearsal of revolution', and coined the neologism 'spectactor' to identify this new participatory role for the audience. In Invisible Theatre the audience must remain unaware that what they are watching is in fact a carefully rehearsed situation that intrudes into real life, such as the verbal sexual abuse of a woman on an underground train. The 'invisible' actors attempt to draw an audience in and encourage them to take sides – a situation of conflict or oppression is therefore chosen to stimulate participation and debate. Newspaper Theatre allows workshop participants to read behind the lines through the enactment of news stories. Image Theatre utilizes symbolic action and gestures rather than text, emphasizing physical rather than verbal processes, with some affinity to **Bertold Brecht**'s notion of *Gestus*. These are just some of the processes which Boal has developed under the umbrella of theatre of the oppressed.

Questions have been asked about the actual efficacy of such techniques and their relationship to real life, with concerns that false hopes might be raised or unrealistic situations presented. Boal's own personal shift into working in politics in Brazil and his current use of Legislative Theatre has not meant the abandonment of these techniques. Instead it can be seen as another means of facilitating the freedom which he seeks for oppressed peoples and encouraging an active dialogue between those with power and those who seemingly have none. The major difference in this latest phase of his work is the emphasis on changing actual legislation rather than changing situations in general.

Bibliography

These ideas are presented in Boal's book, based loosely on Freire. Schutzman and Cohen-Cruz depict wider applications of theatre of the oppressed practices beyond Boal's own work.

Boal, Augusto (1979) *Theatre of the Oppressed*, trans. Charles A. and Maria-Odilia Leal McBride, London: Pluto Press.
Freire, Paolo de (1970) *Pedagogy of the Oppressed*, New York: Seabury.
Schutzman, Mady and Jan Cohen-Cruz (eds) (1994) *Playing Boal: Theatre, Therapy and Activism*, London: Routledge.

TRAINING

Performer training encompasses many disparate processes, even if these often centre on common principles and techniques, as **Eugenio Barba** has attempted to outline with his theory of the pre-expressive and **theatre anthropology**. One fundamental belief in training performers is that, however variable the conditions of performance, especially regarding the unpredictability of **audience** reception, certain skills can be developed to make communication clearer and the experience easier for the performer. In training, the performer usually practises integrating the voice and body, working towards what Phillip Zarrilli has called a body-mind, where impulse leads immediately to action without self-judgement or extended reflection. These principles are also developed by **improvisation**, relaxation and muscular control, ease of breath and an open voice, focus and concentration – fundamental elements of most training systems, depending on the type of theatre that is dominant in any culture. In Euro-American culture, for example, where **naturalist** theatre is still the main form and television and film are so economically significant, most emphasis in training is on vocal delivery of text as well as the invention and psychological interpretation of a character or role, based largely on systems articulated by **Konstantin Stanislavsky** or Lee Strasberg. This is markedly different from an Eastern form such as noh, which emphasizes the complex codified use of the body, all but ignores originality or creativity, employs imitation of a master as its primary teaching mode and considers longevity of training as indispensable.

The time structures in which training happens vary from short workshops measured in days, to lifelong projects as in southern India's Kathakali, where the body is reshaped by vigorous massage – the hips are opened to enable a wide, deep stance. Correspondingly, theatre school communities differ greatly according to their context, from the family-based systems found across Asia, where the school almost replaces the family in the student's life, to the short-lived compressed training of drama or **acting** school programmes familiar to the individualized and commercially oriented approaches found in the West.

For many performance forms, from **circus** and **dance** to **Asian performance**, the need to train is evident. With less skill-based modes, the requirement to train is more debatable, and factors such as charisma and talent can replace system-atically acquired learned knowledge. The explorations of Yvonne Rainer and the **postmodern** dancers of the 1960s in New York, epitomized in a piece like *Trio A* (1966), sanctioned the rejection of technique and turned instead to **everyday** forms like walking (as in Steve Paxton's work). Some **performance artists** deny the need for (or are overtly disinterested in) training, drawing instead on themselves as social rather than trained **performative** beings. Here, autobiography often takes the place of performer craft, though dramaturgical considerations still apply, and there is no question that they are not **performing** – there is simply a different emphasis on the craft. Yet even those like Barba and **Jerzy Grotowski**, who have focused so much of their efforts on establishing discipline and rigorous techniques to help the performer find spontaneity and freedom (a central paradox within performer training), have abandoned training at times or articulated the danger of fixing processes. At one stage Grotowski's Laboratory Theatre gave up their training regime as it had ceased to have any purpose and had become a habitual **ritual**. The primary aim of any training is to go beyond personal and group habits, to explore creatively, and be open to new ways of working. This manifests itself in the sort of receptivity that an audience detect in a group when they appear to be what is called a 'true ensemble'. But such qualities are elusive, and training programmes cannot ensure that such an impression will arise or be perceived within the performance event itself.

The belief that formulaic methodologies simply do not work and that the individual must find his or her own way in relation to the form underpins most models of training in the West. In performance, performers must focus less on technical matters and more on the actor–**spectator** relationship, their relation to other performers working with them, and the performance material they are handling, be it a character, a song, a dance or a piece of text. Of course these cannot be separated from the techniques with which they are enacted, but training and **rehearsal** periods are the time for focusing on the minutiae – be it diction, breath, ways of moving or posture. In the performance, the performer must bring all the separate elements together in a synthesis. Whatever techniques and processes have been explored in training or rehearsal, these skills need to become 'second nature' for the performance. The idea of neutrality as the performer's vital base is central to **Jacques Lecoq**'s training, but the neutral **mask** is just a tool, and is therefore not worn in performance. Performance is pragmatic, and training can only ever be preparation for the high levels of stressful – though also potentially exhilarating – uncertainty that performing entails.

Bibliography

There are few books about theories of actor training in general, but many on specific approaches to acting. Zarrilli and Hodge therefore provide useful collections. Schechner's chapter 'Performer Training Interculturally' outlines some of the functions of training cross-culturally.

Barba, Eugenio and Nicola Savarese (eds) (1991) *A Dictionary of Theatre Anthropology: The Secret Art of the Performer*, London: Routledge.
Hodge, Alison (ed.) (2000) *Twentieth Century Actor Training*, London: Routledge.
Schechner, Richard (1985) *Between Theater and Anthropology*, Philadelphia: University of Pennsylvania Press.
Zarrilli, Phillip B. (ed.) (2002) *Acting (Re)Considered: Theories and Practice*, 2nd edition, London: Routledge.

VISUAL THEATRE AND THEATRE OF IMAGES

Both of these names specify theatre that prioritizes spectacular **scenographic** stage images, presenting visual language as theatre's most important element, and radically challenging Western culture's usual hierarchical, logocentric deference to text and language. Theatre of images can be spectacular in visual content, scale and/or trickery. Magnificent visual content characterizes such work as **Pina Bausch**'s flower-strewn set for *Nelken* (1982), **Tadeusz Kantor**'s performances, and the work of Italy's Sociétas Rafaello Sanzio, which features enormous curtains, on-stage **animals** and unusual bodies, from the anorexic to the obese. **Robert Wilson**'s and **Laurie Anderson**'s performances repeatedly play with scale, introducing outsize costumes, props and instruments. And **Robert Lepage**'s work is notable for its visual trickery, seamlessly transforming a grand piano into a gondola in *Tectonic Plates* (1988), and using **multimedia** projections in *The Seven Streams of the River Ota* (1994) to overlay multiple fictional locations.

Beyond its fundamental political commitment to celebrating the visual, however, the theatre of images ranges widely in its political aims and effects. Writing in 1977, Bonnie Marranca identified the theatre of images of avant-garde American **directors** Robert Wilson, Richard Foreman and Lee Breuer as overtly politicized **postmodern** theatre. It featured non-linear structure, non-representational perfor- mance and flat images, she argued, in order partly to draw metatheatrical attention to how meaning is made through representation. Such work arose from a variety of antecedents, such as **Bertold Brecht**'s use of *Gestus* and tableaux and **Antonin Artaud**'s total theatre. It also owed a debt to the rise of film and television and to the developed visual literacy they produced in their audiences. And its politics extended not only to its aesthetics but also to its processes, since much of it was collectively **devised** and placed equal value on the work of each of its contribut- ing artists, from designer to performer to director. However, while this work bears some potential to be politically challenging, it can also be conservative. Its emphasis on spectacle and entertainment potentially commodifies what it shows. Directors Lepage, **Peter Brook** and Ariane Mnouchkine, for example, have all been criticized, especially in debates on **interculturalism**, for using superficial images of cultural difference to produce visually exotic shows that do not properly represent cultural difference. Wilson, Bausch and the Socíetas Rafaello Sanzio could also be criticized for using unusual bodies as objects for stage pictures rather than as subjects. The dominance of auteur-directors in this field suggests it not only fails to escape theatre's conventional hierarchies but actually reinforces them. Its popularity at international **festivals** is secured by the accessibility of its visual language, but potentially supports the commodification of both the visual and the theatre. The theatre of images pioneered an important cultural and aesthetic re-evaluation of the significance of the visual; what it risks is a capitulation to empty spectacle.

Bibliography

Irvin surveys the work of many influential directors in this area and includes extensive photographs. Marranca collects plays by American directors Foreman, Wilson and Breuer, as well as providing thoughtful contextual analysis. Debord's analysis of the political vacuity of spectacular culture is seminal.

Debord, Guy (1994) *The Society of the Spectacle*, New York: Zone Books.
Irvin, Polly (2003) *Directing for the Stage*, Hove: RotoVision.
Marranca, Bonnie (ed.) ([1977] 1996) *The Theatre of Images*, Baltimore: Johns Hopkins University Press.

A Chronology

Year	World/Performance events	Births	Deaths
1363		Motokiyo Zeami	
1443			Motokiyo Zeami
1863		Konstantin Stanislavsky	
1872		Edward Gordon Craig	
1874		Vsevolod Meyerhold	
1879		Jacques Copeau Rudolf von Laban	
1885		Mikhail Bakhtin	
1896–	The modern Olympics are founded *Ubu Roi*, (director) 'Aurélien Lugné-Poe' Théâtre de l'Oeuvre, Paris	Antonin Artaud	
1898		Bertold Brecht	
1899–1902	Boer War		
1904	*The Cherry Orchard*, Konstantin Stanislavsky, Moscow Art Theatre (MAT), Moscow, Russia		
1912	Titanic disaster	John Cage	
1914–18	First World War		

Year	Event	People
1915		Tadeusz Kantor
1916	Cabaret Voltaire, Zurich, Switzerland	
1917	Russian Revolution	
1919		Merce Cunningham
1920		Victor Turner
1921		Jacques Lecoq
1922		Erving Goffman
1925		Peter Brook
1926	*The Government Inspector*, Vsevolod Meyerhold, Sohn Theatre, Moscow, Russia	
1928		Tatsumi Hijikata
1929	Wall Street Crash – worldwide economic depression	
1931	Balinese dance-theatre, The Dutch Pavilion, Paris Colonial Exposition	Augusto Boal
1933	Hitler leads Germany	Jerzy Grotowski
1934		Richard Schechner
1934		Wole Soyinka
1935		Christo
1935		Jeanne-Claude

continued

Year	World/Performance events	Births	Deaths
1936–9	Spanish Civil War	Eugenio Barba	
1937		Hélène Cixous	
1938			Konstantin Stanislavsky
1939		Tadashi Suzuki	
1939–45	Second World War		
1940		Pina Bausch	Vsevolod Meyerhold
1941		Robert Wilson	
1945	Atom bombs dropped on Japan Holocaust memorials and museums begin to be planned		
1946		Rustom Bharucha Stelios Arcadiou (Stelarc) Marina Abramović	
1947		Laurie Anderson Orlan	
1948			Antonin Artaud
1949	*Mother Courage and Her Children*, Bertold Brecht, Deutsches Theater, Berlin, Germany		Jacques Copeau
1952	*4' 33"*, John Cage, Black Mountain College, North Carolina, USA		

1953	*Waiting for Godot*, Roger Blin, Théâtre de Babylone, Paris		
1954		Annie Sprinkle	
1955		Guillermo Gómez-Peña	
1956		Judith Butler	Bertold Brecht
1957		Robert Lepage	
1958			Rudolf von Laban
1961	US troops enter Vietnam Berlin Wall built	Bread and Puppet Theatre founded	
1962	Cuban missile crisis		
1965	*The Constant Prince*, Jerzy Grotowski, Laboratory Theatre, Wrocław, Poland		Edward Gordon Craig
1966	*Trio A*, Yvonne Rainer, Judson Church, New York		
1968	Riots in Paris and worldwide *Paradise Now*, Living Theatre, Avignon, France *Dionysus in 69*, The Performance Group, New York (to 1969)		
1969	Moon landing		
1973		Bausch founds Wuppertal Dance Theatre	

continued

Year	World/Performance events	Births	Deaths
1974	*Coyote: I Like America and America Likes Me*, Joseph Beuys, René Block Gallery, New York		
1975	*The Dead Class*, Tadeusz Kantor and Cricot 2, Kraków, Poland	Wooster Group founded, New York	Mikhail Bakhtin
1976	Vietnam War finishes *Einstein on the Beach*, Robert Wilson, Avignon Festival, France	Market Theatre founded, Johannesburg, South Africa	
1977	Las Madres de la Plaza de Mayo begin protesting	Sistren founded, Kingston, Jamaica	
1980s–	Raves begin		
1980		Split Britches founded, New York	
1981	*Route 1 & 9 (The Last Act)*, Wooster Group, New York		
1982			Erving Goffman
1983			Victor Turner
1985	*The Mahabharata*, Peter Brook, Les Bouffes du Nord, Paris (to 1988)		
1986			Tatsumi Hijikata

1989	Berlin Wall falls	
	Tiananmen Square demonstrations, Beijing, China	
1990	*The Reincarnation of Saint Orlan* series of operations begins (to 1993)	Tadeusz Kantor
1990–91	Gulf War, Iraq and Kuwait	
1992		John Cage
1994	*The Temple of Confessions*, Guillermo Gómez-Peña and Roberto Sifuentes, toured USA (to 1997)	
1995	Baudrillard's article on Gulf War published	
1997	Lady Diana's funeral, Westminster Abbey, London, England	
1999		Jerzy Grotowski
		Jacques Lecoq
2001	World Trade Towers attacked, New York	
2003	War on Iraq begins	

SELECT BIBLIOGRAPHY

Abramović, Marina (1998) *Artist Body: Performances 1969–1998*, Milan: Charta.

Allain, Paul (1997) *Gardzienice: Polish Theatre in Transition*, Amsterdam: Harwood Academic Publishers.

—— (2002) *The Art of Stillness: The Theatre Practice of Tadashi Suzuki*, London: Methuen.

Alexander, M. Jacqui and Chandra Talpade Mohanty (eds) (1997) *Feminist Genealogies, Colonial Legacies, Democratic Futures*, London: Routledge.

Anderson, Laurie (1994) *Stories from the Nerve Bible: A Retrospective, 1972–1992*, New York: Harper Perennial.

Artaud, Antonin (1970) *The Theatre and Its Double*, trans. Victor Corti, London: Calder and Boyars Ltd.

Aston, Elaine (1995) *An Introduction to Feminism and Theatre*, London: Routledge.

—— and George Savona (1991) *Theatre as Sign System: A Semiotics of Text and Performance*, London: Routledge.

Auslander, Philip (1992) *Presence and Resistance: Postmodernism and Cultural Politics in Contemporary American Performance*, Ann Arbor: University of Michigan Press.

—— (1997) *From Acting to Performance: Essays in Modernism and Postmodernism*, London: Routledge.

—— (1999) *Liveness: Performance in a Mediatized Culture*, London: Routledge.

—— (ed.) (2003) *Performance: Critical Concepts in Literary and Cultural Studies*, 4 vols, London: Routledge.

Austin, John L. (1962) *How to Do Things with Words*, London: Oxford University Press.

Baal-Teshuva, Jacob (1995) *Christo and Jeanne-Claude*, Köln: Benedikt Taschen.

Babbage, Frances (2004) *Augusto Boal*, London: Routledge.

Bakhtin, M. M. (1981) *The Dialogic Imagination*, Michael Holquist (ed.), trans. Caryl Emerson and Michael Holquist, Austin: University of Texas Press.

—— (1984) *Rabelais and His World*, trans. Hélène Iswolsky, Bloomington: Indiana University Press.

Banes, Sally (1987) *Terpsichore in Sneakers*, Hanover: Wesleyan University Press.

—— (1998) *Subversive Expectations: Performance Art and Paratheater in New York 1976–85*, Ann Arbor: University of Michigan Press.

Banham, Martin (ed.) (1995) *The Cambridge Guide to Theatre*, revised edition, Cambridge: Cambridge University Press.

Barba, Eugenio (1968) *Towards a Poor Theatre*, Holstebro: Odin Teatrets Forlag.

—— (1985) *Beyond The Floating Islands*, Denmark: H. M. Bergs Forlag.

—— (1994) *The Paper Canoe – A Guide to Theatre Anthropology*, trans. Richard Fowler, London: Routledge.

——— and Nicola Savarese (eds) (1991) *A Dictionary of Theatre Anthropology: The Secret Art of the Performer*, London: Routledge.

Barker, Clive (1977) *Theatre Games*, London: Eyre Methuen.

Barthes, Roland (1977) *Image Music Text*, ed. and trans. Stephen Heath, London: Fontana.

Bell, John (ed.) (2001) *Puppets, Masks and Performing Objects*, Cambridge, MA: MIT Press.

Benedetti, Jean (1982) *Stanislavski: An Introduction*, London: Methuen.

Bennett, Susan (1997) *Theatre Audiences: A Theory of Production and Reception*, 2nd edition, London: Routledge.

Bentley, Eric (1968) *The Theory of the Modern Drama*, trans. John Willett, London: Penguin.

Bertens, Hans and Joseph Natoli (eds) (2002) *Postmodernism: The Key Figures*, Oxford: Blackwell.

Bharucha, Rustom (1993) *Theatre and the World: Performance and the Politics of Culture*, London: Routledge.

——— (2000) *The Politics of Cultural Practice: Thinking Through Theatre in an Age of Globalization*, London: Athlone.

Bial, Henry (ed.) (2004) *The Performance Studies Reader*, London: Routledge.

Birringer, Johannes (1991) *Theatre, Theory, Postmodernism*, Bloomington and Indianapolis: Indiana University Press.

——— (1998) *Media and Performance: Along the Border*, Baltimore: Johns Hopkins University Press.

——— (2000) *Performance on the Edge: Transformations of Culture*, London: Athlone.

Blau, Herbert (1990) *The Audience*, Baltimore: Johns Hopkins University Press.

Boal, Augusto (1979) *Theatre of the Oppressed*, trans. Charles A. and Maria-Odilia Leal McBride, London: Pluto Press.

——— (1995) *The Rainbow of Desire*, trans. Adrian Jackson, London: Routledge.

——— (1998) *Legislative Theatre*, trans. Adrian Jackson, London: Routledge.

——— (2001) *Hamlet and the Baker's Son: My Life in Theatre and Politics*, trans. Adrian Jackson and Candia Blaker, London: Routledge.

——— (2002) *Games for Actors and Non-Actors*, trans. Adrian Jackson, 2nd edition, London: Routledge.

Bottoms, Stephen, J. (2003) 'The Efficacy/Effeminacy Braid: Unpicking the Performance Studies/Theatre Studies Dichotomy', *Theatre Topics* 13.2.

Bratton, Jacky (2003) *New Readings in Theatre History*, Cambridge: Cambridge University Press.

Braun, Edward ([1979] 1995) *Meyerhold: A Revolution in Theatre*, revised edition, London: Eyre Methuen.

——— (1982) *The Director and the Stage: From Naturalism to Grotowski*, London: Methuen.

Brecht, Bertold (1965) *The Messingkauf Dialogues*, London: Methuen.

——— (1970–present) *Collected Plays*, 10 vols, London: Eyre Methuen.

Brecht, Stefan (1978) *The Theatre of Visions: Robert Wilson*, Frankfurt am Main: Suhrkamp Verlag.

——— (1988) *The Bread and Puppet Theatre*, 2 vols, London: Methuen.

Bremser, Martha (ed.) (1999) *Fifty Contemporary Choreographers*, London: Routledge.

Brockett, Oscar G. and Robert J. Ball (2004) *The Essential Theatre*, 8th edition, Belmont, CA: Wadsworth/Thomson Learning.

Brook, Peter (1968) *The Empty Space*, London: McGibbon and Kee.

—— (1988) *The Shifting Point*, London: Methuen.

—— (1993) *There Are No Secrets: Thoughts on Acting and Theatre*, London: Methuen.

Butler, Judith ([1990] 1999) *Gender Trouble: Feminism and the Subversion of Identity*, revised edition, London: Routledge.

—— (1997) *Excitable Speech: A Politics of the Performative*, London: Routledge.

Cage, John (1967) *A Year from Monday; New Lectures and Writings*, Middletown: Wesleyan University Press.

—— (1968) *Silence: Lectures and Writings*, London: Calder and Boyars.

Caillois, Roger (1979) *Man, Play and Games*, New York: Shocken Books.

Callens, Johan (ed.) (2004) *The Wooster Group and Its Traditions*, Brussels: Peter Lang.

Campbell, Patrick and Adrian Kear (eds) (2001) *Psychoanalysis and Performance*, London: Routledge.

Carlson, Marvin (1989) *Places of Performance: The Semiotics of Theatre Architecture*, Ithaca, NY: Cornell University Press.

—— (1993) *Theories of the Theatre: A Historical and Critical Survey from the Greeks to the Present*, Ithaca, NY: Cornell University Press.

—— (2004) *Performance: A Critical Introduction*, 2nd edition. London: Routledge.

Carr, C. (1993) *On Edge: Performance at the End of the Twentieth Century*, Hanover, NH: Wesleyan University Press.

Carter, Alexandra (ed.) (1998) *The Routledge Dance Studies Reader*, London: Routledge.

Case, Sue-Ellen (1988) *Feminism and Theatre*, New York: Methuen.

—— (ed.) (1990) *Performing Feminisms: Feminist Critical Theory and Theatre*, Baltimore: Johns Hopkins University Press.

—— (ed.) (1996) *Split Britches: Lesbian Practice/Feminist Performance*, London: Routledge.

—— and Janelle Reinelt (eds) (1991) *The Performance of Power: Theatrical Discourse and Politics*, Iowa City: University of Iowa Press.

Chambers, Colin (ed.) (2002) *The Continuum Companion to Twentieth Century Theatre*, London: Continuum.

Charest, Rémy ([1995] 1997) *Robert Lepage: Connecting Flights*, trans. Wanda Romer Taylor, London: Methuen.

Chaudhuri, Una (1997) *Staging Place: The Geography of Modern Drama*, Ann Arbor: University of Michigan Press.

Chinoy, Helen Krich and Linda Walsh Jenkins (1987) *Women in American Theatre*, revised and expanded edition, New York: Theatre Communications Group.

Cleto, Fabio (ed.) (1999) *Camp: Queer Aesthetics and the Performing Subject: A Reader*, Edinburgh: Edinburgh University Press.

Cohen-Cruz, Jan (ed.) (1998) *Radical Street Performance: An International Anthology*, London: Routledge.

Colleran, Jeanne and Jenny S. Spencer (eds) (1998) *Staging Resistance: Essays on Political Theatre*, Ann Arbor: University of Michigan Press.

Counsell, Colin (1996) *Signs of Performance: An Introduction to Twentieth Century Theatre*, London: Routledge.

—— and Laurie Wolf (eds) (2001) *Performance Analysis: An Introductory Coursebook*, London: Routledge.

Craig, Edward Gordon (1911) *On the Art of the Theatre*, New York: Theater Arts Books.

Davis, Tracy C. and Thomas Postlewait (eds) (2004) *Theatricality*, Cambridge: Cambridge University Press.

Delgado, Maria M. and Paul Heritage (eds) (1996) *In Contact with the Gods? Directors Talk Theatre*, Manchester: Manchester University Press.

—— and Caridad Svich (eds) (2002) *Theatre in Crisis? Performance Manifestos for a New Century*, Manchester: Manchester University Press.

Diamond, Elin (ed.) (1996) *Performance and Cultural Politics*, London: Routledge.

—— (1997) *Unmaking Mimesis: Essays on Feminism and Theatre*, London: Routledge.

Dobson, Julia (2002) *Hélène Cixous and the Theatre: The Scene of Writing*, Oxford: Peter Lang.

Dolan, Jill (1988) *The Feminist Spectator as Critic*, Ann Arbor: University of Michigan Press.

—— (2001) *Geographies of Learning: Theory and Practice, Activism and Performance*, Middletown: Wesleyan University Press.

Elam, Keir (2002) *The Semiotics of Drama and Theatre*, 2nd edition, London: Routledge.

Emigh, John (1996) *Masked Performance: The Play of Self and Other in Ritual and Theatre*, Philadelphia: University of Pennsylvania.

Esslin, Martin (1961) *Theatre of the Absurd*, New York: Doubleday.

Etchells, Tim (1999) *Certain Fragments: Contemporary Performance and Forced Entertainment*, London: Routledge.

Fernandes, Ciane (2001) *Pina Bausch and the Wuppertal Dance Theater: The Aesthetics of Repetition and Transformation*, New York: Peter Lang.

Fischer-Lichte, Erika (2004) *Theatre, Sacrifice, Ritual: Exploring Forms of Political Theatre*, London: Routledge.

——, Josephine Riley and Michael Gissenwehrer (eds) (1990) *The Dramatic Touch of Difference: Theatre, Own and Foreign*, Tübingen: Gunter Narr Verlag.

Fleshman, Bob (ed.) (1986) *Theatrical Movement: A Bibliographical Anthology*, Metuchen, NJ, and London: Scarecrow Press, Inc.

Fortier, Mark (2002) *Theory/Theatre*, London: Routledge.

Frith, Simon (1998) *Performing Rites: Evaluating Popular Music*, Oxford: Oxford University Press.

Frost, Anthony and Ralph Yarrow (1990) *Improvisation in Drama*, London: Macmillan.

Fuchs, Anne (2002) *Playing the Market: The Market Theatre, Johannesburg*, revised and updated edition, Amsterdam: Rodopi.

Fusco, Coco (ed.) (2000) *Corpus Delecti: Performance Art of the Americas*, London: Routledge.

Gale, Maggie B. and Viv Gardner (eds) (2000) *Women, Theatre and Performance: New Histories, New Historiographies*, Manchester: Manchester University Press.

—— (eds) (2004) *Auto/Biography and Identity: Women, Theatre and Performance*, Manchester: Manchester University Press.

Garner, Stanton B. (1994) *Bodied Spaces: Phenomenology and Performance in Contemporary Drama*, Ithaca, NY: Cornell University Press.

Geertz, Clifford (1973) *The Interpretation of Cultures*, New York: Basic Books.

Giannachi, Gabriella (2004) *Virtual Theatres: An Introduction*, London: Routledge.

Gilbert, Helen (ed.) (2001) *Postcolonial Plays: An Anthology*, London: Routledge.

Goffman, Erving (1959) *The Presentation of Self in Everyday Life*, New York: Doubleday.

Goldberg, RoseLee (1998) *Performance: Live Art Since the 60s*, London: Thames and Hudson.

—— (2000) *Laurie Anderson*, London: Thames and Hudson.

—— (2001) *Performance Art: From Futurism to the Present*, revised and expanded edition, London: Thames and Hudson.

Gómez-Peña, Guillermo (2000) *Dangerous Border Crossers: The Artist Talks Back*, London: Routledge.

Goodman, Lizbeth (1993) *Contemporary Feminist Theatres: To Each Her Own*, London: Routledge.

—— with Jane de Gay (eds) (1998) *The Routledge Reader in Gender and Performance*, London: Routledge.

—— (eds) (2000) *The Routledge Reader in Politics and Performance*, London: Routledge.

Harding, Frances (ed.) (2002) *The Performance Arts in Africa: A Reader*, London: Routledge.

Hart, Lynda and Peggy Phelan (eds) (1993) *Acting Out: Feminist Performances*, Ann Arbor: University of Michigan Press.

Hartnoll, Phyllis (ed.) (1983) *The Oxford Companion to the Theatre*, 4th edition, Oxford: Oxford University Press.

Harvey, Graham (ed.) (2003) *Shamanism: A Reader*, London: Routledge.

Harvie, Jen (2005) *Staging the UK*, Manchester: Manchester University Press.

Hayward, Philip (ed.) (1998) *Culture, Technology and Creativity in the Late Twentieth Century*, London: John Libbery.

Heathfield, Adrian (ed.) (2004) *Live: Art and Performance*, London: Tate Publishing.

Hodge, Alison (ed.) (2000) *Twentieth Century Actor Training*, London: Routledge.

Holledge, Julie and Joanne Tompkins (2000) *Women's Intercultural Performance*, London: Routledge.

Holmberg, Arthur (1997) *The Theatre of Robert Wilson*, Cambridge: Cambridge University Press.

Howard, Pamela (2002) *What Is Scenography?*, London: Routledge.

Howell, Anthony (1999) *The Analysis of Performance Art: A Guide to Its Theory and Practice*, Amsterdam: Harwood Academic Publishers.

Huizinga, Johan (1970) *Homo Ludens*, New York: Harper.

Huxley, Michael and Noel Witts (eds) (2002) *The Twentieth-Century Performance Reader*, 2nd edition, London: Routledge.

Ince, Kate (2000) *Orlan: Millennial Female*, Oxford and New York: Berg.

Innes, Christopher (ed.) (2000) *A Sourcebook on Naturalist Theatre*, London: Routledge.

Irvin, Polly (2003) *Directing for the Stage*, Hove: RotoVision.

Jackson, Shannon (2003) *Professing Performance: Theatre in the Academy from Philology to Performativity*, Cambridge: Cambridge University Press.

Johnstone, Keith (1981) *Impro: Improvisation and the Theatre*, London: Eyre Methuen.

Jones, Amelia (1998) *Body Art: Performing the Subject*, Minneapolis: University of Minnesota Press.

Kaye, Nick (1994) *Postmodernism and Performance*, London: Macmillan.

—— (1996) *Art into Theatre: Performance Interviews and Documents*, Amsterdam: Harwood Academic Publishers.

Kennedy, Dennis (ed.) (2003) *The Oxford Encyclopedia of Theatre and Performance*, 2 vols, Oxford: Oxford University Press.

Kershaw, Baz (1992) *The Politics of Performance: Radical Theatre as Cultural Intervention*, London: Routledge.

—— (1999) *The Radical in Performance: Between Brecht and Baudrillard*, London: Routledge.

Kirby, Michael, and Victoria Nes Kirby ([1971] 1986) *Futurist Performance*, New York: PAJ Publications.

Kirshenblatt-Gimblett, Barbara (1998) *Destination Culture: Tourism, Museums, and Heritage*, Berkeley: University of California Press.

Klein, Susan Blakley (1988) *Ankokō Buto: The Premodern and Postmodern Influences on the Dance of Utter Darkness*, Ithaca, NY: Cornell University Press.

Kleymeyer, Charles David (ed.) (1994) *Cultural Expression and Grassroots Development: Cases from Latin America and the Caribbean*, Boulder and London: Lynne Rienner.

Klosty, James (ed.) (1975) *Merce Cunningham*, New York: Dutton.

Knowles, Ric (2004) *Reading the Material Theatre*, Cambridge: Cambridge University Press.

Kuhns, David F. (1997) *German Expressionist Theatre: The Actor and the Stage*, Cambridge: Cambridge University Press.

Laban, Rudolf von (1960) *A Life for Dance*, trans. Lisa Ullman, New York: Theatre Arts Books.

Lecoq, Jacques with Jean-Gabriel Carasso and Jean-Claude Lallias (2000) *The Moving Body, Teaching Creative Theatre*, trans. David Bradby, foreword by Simon McBurney, London: Methuen.

Lommel, Andreas (1981) *Masks: Their Meaning and Function*, New York: Excalibur Books.

Longman, Stanley Vincent (ed.) (1998) *Crosscurrents in the Drama – East and West*, Alabama: University of Alabama Press and Southeastern Theatre Conference.

McAuley, Gay (1999) *Space in Performance: Making Meaning in the Theatre*, Ann Arbor: University of Michigan Press.

McGrath, John (1981) *A Good Night Out: Popular Theatre: Audience, Class and Form*, London: Eyre Methuen.

McKenzie, Jon (2001) *Perform or Else: From Discipline to Performance*, London: Routledge.

Mackintosh, Iain (1993) *Architecture, Actor and Audience*, London and New York: Routledge.

McNamara, Brooks and Jill Dolan, (eds) (1986) The Drama Review: *Thirty Years of Commentary on the Avant-Garde*, Ann Arbor: UMI Research Press.

Malkin, Jeanette R. (1999) *Memory-Theater and Postmodern Drama*, Ann Arbor: University of Michigan Press.

Marranca, Bonnie (ed.) ([1977] 1996) *The Theatre of Images*, Baltimore: Johns Hopkins University Press.

—— and Gautam Dasgupta (eds) (1991) *Interculturalism and Performance: Writings from PAJ*, New York: PAJ Publications.

Martin, Carol (ed.) (1996) *A Sourcebook of Feminist Theatre: On and Beyond the Stage*, London: Routledge.

Mayer, David, and Kenneth Richards (eds) (1977) *Western Popular Theatre*, London: Methuen.

Melzer, Annabelle Henkin ([1976] 1994) *Dada and Surrealist Performance*, Baltimore: Johns Hopkins University Press.

Mitter, Shomit (1993) *Systems of Rehearsal*: *Stanislavsky, Brecht, Grotowski and Brook*, London: Routledge.

—— and Maria Shevtsova (eds) (2005) *Fifty Key Theatre Directors*, London: Routledge.

Murray, Timothy (1997) *Drama Trauma: Specters of Race and Sexuality in Performance, Video and Art*, London: Routledge.

Oddey, Alison (1994) *Devising Theatre: A Practical and Theoretical Handbook*, London: Routledge.

Oliveira, Nicolas de, Nicola Oxley and Michael Petry (1994) *Installation Art*, London: Thames and Hudson.

Orlan (1996) *This Is My Body . . . This Is My Software*, London: Black Dog.

—— (2004) *Orlan: Carnal Art*, trans. Deke Dusinberre, Paris: Editions Flammarion.

Parker, Andrew and Eve Kosofsky Sedgwick (eds) (1995) *Performativity and Performance*, London: Routledge.

Pavis, Patrice (1982) *Languages of the Stage*, New York: PAJ Publications.

—— (1992) *Theatre at the Crossroads of Culture*, trans. Loren Kruger, London: Routledge.

—— (ed.) (1996) *The Intercultural Performance Reader*, London: Routledge.

—— (1998) *Dictionary of the Theatre: Terms, Concepts, and Analysis*, trans. Christine Shantz, Toronto: University of Toronto Press.

—— (2003) *Analyzing Performance: Theater, Dance and Film*, trans. David Williams, Ann Arbor: University of Michigan Press.

Pearson, Mike and Michael Shanks (2001) *Theatre/Archaeology*, London: Routledge.

Phelan, Peggy (1993) *Unmarked: The Politics of Performance*, London: Routledge.

—— (1997) *Mourning Sex: Performing Public Memories*, London: Routledge.

—— and Jill Lane (eds) (1998) *The Ends of Performance*, New York: New York University Press.

Pollock, Della (ed.) (1998) *Exceptional Spaces: Essays in Performance and History*, Chapel Hill: University of North Carolina Press.

Postlewait, Thomas and Bruce A. McConachie (eds) (1989) *Interpreting the Theatrical Past: Essays in the Historiography of Performance*, Iowa City: University of Iowa Press.

Read, Alan (1993) *Performance and Everyday Life: An Ethics of Performance*, London: Routledge.

Reinelt, Janelle G. and Joseph R. Roach (eds) (1992) *Critical Theory and Performance*, Ann Arbor: University of Michigan Press.

Riggio, Milla Cozart (2004) *Carnival*, London: Routledge.

Roach, Joseph (1996) *Cities of the Dead: Circum-Atlantic Performance*, New York: Columbia University Press.

——, Janelle Reinelt, Barbara Kirshenblatt-Gimblett, Marvin Carlson, Elin Diamond and Jill Dolan (2001) 'Responses to "Choices Made and Unmade"', *Theater* 31.2: 96–105.

Rubin, Don (general ed.) (1994–2000) *The World Encyclopedia of Contemporary Theatre*, 6 vols, London: Routledge.

Rudlin, John (1986) *Jacques Copeau*, Cambridge: Cambridge University Press.

Sandford, Mariellen (ed.) (1995) *Happenings and Other Acts*, London: Routledge.

Savran, David (1986) *Breaking the Rules: The Wooster Group*, New York: Theatre Communications Group.

Schechner, Richard ([1973] 1994) *Environmental Theater*, New York: Applause Books.

—— ([1977] 1988) *Performance Theory*, London: Routledge.

—— (1985) *Between Theater and Anthropology*, Philadelphia: University of Pennsylvania Press.

—— (1993) *The Future of Ritual: Writings on Culture and Performance*, London: Routledge.

—— (2000) 'Post Post-Structuralism?', *TDR: The Drama Review* 44.3 (T167): 4–7.

—— (2002) *Performance Studies: An Introduction*, London: Routledge.

—— and Willa Appel (eds) (1990) *By Means of Performance: Intercultural Studies of Theatre and Ritual*, Cambridge: Cambridge University Press.

—— and Lisa Wolford (eds) (1997) *The Grotowski Sourcebook*, London: Routledge.

Schechter, Joel (2003) *Popular Theatre: A Sourcebook*, London: Routledge.

Schneider, Rebecca (1997) *The Explicit Body in Performance*, London: Routledge.

—— and Gabrielle Cody (eds) (2002) *Re:Direction: A Theoretical and Practical Guide*, London: Routledge.

Schutzman, Mady and Jan Cohen-Cruz (eds) (1994) *Playing Boal: Theatre, Therapy and Activism*, London: Routledge.

Servos, Norbert (1984) *Pina Bausch Wuppertal Dance Theater, or, the Art of Training a Goldfish: Excursions into Dance*, trans. Patricia Stadié, Cologne: Ballett-Bühnen Verlag.

Shank, Theodore (2002) *Beyond the Boundaries: American Alternative Theatre*, revised and updated edition, Ann Arbor: University of Michigan Press.

Shepherd, Simon and Mick Wallis (2004) *Drama/Theatre/Performance*, London: Routledge.

Shyer, Laurence (1989) *Robert Wilson and His Collaborators*, New York: Theatre Communications Group.

Smith, Sidonie and Julia Watson (eds) (2002) *Interfaces: Women/Autobiography/Image/ Performance*, Ann Arbor: University of Michigan Press.

Soyinka, Wole (1988) *Art, Dialogue and Outrage: Essays on Literature and Culture*, London: Methuen.

Sprinkle, Annie (1998) *Annie Sprinkle, Post-Porn Modernist: My Twenty-Five Years as a Multimedia Whore*, revised and updated edition, San Francisco: Cleis Press.

—— (2001) *Hardcore from the Heart: The Pleasures, Profits and Politics of Sex in Performance: Annie Sprinkle: Solo*, Gabrielle Cody (ed.), London: Continuum.

Stanislavski, Konstantin (1924) *My Life in Art*, trans. J. J. Robbins, London: Geoffrey Bles.

Stanton, Sarah and Martin Banham (eds) (1996) *The Cambridge Paperback Guide to the Theatre*, Cambridge: Cambridge University Press.

States, Bert O. (1985) *Great Reckonings in Little Rooms: On the Phenomenology of Theater*, Berkeley and Los Angeles: University of California Press.

Stiles, Kristine *et al.* (1998) *Out of Actions: Between Performance and the Object, 1949–1979*, London: Thames and Hudson.

Striff, Erin (ed.) (2003) *Performance Studies*, London: Palgrave Macmillan.

Stucky, Nathan and Cynthia Wimmer (eds) (2002) *Teaching Performance Studies*, Carbondale: Southern Illinois University Press.

Suzuki, Tadashi (1986) *The Way of Acting*, New York: Theatre Communications Group.

Taylor, Diana (1997) *Disappearing Acts: Spectacles of Gender and Nationalism in Argentina's 'Dirty War'*, Durham: Duke University Press.

Turner, Victor (1969) *The Ritual Process*, Chicago: Aldine.

—— (1974) *Drama, Fields and Metaphors: Symbolic Action in Human Society*, Ithaca, NY: Cornell University Press.

—— (1982) *From Ritual to Theatre: The Human Seriousness of Play*, New York: Performing Arts Journal Press.

—— (1986) *The Anthropology of Performance*, New York: PAJ Publications.

Ubersfeld, Anne (1999) *Reading Theatre*, trans. Frank Collins, Toronto: University of Toronto Press.

Viala, Jean and Nourit Masson-Sekine (eds) (1988) *Butoh: Shades of Darkness*, Tokyo: Shufunotomo Co. Ltd.

Warr, Tracey (ed.), survey by Amelia Jones (2000) *The Artist's Body*, London: Phaidon.

Waters, Erika J. and David Edgecombe (eds) (2001) *Contemporary Drama of the Caribbean*, Kingshill, St Croix: The Caribbean Writer.

Watson, Ian and colleagues (2002) *Negotiating Cultures – Eugenio Barba and the Intercultural Debates*, Manchester: Manchester University Press.

Wiles, David (2003) *A Short History of Western Performance Space*, Cambridge: Cambridge University Press.

Willett, John (ed.) (1964) *Brecht on Theatre*, London: Methuen.

Williams, David (ed.) (1991) *Peter Brook and* The Mahabharata*: Critical Perspectives*, London: Routledge.

Worthen, W. B. (1995) 'Disciplines of the Text/Sites of Performance', *TDR: The Drama Review: The Journal of Performance Studies* 39.1: 13–28.

Zarrilli, Phillip B. (ed.) (2002) *Acting (Re)Considered: A Theoretical and Practical Guide*, 2nd edition, London: Routledge.

SELECT JOURNALS

Contemporary Theatre Review
TDR: The Drama Review: The Journal of Performance Studies
The Journal of Dramatic Theory and Criticism
Modern Drama
NTQ: New Theatre Quarterly
PAJ: Performing Arts Journal
Performance Research
Theater
Theatre Journal
Theatre Research International
Theatre Topics

INDEX